VINTAGE

INTERNATIONAL

BOOKS BY EUDORA WELTY

The Eye of the Story

Vintage International
Vintage Books
A Division of Random House, Inc.
New York

The Eye
of the Story

SELECTED ESSAYS
AND REVIEWS

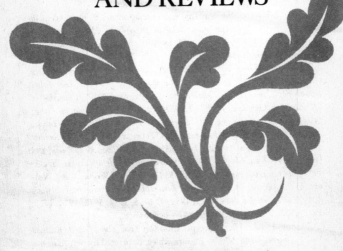

EUDORA
WELTY

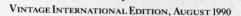

VINTAGE INTERNATIONAL EDITION, AUGUST 1990

Grateful acknowledgment is made to the following:

The Yale Review, *The Southern Review*, The Symphony League of Jackson, *Mademoiselle*, *The Mississippi Quarterly*, *The Atlantic Monthly*, Mississippi Historical Society, University of Nebraska Press, *Harper's Bazaar*, *The New Republic*, *Accent*, *The Virginia Quarterly Review*, *The Hudson Review*, *Esquire*, *Critical Inquiry*, *Cornell Review*.

Little, Brown and Company in association with The Atlantic Monthly Press: Excerpt from *Atlantic Brief Lives* edited by Louis Kronenberger. Copyright © 1968 by Little, Brown and Company. Reprinted by permission.

The New York Times: For the following Eudora Welty pieces: *Charlotte's Web*, October 19, 1952; *Marianne Thornton*, May 27, 1956; *Last Tales*, November 3, 1957; *Granite and Rainbow*, September 21, 1958; *The Most of S.J. Perelman*, October 12, 1958; *The Western Journals of Washington Irving*, December 24, 1944; *Names on the Land*, May 6, 1945; *Baby, It's Cold Inside*, August 30, 1970; *The Underground Man*, February 14, 1971; *The Saddest Story: A Biography of Ford M. Ford*, May 2, 1971; *The Life to Come, and Other Short Stories*, May 13, 1973; *Pictures and Conversations*, January 5, 1975; *The Cockatoos*, January 19, 1975; *The Letters of Virgina Woolf*, Volume II, November 14, 1976; *Selected Letters of William Faulkner*, February 6, 1977. Copyright 1944, 1945, 1952, © 1956, 1957, 1958, 1970, 1971, 1973, 1975, 1976, 1977. Reprinted by permission.

Random House, Inc.: Excerpts from *One Time, One Place* by Eudora Welty. Copyright © 1970 by Eudora Welty. Reprinted by permission.

LIBRARY OF CONGRESS CATALOGING IN PUBLICATION DATA
Welty, Eudora, 1909–
The eye of the story.
I. Title
PS3545.E6E91979   820'.9   89-40721
ISBN 0-679-73004-4

To Kenneth Millar

Contents

I

ON WRITERS

The Radiance of
Jane Austen

Jane Austen will soon be closer in calendar time to Shakespeare
than to us. Within the reading life of the next generation, that
constellation of six bright stars will have swung that many years
deeper into the one sky, vast and crowded, of English literature. Will these future readers be in danger of letting the novels
elude them because of distance, so that their pleasure will not
be anything like ours? The future of fiction is a mystery; it is
like the future of ourselves.

But, we ask, how could it be possible for these novels to
seem remote? For one thing, the noise! What a commotion
comes out of their pages! Jane Austen loved high spirits, she
had them herself, and she always rejoiced in the young. The
exuberance of her youthful characters is one of the unaging
delights of her work. Through all the mufflings of time we
can feel the charge of their vitality, their happiness in doing,
dancing, laughing, in being alive. There is always a lot of
jumping; that seems to vibrate through time. Motion is constant—indeed, it is necessary for communication in the country.
It takes days to go some of the tiny distances, but how the
wheels spin! The sheer velocity of the novels, scene to scene,
conversation to conversation, tears to laughter, concert to picnic
to dance, is something equivalent to a pulsebeat. The clamorous

griefs and joys are all giving voice to the tireless relish of life. The novels' vitality is irresistible for us. Surely all this cannot fade away, letting the future wonder, two hundred years from now, what our devotion to Jane Austen was all about.

For nearly this long already the gaiety of the novels has pervaded them, the irony has kept its bite, the reasoning is still sweet, the sparkle undiminished. Their high spirits, their wit, their celerity and harmony of motion, their symmetry of design appear still unrivaled in the English novel. Jane Austen's work at its best seems as nearly flawless as any fiction could be.

Of course, this in itself may create a gentle threat to the reader's mood of understanding today. This is possible even while we are still able to like, and to turn to, that which we know to be better than *we* could do. And besides writing perfectly, she did so not in the least by accident; the oddness is compounded. Her intelligence was formidable, and it was well nourished by an understanding family. She was beautifully educated at home, was always well read, "intimately acquainted with the merits and defects of the best essays and novels in the English language," Henry Austen has told us in the Biographical Notice, and "her memory [was] tenacious." Best of all, she had been born, or rewarded, with fairy gifts—not one, but two entirely separate ones. She had the genius of originality, and she had the genius of comedy. And they never fought each other at all, but worked together in a harmony that must have delighted her in a way we rejoice to think about, and a way particularly belonging to the eighteenth century, whose spiritual child she was.

She was, of course, from the first, a highly conscious artist. This the writer of comedy indeed must be, and in comedy was she not supreme? We know, too, from her own remarks, that she looked on the novel as a work of art, and that she gave it the concentration, the devotion, of all her powers.

But it is further well known that Jane Austen's life was not only unusual for an author's, it was unique. And for this, will the future treat her as blindly as we have been known to treat her and take her down because she was a spinster who—having never lived anywhere outside her father's rectory and the later family homes in Bath, Southampton, and Chawton, whose notion of travel was an excursion to Lyme Regis—could never have got to know very much about life? Will they wish to call her a snob?—her life touched intimately only that of the other country gentry in the neighborhood. Or a butterfly?—gossip comes down through all these years that she couldn't do at all without dancing. Her detractors have also declared that even the Battle of Waterloo went by without her notice, so remote was her life; although a novel called *Emma*, published of course anonymously like her others, came out dedicated to the Prince Regent soon after his victory "by His Royal Highness's dutiful and obedient servant, the author." It might be that dedication page that will puzzle the far future: readers of *Emma* may wonder what it was that the Prince Regent had done that was so deserving.

But what must be indelibly certain is that never did it escape Jane Austen that the interesting situations of life can take place, and notably do, at home. The dangerous confrontations and the decisive dialogues can very conveniently happen in country parsonages. The novels she wrote were, in themselves, remarkable examples of this very phenomenon.

Each novel is a formidable engine of strategy. It is made to be—a marvel of designing and workmanship, capable of spontaneous motion at the lightest touch and of travel at delicately controlled but rapid speed toward its precise destination. It could kill us all, had she wished it to; it fires at us, all along the way, using understatements in good aim. Let us be thankful it is trained not on our hearts but on our illusions and our vanities. Who among novelists ever more instantly recognized the absurd when she saw it in human behavior, then polished it off to more devastating effect, than this young daughter of a Hampshire rectory, who as she finished the chapters enjoyed reading them to her family, to whom she also devoted her life?

She could be our Waterloo; she *is* our Waterloo. We pray that those readers of the future will not lose or throw away their heritage of absurdity; this alone would render them incapable of knowing what her novels "are all about," and would probably make them hopeless as human beings in the process.

Reading those chapters aloud to her own lively, vocative family, on whose shrewd intuition, practiced estimation of conduct, and seasoned judgment of character she relied almost as well as on her own, Jane Austen must have enjoyed absolute confidence in an understanding reception of her work. The novels still have a bloom of shared pleasure. And the felicity they have for us must partly lie in the confidence they take for granted between the author and her readers—at the moment, ourselves. Odd to our own twentieth-century expectations as this trust may be, it is unshakably effective to this day.

This young novelist's position was in every respect clear. As all her work testifies, her time, her place, her location in society are in no more question than the fact that she was a woman. She wrote from a perfectly solid and firm foundation, and her work is wholly affirmative.

There is probably some connection between this confidence, this positivity, and the flow of comedy. A novelist may be strictly satiric in the presence of strangers, encouraged to more acidity still by a ring of sworn enemies. But when the listeners all have bright faces, ready minds, teasing and affectionate dispositions, mimicking ways, and kindred ears, it would have been hard, even had it occurred to her, to keep up hauteur, to give in to sentimentality, to plunge into unconfined melodrama, to pause for too many sermons along the way. Comedy is sociable and positive, and exacting. Its methods, its boundaries, its *point*, all belong to the familiar.

Jane Austen *needed* very little space, very limited material, to work with; asking for little seems immoderate to us. Given: a household in the country, then add its valuable neighbor—and there, under her hands, is the full presence of the world. As if coming in response to a call for good sense, life is at hand and astir and in strong vocal power. At once there is convenient and constant communication between those two houses. The day, the week, the season fill to repletion with news, arrivals, speculation, and fresh strawberries, with tumult and crises, and the succeeding invitations. Everybody doing everything together—what mastery she has over the scene, the family scene! The dinner parties, the walking parties, the dances, picnics, concerts, excursions to Lyme Regis and sojourns at Bath, all give their testimony to Jane Austen's ardent belief, —which our century's city dwellers find odd—that the unit of everything worth knowing in life is in the family, that family relationships are the natural basis of all other relationships.

Her world, small in size but drawn exactly to scale, may of course easily be regarded as a larger world seen at a judicious distance—it would be the exact distance at which all haze evaporates, full clarity prevails, and true perspective appears. But it would be more to the point to suppose that her stage was small because such were her circumstances and that, in fact, she was perfectly equipped to recognize in its very dimensions the first virtue and principle of comedy. The focus she used was for the same end: it was central. A clear ray of light strikes full upon the scene, resulting in the prism of comedy.

And of this prerequisite world she sees and defines both sides—sensibility as well as sense, for instance—and presents them in their turns, in a continuing state of balance: moral, esthetic, and dramatic balance. This ingenuity in the way of narrative (not to put it too strongly) and this generosity of understanding could be seen in their own brilliant way as other manifestations of her comic gift. The action of her novels is in itself a form of wit, a kind of repartee; some of it is the argument of souls.

Her habit of mind of seeing both sides of her own subject —of seeing it indeed in the round—is a little unusual, too, to writers and readers of our day. And it offers one more good reason, perhaps, why there is little comedy being written now; what is shaped from a single point of view and grows heavily weighted to one side is more likely to turn out a tragedy, or a tragedy by courtesy. But it cannot be allowed that there is any less emotional feeling contained in the novels of Jane Austen because they are not tragedies. Great comic masterpieces that they are, their roots are nourished at the primary sources. They are profound in emotion. Jane Austen was by declared intention a moral, even "improving," writer; if she could have improved us at all, at this far reach, it must be doubted that she would have hesitated. Nor did moralizing keep out life. In her novels the strong feelings she knew, respected, and made evident in her characters and their situations were given their full weight. Far from denying the emotions their power, she used her intuitive and narrative restraint and employed it to excellent advantage. Nothing of feeling has been diminished. There is passion, the stronger for being concealed until it can be concealed no longer; there is desperation, intense suffering such as Marianne Dashwood's and Jane Fairfax's. But the effect of the whole is still that of proportions kept, symmetry maintained, and the classical form honored—indeed, celebrated. And we are still within the balustrades of comedy.

All the differences between people then and people now are not external, of course—differences never are. In Jane Austen's time they quite literally saw the world differently.

She was "a warm and judicious admirer of landscape," says Henry Austen's Biographical Notice; and for Jane Austen the novelist "judicious" can be taken to mean that landscape was appraised for its suitability in the calendar of events, when excursions called for fine prospects as they did for cold collations. In the novels everything keeps its place, and the place of landscape is in the middle background, in size proportionally small, but drawn and furnished to specification, as truly as was Northanger Abbey built for Catherine Morland to read Mrs. Radcliffe in.

Landscape may be simply a setting, convenience laid out. There is Elizabeth's favorite grove in *Pride and Prejudice*; it is the one Mr. Darcy walks in—and walks for some time—in the hope of meeting Elizabeth in order to give her, with his look of haughty composure, the letter he wrote her at eight o'clock—those two pages written in a very close hand and beginning "Be not alarmed, Madam." As a grove it is not visible, rather it is suitable. Lady Catherine de Bourgh, paying her call upon the Bennets, condescends to say, "Mis' Bennet, there seemed to be a prettyish kind of a little wilderness on one side of your lawn. I should be glad to take a turn in it." And here, on the other hand, is Lady Catherine de Bourgh's park: "Every park has its beauty and its prospects; and Elizabeth saw much to be pleased with, though she could not be in such raptures as Mr. Collins expected the scene to inspire, and was but slightly affected by his enumeration of the windows in front of the house, and his relation of what the glazing altogether had originally cost Sir Lewis De Bourgh."

Between Jane Austen's time and ours lies the Romantic Movement, but it doesn't matter: it does not lie between her page and our minds. She has command over our vision, and any description of the surround is irrelevant to *Pride and Prejudice*: what we are being afforded are views of character. Thus landscape provides an excuse to Mrs. Elton for bringing her brother Mr. Suckling's barouche-landau into the conversation. The seaside is the cause of rapture in Louisa Musgrove's breast, so that she has to be jumped down the steps by Captain Wentworth, to unlooked-for misinformation.

But it may be harder for us to see what she wants us to when she shakes her finger in our faces. She moralized; she could also be cynical, even at the rare moment coarse—she was, once again, of her day. (And the coarseness of an earlier age shocks the later, perhaps because an ugliness that isn't our own seems to have been something unintentional.) But in her writing there deeply lies, as deeply as anything in her powers, a true tenderness of feeling. Though it could be at the odd moment turned into the other thing, even into cruelty, seldom indeed did it suffer the fatal lapse into what is unlifelike. But our occasional blank aversion from her, now, shows us simply how precarious is the passage of time.

The century that produced Jane Austen was even seamier and more brutal in many ways than our own, and although we, too, boast of an opposite extreme, ours is not *their* opposite extreme: we have nothing in our own best that corresponds to the orderliness, the composure, of that life, or that meets its requirements of the small scale, the lovely proportions, the intimacy, the sense of personal security. And not only is our fare different, our palate is different.

Think of today's fiction in the light of hers. Does some of it appear garrulous and insistent and out-of-joint, and nearly all of it slow? Does now and then a novel come along that's so long, arch, and laborious, so ponderous in literary conceits and so terrifying in symbols, that it might have been written (in his bachelor days) by Mr. Elton as a conundrum, or, in some prolonged spell of elevation, by Mr. Collins in a bid for self-advancement? Yes, but this is understandable. For many of our writers who are now as young as Jane Austen was when she wrote her novels, and as young as she still was when she died, at forty-one, ours is the century of unreason, the stamp of our behavior is violence or isolation; non-meaning is looked upon with some solemnity; and for the purpose of writing novels, most human behavior is looked at through the frame, or the knothole, of alienation. The life Jane Austen wrote about was indeed a different one from ours, but the difference was not as great as that between the frames through which it is viewed. Jane Austen's frame was that of *belonging to her world*. She could step through it, in and out of it as easily and unselfconsciously as she stepped through the doorway of the rectory and into the garden to pick strawberries. She was perfectly at home in what she knew, as well as knowledgeable of precisely where she was on earth; she even believed she knew why she was here.

Nothing can change his own life for the writer. Reading can roam the centuries and pleasure itself at will, but writing, the writing of novels, is of its own time only. To each of us alive, our own world is with us, as was Jane Austen's world entirely with her. To any novelist, that which is less important than his own world's presence—its ruthless presence, its blotting-out nearness and newness—is simply irrelevant.

Yet there is left the reconcilable element. Pride and Prejudice, Sense and Sensibility, Persuasion: looked at not only as titles but as the themes they are, they might be called simple, but it is more accurate to call them basic. They are lustrous with long and uninterrupted use. Though at first glance they might not be recognized, it is possible to see most of them today in their newest incarnations. They are beyond time, because they pertain not to the outside world but to the interior, to what goes on perpetually in the mind and heart.

The contemporary mood, temperament, force of habit, or even the elbow-nudge of a passing fashion can affect the way we see life but not the way we *know* it. This is personal and singular and obstinate and hard to kill. The novelist writes as his own person. And so he reads. In reading a novel, as in experiencing our own life, it is what people say and what they do and the way in which they say and do it that tells us the most about them. There is nothing in Jane Austen's work to let us imagine we have learned any more about human character and behavior than she knew; indeed, part of what we know today may well have come to us through reading and rereading her novels.

We have our own charts of the mind and diagnoses of the heart, but they are still the same dangerous territories that Jane Austen knew as well as the shrubbery at Steventon. And here it is their unchangeableness that gives us the shock of pleasure when we read her novels. How familiar, after all, and how inevitable is the motivation of man. His deeds by now may be numberless, but this is in contrast to the very small range of the feelings that drive him. He may fly to the moon at any moment, but at home on earth his motives can still be counted on his fingers. They have not increased or altered yet, and so, for some centuries to come, people may go on saying of Jane Austen, How really *modern* she is, after all.

What is the real secret of the novels' already long life? The answer seems to be: life itself. The brightness of Jane Austen's eye simply does not grow dim, as have grown the outlines and colors of the scene she saw herself while she wrote—its actualities, like its customs and clothes, have receded from us forever. But she wrote, and her page is dazzlingly alive. Her world seems not only accessible but near, for under her authority and in her charge, all its animation is disclosure.

And toward this life is directed a point of view that is not quite like that of any other novelist at any time on earth. In this point of view she speaks to us, or a voice speaks: it is the author's, and possibly not the same voice that the family heard; but we cannot mistake it; it is her own. It must be the most personal expression of her own true and original mind. And it is inimitable, forever so.

Then will her novels not always catch up with her readers as the generations fly? To the farthest future, we might wonder if at least some of the characters might not safely travel— especially some of the great secondary characters: the eccentrics, like Mr. Woodhouse, but he is already feeling the draft; or the steady talkers, like Miss Bates, who has just recollected what she was talking *about*, her mother's spectacles. But it is already clear what Jane Austen's characters are made of: they are made of the novel they are in, and never can they come away from their context. Miss Bates, though always so ready to go anywhere, is not movable; she is part of *Emma*.

It might even be the case that the more original the work of imagination, the greater the danger of its succumbing to the violence of transportation. Insomuch as it is alive, it must remain fixed in its own time and place, whole and intact, inviolable as a diamond. It abides in its own element, and this of course is the mind.

No, Jane Austen cannot follow readers into any other time. She cannot go into the far future, and she never came to us. She is there forever where she wrote, immovable to the very degree of her magnitude. The readers of the future will have to do the same as we ourselves have done, and with the best equipment they can manage, make the move themselves. The reader is the only traveler. It is not her world or her time, but her art, that is approachable, today or tomorrow. The novels in their radiance are a destination.

(1969)

Henry Green:
Novelist of the Imagination

Through the novels of Henry Green from *Living* on, a strong originality has poured in a stream at once pure and changing. Other good novelists in England who were brought up at the same time and in the same mold of home and school and university wrote and still write at times rather like one another, but not one has produced one novel that in the conception or in the writing seems now in the same world of art with *Living* or *Party Going* or *Caught* or *Loving* or *Back* or *Concluding* or *Nothing* or *Doting* or, in quite the same way these novels seem, in the world with us. His novels are not only unlike those of other writers, they are to an unusual degree unlike one another, and while each has been made to stand as clear as possible out in space, yet there could be above all no mistaking of the hand. The intelligence, the blazing gifts of imagery, dialogue, construction, and form, the power to feel both what can and what never can be said, give Henry Green's work an intensity greater, this reader believes, than that of any other writer of imaginative fiction today. For thirty years the nature of each next work has been unpredictable, and this is still the case. His remains the most interesting and vital imagination in English fiction in our time.

He brings to bear on that imagination a knowledge of the

wide world as intimate as Jane Austen enjoyed of her own. To be sure, their sex and their centuries divide them, as does the different order and play of their powers, but any two unfooled novelists may meet somewhere, and it is no little thing to have a sense of the absurd in common. While they could meet as wits, and he could get away as she passes judgment, it would be he who finds human behavior extraordinary and she who finds it not too different from what she'd expected. The at-homeness possible to him in the wider world allows him irony and apprehension as well, and has made him richly aware of the comic and also of the outrageous, the bizarre, the awful, the inhuman—all that "home" is not. She merely approved of the landscape which has so often carried him away; with her own good eyes she was as innocent of that world as she was of the symbolic that he can also see. And then another divider would have opened between them, this time the true Grand Canyon, love. Without ever taking us back, this not being his direction, Henry Green may seem more congenial in mind, perhaps, with a century of order, form, and reason than he does with ours, and a sense of order appears to lie deep in his writing; nevertheless we may feel that it is not so deep as where the spring rises.

For his seems a lyric voice that first and last praises the phenomenon of life, and the effect of his fiction is that we have been charged in various and astonishing ways with seeing the phenomenon and in time, before its radiance is spent. And in this he is not typical of our century either; indeed, he is nowhere this.

You could say that he starts with the visible and present world, the variety of its people, and time. Then you could take one theme of his to be the extreme, almost triumphant vulnerability of man to this mortal world and variety, what with the power of the feelings and fates and the plain nuisances that come in the course and confinement of time to assail him. The characters in his novels live to a degree aware of their own exposure even when not too steadily aware of the world, even when deaf and blind to it. A character with defenses up on three sides will be found in the end helpless as a baby on the fourth side; and generally—here is a mark of this writer—feeling the better for it. Vulnerability is a personal and valuable and selfish possession—perhaps more; perhaps in effect it is the self. At any rate, tolerance for the condition comes not too hard.

Signs, omens, charms and works, hopes, confidences, deceptions and self-deceptions, truth and lies, loving and harm-doing, everything sweet or formidable that we go provided with, all in the end will tell what we tried to provide against. All, down to the most frittering talk and most antic behavior of daily living, are eloquent of the complicated, almost oriental threats that are constantly being made against our living at all. Death by inches is waiting just beyond the door, and someday the dead pigeon, or the fire bomb, will come tumbling down from the sky straight for somebody's head.

For of course he is writing against death, and this the artist whose medium is the word is always doing. A painter *may* paint merely against boredom and come up with a masterpiece —we have read that. But whoever turns to incantation, just as whoever turns to reasoning, seizes the word. (And might it not be that all Mr. Green's titles go back in turn to one word, that *Living* is the generic title of all his work?) With its vigor, its true gaiety, its satire quick as a nerve, with its tireless glow of beauty, with its blessed oddity, work which has many a strange and never a ponderous line in it, you are left free to find as you will: it is presented as and for itself only, and this to me fills it to the brim with "what it means": itself.

Here the world is always right up against our eyes. The characters are shown doing the daily kind of thing, dining, working, bathing, sleeping, dancing (they can nearly all dance, barring a missing leg, and you know they are going to keep on dancing), making love, sitting in pubs and nightclubs and movies, meeting, talking, talking, but nearly always failing to get much further along with it. As Henry Green proceeds with them we are given matchless descriptions of indolence itself, of sleep itself, of moving through woods, through streets of cities, through rooms and gardens of houses, through times of secrecy and of driving emotion, of hallucination, of pain and plain giddiness, through a dream or a factory, a toy shop or a railway station, through fire. What is typical and what is incalculable about people are set forth with no favoritism shown. Mr. Green has imagined characters of a free range in kind and sensibilities and age, of an average sanity (some at both ends), and all of them—Birmingham factory workers, the young of Mayfair, the men of the Auxiliary Fire Service, the servants in an Irish castle, the bereaved soldier coming back to life from the war, tomorrow's forgotten sage surrounded by schoolmistresses of the State and schoolgirls lost or hiding in the wild—all these are people who are ordinary inside their world and might have stepped into being as part of their year of origin. Though *Party Going* may happen in Limbo, and *Concluding*—that novel of projections, protractions, long shots, and shadows flying ahead, a slow fall—does happen, we are told (1948) in the near future, these obliquely seen settings only increase the sense of *today's* life dying. In these novels— and only their titles can, and do, begin to describe them—place and time are mortally real, and the characters and happenings of the imagination rise up by the grace of the time and place, but their life is on the instant their own, each is a single and separate spirit, and in much the same way the life of each novel is peculiarly and intensely its own. How strong everywhere do we feel the power of the personal, its power all but incredible. When London starts to burn at the end of *Caught*, with the holocaust in our faces, what we cry is "At last!" for Richard Roe.

Mr. Green takes delight in his characters, and it is not more than we take. He explains none, exploits none; he is just without solemnity, satirical without malice; he never deprecates them or sums them up, doesn't inflate them, diminishes nothing that they feel, he can be at one with their spirits, he is at home with them all. He seems equally free of bitterness, boyishness, ridicule, and religious pranks where they are concerned. His sympathy is even quicker than his wit, not to be caught up with. Only a man of reason, we feel, is likely to be so aware of and so fascinated by the irrational in human motive and behavior; only an artist could show the extraordinary aspects of behavior in ordinary people and suggest, without robbing them at all, where they keep the kernel of their singularity, which as in the fairy tales is well guarded but not too well guarded.

The events in these novels could be said to hang upon how well the characters find out and keep hold of who they are, often by feeling where it hurts or how it pinches; whereupon they take up some fresh responsibility for the self to the self and (always) at least one other; and not a man among them will so slip as to do this heroically, but rather by the accident of circumstance, by the pull of the instinct of self-preservation, by falling for a girl.

In each novel, the characters within its world are busy, no matter what happens, *making* a world—with the hands perhaps, but certainly with the emotions; something will get positively pulled into shape, patched together, to hold on to against time and death. The characters would like well enough to speak to each other, but most of them are like us, not good at it. But they can create. To create is, after all, easier than to communicate—fantastic truth. Even if it is a creation of self-deception, they can throw together for the time being a little peace, goodness, gaiety, creature comfort, they can feather the nest, and this success is the sweeter because it is loneliness that is getting cheated and what they are making turns out, some way, to be love. They can make at least a partial settlement with life, on the basis that intimacy comes to be a fair substitute for understanding.

Even when the events in their lives are themselves of frail import, what underlies these is major, some plain deal from what life has in store. This may be unstated, may be ambiguous, and ambiguity may be the novel's origin, as in *Back*. Always at the core of the book is common experience, mystifying or not—but then, it always will be, for in every novel it is given that much powerful immediacy.

There is no lack of the sinister in Henry Green's work, of horror and violence; they are present as the fact that the day brings forth, the fiction showing the characters' response to the daily fact. Their horror as well as their delight can tell what they feel they are looking for, the implication they find or miss or lose and mourn, how much they can resist or share or get the better of. Their tragedy this writer knows and accommodates, their comedy he runs out to meet.

Henry Green has shown to what lasting pleasure that nothing about the revelation of humankind requires that it be solemn. Some of his most brilliant insight makes for highest comedy. Nor is the comic confined to the novels of comedy; he makes it appear to enter at will, its own, as in life, and even in the midst of horror we will meet with an insight of such intensity that it could have come in at that moment by no other door. Humor is not a relief, as beauty is not a decoration; all that can be said is that there occur, when these qualities appear, highly sensitive spots where you are surest to hear the pulsebeat of the fiction.

In his love scenes, and there have been many of many kinds since Lily began beating time on Mr. Dale's arm to the cinema band in *Living*, there is never any question as to love's presence. How well he can convey pleasure and pain and the suspense both carry! Love and anger, at the moment we confront them in everyday life, are apt to seem as experiences brand-new; and *were* they so, they could not half so seriously challenge the novelist. Perhaps what Henry Green is able to do, through some power of concentration, is to *see* them new. In his scenes, when emotion strikes us, it may be by the shock of what first seems new that we are led so truly to recognize the familiar.

There is nothing mystical but everything mysterious in what

this writer sees and makes of a given set of experiences. For it is a fact in life, certainly, and is Richard Roe's complaint when he tries to describe the blitz on London to his sister-in-law: you can't explain "difficult" things "ordinarily." And what is not difficult? The Green characters in their experiences—some that hurt or try to walk over them, some that hold out promise of comfort and change and, who knows, maybe more —live through fits and starts, fevers, caprices, dreams and terrors and chases and obsessions, oblivion malign or benign, while simply doing the daily thing. And there is always a wild appropriateness about the business. Nobody steps out of line for long to take a roaring stand or to wave his fist, hardly anybody is going to make that kind of fool of himself. I suppose failure of the understanding is what they go on enjoying or suffering from—a wasting disease: we have it. It's like vulnerability, though—being our own private complaint, it has its charms. But meanness of heart, inhumanity, is the foe, the real and awesome foe; it is all the dangers of the future in one, and so real at any given moment as to all but paralyze the spirit— yet so far, we can still cheat paralysis. Whether it be from the inhumanity of the war in *Caught* or from that of hateful, withered Miss Edge in *Concluding*, something is saved. Native, cranky, frolicking, magnificent willfulness has been our blessing. And the pet peeve, the private joke shared, the hope of a stolen kiss, like the thought of tomorrow, is as hard to dislodge as any passion.

Henry Green seems to me to be a romantic artist who has chosen to write from inside the labyrinth of everyday life, whose senses and whose temperament are and have remained romantic and whose reason and experience are lying in wait for the romantic at every turn. So all the novels make new departures. Too much must have always been at stake to stop for the conventions of the novel, and he has done away with scaffolding, with one prop after another, as rapidly as his contemporaries seem to have added them, as promptly as he disposed of the "the" in *Living*. (A still earlier novel, begun while he was at Eton, was published while he was still up at Oxford, not available here as far as I know, but with the title one whale of a prop went down: *Blindness*.) What matters most is that the feeling which the early *Living* revealed must have already been more than he could use; but for the feeling, there could never have come the need that has kept pressing this writer to experiment again. For what he wanted in writing his fiction was to communicate: "Prose is not to be read aloud but to oneself alone at night, and it is not quick as poetry, but rather a gathering web of insinuations which go further than names however shared can ever go. Prose should be a long intimacy between strangers with no direct appeal to what both have known. It should slowly appeal to feelings unexpressed, it should in the end draw tears out of the stone."

After a rapid-fire quintet of almost uncannily *seen* novels, each a major work of his, and how dissimilar they are—*Party Going, Loving, Caught, Back, Concluding*—the next, and then the last so far, are provided with key settings and then the characters open their mouths and raise their novels from scratch. Henry Green can do this because, for all his justly renowned ear for the way people talk, he has the gift beyond that of turning what people say into the fantasy of what they are telling each other, at the same time calling up out of their own mouths their vital spirit. His ear is the organ of his sense of comedy as, it might be imagined, his eye is that of tragedy. And how well this novelist knows and conveys what is wordless, as he makes us aware of those tracts in mind and heart too dark since the beginning for eye to see into. His novels are as charged with feeling beyond the feeling stated as their landscapes are alive with birds.

I seem to remember that readers who only wanted *Loving* again said that *Nothing* and *Doting*, when they appeared, were frivolous novels. But aren't these novels *about* frivolity, which is part of the everyday world along with the murder in the next street and the rose in the garden—with us, within us. As when in *Caught* Henry Green makes a tragic novel out of wartime London and its night lit by unnatural passion and inhuman fire and "the intense impartiality of moonlight," in *Nothing* and *Doting* he makes comic novels out of the pinch and press of a postwar middle age. The working class was unfamiliar matter for a novel too, in 1931, when *Living* rushed forth like a pear tree into bloom on a black morning. It was from this novel, set as it was in drabness and monotony, that it became clear that Henry Green had a gift of gaiety more dazzling than any of his contemporaries, and more dazzling than his youngers have today, I think.

Different as they are from one another, all Henry Green's novels are likely on first impact to seem at once odd and oddly familiar. One reason must be that they touch, as they always do, uncommonly close to the quick of experience. Another reason may be that when after moving you as they do they come to an end, they do not (I think) release you, like the more orthodox novels and like the greatest novels. Particularly do you stand a chance of being left in the power of *Concluding* —of all that has deliberately not been said, has been mysteriously implied. The spell comes each time from his style, a fact which explains nothing, for style is as mysterious a thing as any spell.

The structure of a Green sentence is as eccentric and as purposeful as a Faulkner sentence. But the physical character of Henry Green's prose is no more like William Faulkner's than it is like anybody else's. The short, spare, dealing-out sentences, made up of one- and two-syllable words, the only long words being perhaps the given names of women or the young, are designed to convey what is happening in the action, of course, but designed just as often to convey emotion. The sentences are short but they are glancing—the effect can be magically exhilarating: as when the knife thrower does not pierce but surrounds the living target, and it is the reader whose heart is thereby found. If these short sentences have the look of simplicity, let no simplifier try to copy what they do. And the long sentences, lengthy with unsimple modifications and qualifications, that this master of imagery constructs with hardly ever a use of the word "like," are above all *precise* in their ordering. He has shown best of any writer I know that no power may be exercised with greater precision than the power of suggestion. Henry Green's imagery is evocation by precision and also by grace of daring, which as in every true artist's case may be the ordinary act of the passion to see. Not to copy what is there to his knowledge, but to show you what is there as alive, basically inviolate, a person or a moment in time—this is what he does in prose, and to show you a thing this tender and fragile is to invite disaster and to escape it by a hairsbreadth. Yet novels that have been this risky for the writer to write seem in an odd way so reliable for the reader to read, the only safe place to lay some faith in this world, and I find in the paradox something characteristic of Henry Green.

Certainly he risks more than we readers can know. (Indeed, it goes without saying, there is a superb lack of fuss in any of his work.) *Party Going* is a novel that might be all an image in itself, satirically conceived, mysteriously complicated, held like the long breath of enchantment. The shape of it might be a turning arabesque, delicate and shimmering as the threads in the stem of a wineglass, that, after the novel becomes part of your memory, seems as sobering and sad as a monument destined to stand in its lonely park after you have passed by. You may look back on this satiric yet tender story of the young and gilded and see the monument in it, raised indeed to their "going," and since you have been inside you know the interior vistas, whose dimensions may take on more and more a Piranesian scale.

While *Party Going* is a continuous visual experience, *Nothing* (which might be about some of *Party Going*'s characters twenty years later—this is where they went) and then *Doting* assume forms you are aware of almost kinetically, as you are of the juggling act in *Doting*. In this latest novel of Mr. Green's, through dialogue alone, one pair of characters, now another, are set in bantering motion, at the right moment

the odd third is introduced, then the even fourth gently insinu-
ated, and presently the whole set are brought into play with a
brilliant finale that recalls and smiles back on the beginning.
(Arthur Middleton has only to make one spill to bring down
the whole thing and he is allowed precisely the moment to do
it.)

We may not be used even yet to imagery that can be small
as a proper name, large as a whole novel, or even something we
cannot see; to forms of construction as fully and subtly realized; to symbols as looming or as fleeting or as weightless and
free as his, and as subject to mutation; even to the sources he
so readily takes them from—geography, the animal kingdom,
the machine parts in a factory, anywhere but out of a book.
There are some of great power that are more felt than seen,
that are so strong that the curiosity is stirred as to whether
these might be not too far removed from those first pictures
in the mind that later became the novels.

In all that he writes the senses play their part, and a great
one. Amabel coming out of her bath in the station hotel in
Party Going is something that on the face of it I feel Colette
has never done better, yet Colette, I believe, at such moments
submerges identity when Henry Green intends to state it. He
can walk through walls of consciousness and down the corri-
dors of the senses, as it is obvious he can walk through walls
of class in English society, with a step so light that it is like
the future's, and nothing in the novel appears altered by it;
his regard goes in, his word comes out, the effect is of transmu-
tation.

He has both solved and set up a fair number of problems in
the novel, along his way. He leaves out a good deal that we are
accustomed to, such as omniscient explanations of motive in
the characters; and human behavior thereby seems for the
moment as phenomenal as it must be in truth. The moon seen
in partial eclipse tells us something moonlike that the big broad
shiner doesn't, and the phenomenal is simply the usual on view
with the coziness sheared off. Mr. Green does not tell you

what his characters think nor assume their points of view; he sees through no single mind. (Yes, in *Back* he does—do not generalize about this author; but the mind of Charley Summers, that the war has set to working in strange ways, is that novel's territory, is back of *Back*.)

And all the time, with all his resources, he is telling us, I think, how extraordinarily different all ordinary human beings can be from one another. It takes the extraordinary writer to tell us this, and never to mention it in words; but indeed it is only as long as there are writers like himself able to imply that the unique is blessed and gives us blessing, that life on earth is still being celebrated.

What is unmistakable is that Henry Green is inside his character's *world*, totally and literally, down to the last inch they fill up in their boots and from the moment they open their nearly always big eyes. In *Loving*, the landscape pulses with a fairy-tale glow and the characters, themselves aglow, rarely even see it. The sinister world of *Concluding* is, if possible, still more beautiful, side-lit and colored like an undersea kingdom (it is the welfare state of the future)—and Mr. Rock sees it, as with the finally satisfied gaze of farewell; but *Loving*, in scene after scene spread as at the strokes of a wand, is the seducing one; and it is through your eyes you know it for the world of *sans souci*. *Loving*'s own characters simply respond to it—in play, through the motions of a dream or game of blindfold, in dancing together, or perhaps in the sandy-eyed oblivion of a picnic by the edge of the sea; on further thought, it's a hundred times better than that: Edith, when she looks out on the morning, "the soft bright morning that struck her dazzled dazzling eyes," is at least near to being herself what that world is.

There is no need to say whether such writing is of the exterior or the interior world. With the old man of *Concluding*, his granddaughter, and the starlings at evening, with "the enormous echo of the blood, or of the sea," where does the line come? What the poet, and he is this, has found most explicit about life was clear to him before the line between exterior and interior was ever invented.

You never see Henry Green, he takes up no space as the author. But though he has never intruded the self, you feel his authorship continuously and pervasively because his novels have a mind—an acute, subtle, impartial mind, a partial disposition, and a temperament that streaks the most marvelous color through the work. He is there at the center of what he writes, but in effect his identity has turned into the fiction. And while you the reader know nothing of Mr. Henry Green's life, as he has taken good care to see to, in the long run a life's confidence is what you feel you have been given.

This author seems to say: if the transitory cannot be held fast, it can be made to seem more itself, can have its intensity matched in words, to persist there. He uses artifice, uses "naturalism," symbols, every device at his command and there are many, but his work in long and best result lies at the other extreme from the artificial, in the open country of poetry. In *Pack My Bag*, the "self-portrait" from which came the lines quoted above, the author suggests it is the common memory he addresses himself to and that will respond. Surely his concern, like his delight, his hope implied, his deepest feeling, seems to abide in indelibility in the face of chaos, and through his novels, in every one, a shape for indelibility is what he has made.

And this, discovering a shape or pattern to some set of experiences, is the way we all take of imagining what life is up to. I think the novelist through the long act of writing evolves his pattern, and it is this resulting and unpredictable thing, which was intuitive but discernible only through art, that is impressed, without announcement, on the mind of the reader in a way not to be put into words but all the more greatly to be felt. Indelibility itself is subjective, is an image; and with the kite up it is so much better not to talk kite at all. Because if it flies, a marvelous one-time-only construction in thin air, that is everything, that is enough.

It is true that passages like the one about Mr. Rock and the starlings at evening are not only indelible in themselves, they have the aura of indelibility about them. The ears seem to ring when we come to them on the page. They seem frank soaring over and above the thing at hand, intensifications both deliberate and justified; not showing off, though who else could write them, but serving a purpose, the most serious. Virtuosity, unless it move the heart, goes at the head of the whole parade to dust. With Henry Green we always come back to this: this work is so moving. Some scenes and paragraphs have a quality of being offered—to the moment itself? To life?

Surely each novel written stands as something of a feat. For what has been done? First ask, what was the heart's desire? Not the creating of an illusion, but the restoring of one; something brought off. We are not children once we have pasts; and now as we come looking in fiction with more longing than in any experience save love, but to which love adds, looking for reflections and visions of all life we know compounded through art, performance itself is what we ask for. We ask only that it be magic. Good fiction grants this boon, bad denies it. And performance is what the novelist would like to give— a fresh performance; not to show off skill, which would be (as obviously in the case of the pseudonymous Henry Green) a thing to be despised, but, out of respect, love, and fearlessness for all that may be tried, to command the best skill.

As told in *Pack My Bag*, Henry Green was born in 1905; this is only 1961. His novels so far are dissimilar enough to suggest that their whole, whenever he chooses to draw this line, which one hopes is a time out of sight, will have a meaning then to be looked at for the whole; yet it has always seemed that his whole meaning expressed will be more than the sum of its parts. These eight together make it plain that his focus, instantaneously seen to be sharp and clear, is also wide and clear; they show us the sweep of his sympathies and the drive and control of his feelings, and we know that there has been no stopping of him technically. His grasp of imaginative construction alone is altogether astonishing. He has not shown a sign of repeating himself, unless this could be said in some respects of *Nothing* and *Doting*, and it was said; even so, the repeat in itself is remarkable, as if Daniel had got out of the lions' den twice in a row.

As to what his work is doing all along for the development of the novel, I doubt if it is able to do much. And why would we think this an additional good? Better than any influence is the living artist, and we here are the ones who can now read. The novel will take care of itself, or else it will perish. And it is for themselves to tell what the readers of the future will think of Henry Green. But a writer so consistently intuitive does seem to have a good chance of speaking to the future, and one so original, it is to be hoped, will to any generation have something to say. It can be believed that he will if *they* have something to say. This much can also be remarked now, that from the first his best has stood for experiment and must continue to stand for this, that it will not be on Henry Green's head if the novel for its life does not look to its own future rather than to its past.

Reading and writing can each teach us something, eventually, about the other, though it is nothing to brag about. Because fiction flows so close by our door, jumping with words that we use every day and all of them to do with men and women like ourselves, there is too much thanking heaven for the novel as one art that is easy to understand, to explain, even explain away. But a novel ought to at least start out by being able to stump us. As for explaining one, I could say that *Concluding* is like Venus on a clear evening going down over water, and if you agreed—still worse if you disagreed—where are we now? No, we must go back into the pages of the book to recognize it. A novel outside its own terms, which never were explanatory, no longer exists; in the course of being written it apprehended all the reality it could, drank up all the existence around it. Further words, even the author's, could add nothing to what is now complete, any more than they could by being hung around the neck of a statue. Reading can teach us something, and it is endless, about *reading*, about meeting with art.

After Monet was impelled to break up pigment to convey light, so that a new kind of color poured alive through those fissured walls, now a Monet painting is a place you can never go. And neither is a novel by Henry Green the land you thought you knew. His work indeed does not represent life, it presents life. What you discover about it is not the "key" to it, not the "secret" of his work, which is his only, anyway, but the experience of giving your regard to beauty, to wonder. There you have come slap up against the reality of fiction.

And everybody who can read knows that by fishing a sentence out of a novel, to spread like a captured sea serpent on the bank with the color going out of it, the creature's scales can be counted; but in the element where it lived it was, to begin with, not a monster. The element is illusion, the words that bathed in it were induced into these waters at the source, and these brought the river with them. And the landscape as far as you can see it is its dream.

Now that each passing day makes some threat or other not only against continuing reality on earth but against our illusion of it, it is the reading of novels by one of ourselves that we live on as never before, and this is not absurd, for in novels, if they are good, life on earth is intensified in its personal meaning, and so restored to human terms. We are surer of the existence of our world for the thousand evidences to which Henry Green swears in his fiction, and I think swears is not too strong a word. Also, we are that much surer of what we can laugh about. For at least our lifetime, and who can say further about the roof we sit under to read, his fiction will be part of the mind; it will travel as fast as we do, as far as we go, in its excellence and delight and beauty.

(1961)

Katherine Anne Porter: The Eye of the Story

~§

In "Old Mortality" how stirring the horse race is! At the finish the crowd breaks into its long roar "like the falling walls of Jericho." This we hear, and it is almost like seeing, and we know Miss Lucy has won. But beyond a fleeting glimpse—the "mahogany streak" of Miss Lucy on the track—we never get much sight of the race with our eyes. What we see comes afterward. Then we have it up close: Miss Lucy bleeding at the nose. For Miranda has got to say "That's winning too." The race would never have got into the story except that Miranda's heart is being prepared to reject victory, to reject the glamour of the race and the cheering grandstand; to distrust from now on all evidence except what she, out of her own experience, can testify to. By the time we *see* Miss Lucy, she is a sight for Miranda's eyes alone: as much symbol as horse.

Most good stories are about the interior of our lives, but Katherine Anne Porter's stories take place there; they show surface only at her choosing. Her use of the physical world is enough to meet her needs and no more; she is not wasteful with anything. This artist, writing her stories with a power that stamps them to their last detail on the memory, does so to an extraordinary degree without sensory imagery.

I have the most common type of mind, the visual, and when first I began to read her stories it stood in the way of my trust in my own certainty of what was there that, for all my being bowled over by them, I couldn't see them happening. This was a very good thing for me. As her work has done in many other respects, it has shown me a thing or two about the eye of fiction, about fiction's visibility and invisibility, about its clarity, its radiance.

Heaven knows she can see. Katherine Anne Porter has seen all her life, sees today, most intimately, most specifically, and down to the bones, and she could date the bones. There is, above all, "Noon Wine" to establish it forever that when she wants a story to be visible, it is. "Noon Wine" is visible all the way through, full of scenes charged with dramatic energy; everything is brought forth into movement, dialogue; the title itself is Mr. Helton's tune on the harmonica. "Noon Wine" is the most beautifully objective work she has done. And nothing has been sacrificed to its being so (or she wouldn't have done it); to the contrary. I find Mr. Hatch the scariest character she ever made, and he's just set down there in Texas like a chair. There he stands, part of the everyday furniture of living. He's opaque, and he's the devil. Walking in at Mr. Thompson's gate —the same gate by which his tracked-down victim walked in first—he is that much more horrifying, almost too solid to the eyes to be countenanced. (So much for the visual mind.)

Katherine Anne Porter has not in general chosen to cast her stories in scenes. Her sense of human encounter is profound, is fundamental to her work, I believe, but she has not often allowed it the dramatic character it takes in "Noon Wine." We may not see the significant moment happen within the story's present; we may not watch it occur between the two characters it joins. Instead, a silent blow falls while one character is alone—the most alone in his life, perhaps. (And this is the case in "Noon Wine" too.) Often the revelation that pierces a character's mind and heart and shows him his life or his death comes in a dream, in retrospect, in illness or in utter defeat, the moment of vanishing hope, the moment of dying. What Miss Porter makes us see are those subjective worlds of hallucination, obsession, fever, guilt. The presence of death hovering about Granny Weatherall she makes as real and brings as near as Granny's own familiar room that stands about her bed—realer, nearer, for we recognize not only death's presence but the character death has come in for Granny Weatherall.

The flash of revelation is revelation but is unshared. But how unsuspecting we are to imagine so for a moment—it *is* shared, and by ourselves, her readers, who must share it feeling the doubled anguish of knowing this fact, doubled still again when it is borne in upon us how close to life this is, to *our* lives.

It is to be remembered that the world of fiction is not of itself visible. A story may or may not be born in sensory images in a given writer's mind. Experience itself is stored in no telling how many ways in a writer's memory. (It was "the sound of the sea, and Beryl fanning her hair at the window" that years later and thousands of miles away brought Katherine Mansfield to writing "At the Bay.") But if the physical world *is* visible or audible in the story, it has to be made so. Its materialization is as much a created thing as are the story's characters and what they think or do or say.

Katherine Anne Porter shows us that we do not have to see a story happen to know what is taking place. For all we are to know, she is not looking at it happen herself when she writes it; for her eyes are always looking through the gauze of the passing scene, not distracted by the immediate and transitory; her vision is reflective.

Her imagery is as likely as not to belong to a time other than the story's present, and beyond that it always differs from it in nature; it is *memory* imagery, coming into the story from memory's remove. It is a distilled, a re-formed imagery, for it is part of a language made to speak directly of premonition, warning, surmise, anger, despair.

It was soon borne in upon me that Katherine Anne Porter's moral convictions have given her readers another way to see.

Surely these convictions represent the fixed points about which her work has turned, and not only that, but they govern her stories down to the smallest detail. Her work has formed a constellation, with its own North Star.

Is the writer who does not give us the pictures and bring us the sounds of a story as it unfolds shutting out part of life? In Katherine Anne Porter's stories the effect has surely been never to diminish life but always to intensify life in the part significant to her story. It is a darkening of the house as the curtain goes up on this stage of her own.

Her stories of Mexico, Germany, Texas all happen there: where love and hate, trust and betrayal happen. And so their author's gaze is turned not outward but inward, and has confronted the mysterious dark from her work's beginning.

Since her subject is what lies beneath the surface, her way—quite direct—is to penetrate, brush the stuff away. It is the writer like Chekhov whose way of working is indirect. He moved indeed toward the same heart and core but by building up some corresponding illusion of life. Writers of Chekhov's side of the family are themselves illusionists and have necessarily a certain fondness for, lenience toward, the whole shimmering fabric as such. Here we have the professional scientist, the good doctor, working with illusion and the born romantic artist—is she not?—working without it. Perhaps it is always the lyrical spirit that takes on instantaneous color, shape, pattern of motion in work, while the meditative spirit must fly as quickly as possible out of the shell.

All the stories she has written are moral stories about love and the hate that is love's twin, love's impostor and enemy and death. Rejection, betrayal, desertion, theft roam the pages of her stories as they roam the world. The madam kicking the girl in "Magic" and the rest of the brutality in the characters' treatment of one another; the thieving that in one form or another infects their relationships; the protests they make, from the weakness of false dreams or of lying down with a cold cloth over the eyes, on up to towering rages—all this is a way of showing to the inward eye: Look at what you are doing to human love.

We hear in how many more stories than the one the litany of the little boy at the end of "The Downward Path to Wisdom," his "comfortable, sleeping song": "I hate Papa, I hate Mama, I hate Grandma, I hate Uncle David, I hate Old Janet, I hate Marjory, I hate Papa, I hate Mama . . ." It is like the long list of remembered losses in the story "Theft" made vocal, and we remember how that loser's decision to go on and let herself be robbed coincides with the rising "in her blood" of a "deep almost murderous anger."

"If one is afraid of looking into a face, one hits the face," remarked W. B. Yeats, and I think we must conclude that to Katherine Anne Porter's characters this face is the challenging face of love itself. And I think it is the faces—the inner, secret faces—of her characters, in their self-delusion, their venom and pain, that their author herself is contemplating. More than either looking at the face or hitting it, she has made a story out of her anger.

If outrage is the emotion she has most strongly expressed, she is using outrage as her cool instrument. She uses it with precision to show what monstrosities of feeling come about not from the lack of the existence of love but from love's repudiation, betrayal. From which there is no safety anywhere. Granny Weatherall, eighty, wise, affectionate and good, and now after a full life dying in her bed with the priest beside her, "knew hell when she saw it."

The anger that speaks everywhere in the stories would trouble the heart for their author whom we love except that her anger is pure, the reason for it evident and clear, and the effect exhilarating. She has made it the tool of her work; what we do is rejoice in it. We are aware of the compassion that guides it, as well. Only compassion could have looked where she looks, could have seen and probed what she sees. Real compassion is perhaps always in the end unsparing; it must make itself a part of knowing. Self-pity does not exist here;

these stories come out trenchant, bold, defying; they are tough as sanity, unrelinquished sanity, is tough.

Despair is here, as well described as if it were Mexico. It is a despair, however, that is robust and sane, open to negotiation by the light of day. Life seen as a savage ordeal has been investigated by a straightforward courage, unshaken nerve, a rescuing wit, and above all, with the searching intelligence that is quite plainly not to be daunted. In the end the stories move us not to despair ourselves but to an emotion quite opposite because they are so seriously and clear-sightedly pointing out what they have been formed to show: that which is true under the skin, that which will remain a fact of the spirit.

Miranda, by the end of "Old Mortality" rebelling against the ties of the blood, resenting their very existence, planning to run away now from these and as soon as she can from her own escape into marriage, Miranda saying "I hate loving and being loved," is hating what destroys loving and what prevents being loved. She is, in her own particular and her own right, fighting back at the cheat she has discovered in all that's been handed down to her as gospel truth.

Seeing what is not there, putting trust in a false picture of life, has been one of the worst nightmares that assail her characters. "My dreams never renege on me, Mr. Richards. They're all I have to go by," says Rosaleen. (The Irish are no better than the Southerners in this respect.) Not only in the comic and touching Rosaleen, the lovely and sentient and tragic Miranda, but in many other characters throughout the stories we watch the romantic and the anti-romantic pulling each other to pieces. Is the romantic ever scotched? I believe not. Even if there rises a new refrain, even if the most ecstatic words ever spoken turn out to be "I hate you," the battle is not over for good. That battle is in itself a romance.

Nothing is so naturally subject to false interpretation as the romantic, and in furnishing that interpretation the Old South can beat all the rest. Yet some romantic things happen also to be true. Miss Porter's stories are not so much a stand against the romantic as such, as a repudiation of the false. What alone can instruct the heart is the experience of living, experience which can be vile; but what can never do it any good, what harms it more than vileness, are those tales, those legends of more than any South, those universal false dreams, the hopes sentimental and ubiquitious, which are not on any account to be gone by.

For there comes a confrontation. It is then that Miss Porter's characters, behaving so entirely like ourselves, make the fatally wrong choice. Enter betrayal. Again and again, enter betrayal. We meet the betrayal that lies in rejection, in saying No to others or No to the self, or that lies with still more cunning in saying Yes when this time it should have been No.

And though we are all but sure what will happen, we are possessed by suspense.

It appears to me irrelevant whether or not the story is conceived and put down in sensory images, whether or not it is dramatic in construction, so long as its hold is a death-grip. In my own belief, the suspense—so acute and so real—in Katherine Anne Porter's work never did depend for its life on disclosure of the happenings of the narrative (nothing is going to turn out very well) but in the writing of the story, which becomes one single long sustained moment for the reader. Its suspense is one with its meaning. It must arise, then, from the mind, heart, spirit by which it moves and breathes.

It is a current like a strand of quicksilver through the serenity of her prose. In fiction of any substance, serenity can only be an achievement of the work itself, for any sentence that is alive with meaning is speaking out of passion. Serenity never belonged to the *now* of writing; it belongs to the later *now* offered its readers. In Katherine Anne Porter's work the forces of passion and self-possession seem equal, holding each other in balance from one moment to the next. The suspense born of the writing abides there in its own character, using the story for its realm, a quiet and well-commanded suspense, but a genie.

There was an instinct I had, trustworthy or not, that the matter of visibility in her stories had something to do with time. Time permeates them. It is a grave and formidable force.

Ask what time it is in her stories and you are certain to get the answer: the hour is fateful. It is not necessary to see the hands of the clock in her work. It is a time of racing urgency, and it is already too late. And then recall how many of her characters are surviving today only for the sake of tomorrow, are living on tomorrow's coming; think how we see them clearest in reference to tomorrow. Granny Weatherall, up to the last—when God gives her no sign acceptable to her and jilts her Himself—is thinking: "There was always so much to be done, let me see: tomorrow." Laura in "Flowering Judas" is "waiting for tomorrow with a bitter anxiety as if tomorrow may not come." Ordinary, self-respecting and—up to a certain August day—fairly well blessed Mr. Thompson, because he has been the one to kill the abominable Mr. Hatch, is self-tried, self-pleaded for, and self-condemned to no tomorrow; neither does he leave his sons much of a tomorrow, and certainly he leaves still less of one to poor, red-eyed Mrs. Thompson, who had "so wanted to believe that tomorrow, or at least the day after, life, such a battle at best, was going to be better." In "Old Mortality" time takes Miranda by the hand and leads her into promising herself "in her hopefulness, her ignorance": "At least I can know the truth about what happens to me." In "Pale Horse, Pale Rider" the older Miranda asks Adam, out of her suffering, "Why can we not save each other?" and the straight answer is that there is no time. The story ends with the unforgettable words "Now there would be time for everything" because tomorrow has turned into oblivion, the ultimate betrayer is death itself.

But time, one of the main actors in her stories—teacher, fake healer, conspirator in betrayal, ally of death—is also, within the complete control of Miss Porter, with his inimical powers made use of, one of the movers of her writing, a friend to her work. It occurred to me that what is *seeing* the story is the dispassionate eye of time. Her passionate mind has asked itself, schooled itself, to use time's eye. Perhaps Time is the genie's name.

Laura is stuck in time, we are told in "Flowering Judas"— and told in the timeless present tense of dreaming, a brilliant working upon our very nerves to let us know precisely Laura's dilemma. There is in all Katherine Anne Porter's work the strongest sense of unity in all the parts; and if it is in any degree a sound guess that an important dramatic element in the story has another role, a working role, in the writing of the story, might this not be one source of a unity so deeply felt? Such a thing in the practice of an art is unsurprising. Who can separate a story from the story's writing?

And there is too, in all the stories, a sense of long, learning life, the life that is the story's own, beginning from very far back, extending somewhere into the future. As we read, the initial spark is not being struck before our eyes; the fire we see has already purified its nature and burns steadied by purpose, unwavering in meaning. It is no longer impulse, it is a signal, a beacon.

To me, it is the image of the eye of time that remains the longest in the mind at her story's end. There is a judgment to be passed. A moral judgment has to be, in all reason, what she has been getting at. But in a still further act of judiciousness, I feel, she lets Time pass that judgment.

Above all, I feel that what we are responding to in Katherine Anne Porter's work is the intensity of its life, which is more powerful and more profound than even its cry for justice.

They are excoriating stories. Does she have any hope for us at all? Well, do we not feel its implication everywhere—a desperate hope for the understanding that may come, if we use great effort, out of tomorrow, or if not then, maybe the day after? Clearly it has to become at some point an act of faith. It is toward this that her stories all point: here, it seems to me, is the North Star.

And how calm is the surface, the invisible surface of it all!

In a style as invisible as the rhythm of a voice, and as much her own as her own voice, she tells her stories of horror and humiliation and in the doing fills her readers with a rising joy. The exemplary prose that is without waste or extravagance or self-indulgence or display, without any claim for its triumph, is full of pride. And her reader shares in that pride, as well he might: it is pride in the language, pride in using the language to search out human meanings, pride in the making of a good piece of work. A personal spell is about the stories, the something of her own that we refer to most often, perhaps, when we mention its beauty, and I think this comes from the *making* of the stories.

Readers have long been in the habit of praising (or could it be at times reproaching?) Katherine Anne Porter by calling her a perfectionist. I do not agree that this is the highest praise, and I would think the word misleading, suggesting as it does in the author a personal vanity in technique and a rigidity, even a deadness, in her prose. To me she is something more serious than a perfectionist. I celebrate her for being a blessed achiever. First she is an artist, of course, and as an artist she is an achiever.

That she hasn't wasted precious time repeating herself in her stories is sign enough, if it were needed, that she was never interested in doing the thing she knew already that she was able to bring off, that she hasn't been showing off for the sake of high marks (from whom?), but has patiently done what was to her her born necessity, quietly and in her own time, and each time the way she saw fit.

We are left with a sense of statement. Virginia Woolf set down in her diary, on the day when she felt she had seen that great brave difficult novel *The Waves* past a certain point in the writing: "But I think it possible that I have got my statues against the sky." It is the achieving of this crucial, this monumental moment in the work itself that we feel has mattered to Katherine Anne Porter. The reader who looks for the flawless result can find it, but looking for that alone he misses the true excitement, exhilaration, of reading, of rereading. It is the achieving—in a constant present tense—of the work that shines in the mind when we think of her name; and in that achieving lies, it seems to me, the radiance of the work and our recognition of it as unmistakably her own.

And unmistakable is its source. Katherine Anne Porter's deep sense of fairness and justice, her ardent conviction that we need to give and to receive in loving kindness all the human warmth we can make—here is where her stories come from. If they are made by the mind and address the mind, they draw their eloquence from a passionate heart. And for all their pain, they draw their wit, do they not, from a reserve of natural gaiety? I have wondered before now if it isn't those who were born gay who can devote themselves most wholeheartedly in their work to seriousness, who have seriousness to burn. The gay are the rich in feeling, and don't need to save any of it back.

Unmistakable, too, is what this artist has made. Order and form no more spring out of order and form than they come riding in to us upon seashells through the spray. In fiction they have to be made out of their very antithesis, life. The art of making is the thing that has meaning, and I think beauty is likely to be something that has for a time lain under good, patient hands. Whether the finished work of art was easy or hard to make, whether it demanded a few hours or many years, concerns nobody but the maker, but the making itself has shaped that work for good and all. In Katherine Anne Porter's stories we feel their making as a bestowal of grace.

It is out of the response to her particular order and form that I believe I may have learned the simplest and surest reason for why I cannot see her stories in their every passing minute, and why it was never necessary or intended that a reader should. Katherine Anne Porter is writing stories of the spirit, and the time that fills those moments is eternity.

(1965)

The House
of Willa Cather

ം

"More than anything else I felt motion in the landscape; in the fresh, easy-blowing morning wind, and in the earth itself, as if the shaggy grass were a sort of loose hide, and underneath it herds of wild buffalo were galloping, galloping . . ." All Willa Cather's prose, like this passage in *My Ántonia*, speaks of the world in a way to show it's alive. There is a quality of animation that seems naturally come by, that seems a born part of every novel. Her own living world is around us as we read, present to us through our eyes and ears and touch.

Of course, it doesn't escape us that this physical landscape is brought home to us in a way that is subjective. "Overhead the stars shone gloriously. It was impossible not to notice them." "The summer moon hung full in the sky. For the time being it was the great fact in the world." Willa Cather would like our minds to receive what she is showing us not as its description—however beautiful—but as the thing described, the living thing itself. To this end she may eliminate its picture, the better to make us see something really there. It was her observation that "whatever is felt upon the page without being specifically named there—that, one might say, is created." "There were none of the signs of spring for which I used to watch in Virginia," says the narrator of *My Ántonia*. "There was only spring itself, the throb of it . . . If I had been tossed down blindfolded on that red prairie, I should have known that it was spring."

And so the texture, that informs us of so much in her prose, owes more than a little to its function. "It was over flat lands like this . . . that the larks sang." Now we see the land. And hear the lark.

What she has given us is, of course, not the landscape as you and I would see it, but her vision of it; we are looking at a work of art.

There is something very special, too, about its composition. Look at the Nebraska of her novels as a landscape she might have addressed herself to as an artist with a pencil or a brush. There is the foreground, with the living present, its human figures in action; and there is the horizon of infinite distance, where the departed, now invisible ancients have left only their faint track, cliff dwellings all but disappeared into thin air, pure light. But there is no intervening ground. There is no generation preceding the people now here alive to fill up the gap between, to populate the stretch of emptiness. Nobody we can see, except the very youngest child, has been born here. Fathers and mothers traveled here, a few hardy grandparents who kept up will survive the life a little while too, and the rest of the antecedents have been left in their graveyards the width of the continent behind.

In this landscape we are made as aware of what isn't as of what is. There is no recent past. There is no middle distance; the perspectives of time and space run unbroken, unmarked, unmeasured to the vanishing point. With nothing in between, the living foreground and that almost mythological, almost phantasmagorial background are all but made one, as in a Chinese painting—and exactly as in one of the mirages that Willa Cather's people often meet, quite casually, in the desert:

> . . . a shallow silver lake that spread for many miles, a little misty in the sunlight. Here and there one saw re-

flected the image of a heifer, turned loose to live upon the sparse sand grass. They were magnified to a preposterous height and looked like mammoths, prehistoric beasts standing solitary in the waters that for many thousands of years actually washed over that desert: the mirage itself may be the ghost of that long-vanished sea.

Or that ancient life may be discovered through profound personal experience, through one of her "opening windows." Willa Cather brought past and present into juxtaposition to the most powerful effect. And the landscape itself must have shown her this juxtaposition. It existed in the world where she lived, she had eyes to see it, and she made it a truth of her art. When the sword of Coronado and the plow against the sun are fused into one in *My Ántonia*, we are seeing another vision of it.

The past can be seen—she lets us see it—in physical form. It can be touched—Thea can flake off with her thumb the carbon from the rock roof that came from the cooking stove of the Ancient People. Thea comes to have intuitions about their lives so close to heart that she could walk the trail like the women whose feet had worn it, "trying to walk as they must have walked, with a feeling in her feet and loins which she had never known before . . . She could feel the weight of an Indian baby hanging to her back as she climbed."

And so Neil, of a later day, in *A Lost Lady*, feels in saying goodbye to it:

He had seen the end of an era, the sunset of the pioneer. He had come upon it when already its glory was nearly spent. So in the buffalo times a traveller used to come upon the embers of a hunter's fire on the prairie, after the hunter was up and gone; the coals would be trampled out, but the ground was warm, and the flattened grass where he had slept and where his pony had grazed, told the story.

She saw the landscape had mystery as well as reality. She was undaunted by both. And when she writes of the vast spaces of the world lying out in the extending night, mystery comes to her page, and has a presence; it seems to me a presence not too different from that called up by Turgenev in his magical "Behzin Meadow."

Willa Cather saw her broad land in a sweep, but she saw selectively too—the detail that made all the difference. She never lost sight of the particular in the panorama. Her eye was on the human being. In her continuous, acutely conscious and responsible act of bringing human value into focus, it was her accomplishment to bring our gaze from that wide horizon, across the stretches of both space and time, to the intimacy and immediacy of the lives of a handful of human beings.

People she saw slowly, with care, in their differences: her chosen characters. They stood up out of their soil and against their sky, making, each of them and one by one, a figure to reckon with.

"For the first time, perhaps, since that land emerged from the waters of geologic ages," she says of Alexandra in that memorable passage in *O Pioneers!*, "a human face was set toward it with love and yearning. It seemed beautiful to her, rich and strong and glorious. Her eyes drank in the breadth of it, until her tears blinded her. Then the Genius of the Divide, the great, free spirit which breathes across it, must have bent lower than it ever bent to a human will before. The history of every country begins in the heart of a man or a woman."

And the farther and wider she could see when she started out, the closer it brought her, we feel, full circle—to the thing she wanted, the living, uncopyable *identity* of it, that all her working life she wrote in order to meet, to face, to give us as well as she knew it in stories and novels.

The lack of middle distance may have something to do with the way the characters in the foreground cast such long, back-reaching shadows. In that lonely stretch of empty and waiting space, they take on heroic stature. And so, Jim Burden tells us—and this has been earned; we have almost reached the end of her novel:

Ántonia had always been one to leave images in the mind that did not fade—that grew stronger with time . . . She lent herself to immemorial human attitudes which we recognize by instinct as universal and true. She was a battered woman now, not a lovely girl; but she still had that something which fires the imagination, could still stop one's breath for a moment by a look or a gesture that somehow revealed the meaning in common things. She had only to stand in the orchard, to put her hand on a little crab tree and look up at the apples, to make you feel the goodness of planting and tending and harvesting at last. All the strong things of her heart came out in her body . . . She was a rich mine of life, like the founders of early races.

A writer uses what he's been given. The work of William Faulkner—another writer of Southern origin, who was destined himself to live in the thick of his background and who had his own abiding sense of place and time and history—is packed most densely of all at the middle distance. The generations clustered just behind where the present-day characters are in action are in fact the tallest—and the most heavily burdened with that past. Faulkner's ancient peoples, his Indians, whose land was taken away by unjust treaty, who were expelled from their own, their race dispersed and brought to nothing, have made the land inimical to the white man. The slave has cursed him again. History for Faulkner is directly inherited; it has come down to the present with the taint of blood and the shame of wrongdoing a part of it. Along with the qualities of nobility and courage and endurance, there were for him corresponding qualities of guilt; there is torment in history and in Faulkner's wrestling with it, in his interpretation of it. Willa Cather's history was not thus bonded to the present; it did not imprison the present, but instructed it, passed on a meaning. It was pure, remained pure, and in its purity could come and go in crystal air. It had the character and something of the import of a vision. The spirit, and not the blood, received it.

In the world of her novels, history lies in persistence in the memory, in lost hidden places that wait to be found and to be known for what they are. Such history is barely accessible, the shell of it is only fraily held together, it will be loseable again. But the continuity is *there*.

Where does the continuity lie, then? It is made possible, it is carried out, is lived through, by the pioneer. And it is perceived by the artist. And even more profoundly, it exists, for Willa Cather, as a potential in the artist himself; it is his life's best meaning, his own personal, and responsible, connection with the world.

Thea is meditating in Panther Cañon:

That stream was the only thing left of the drama that had been played out in the cañon centuries ago. In the rapid, restless heart of it, flowing swifter than the rest, there was a continuity of life that reached back into the old time . . . The stream and the broken pottery: what was any art but an effort to make a sheath, a mould in which to imprison for a moment the shining, elusive element which is life itself—life hurrying past us and running away, too strong to stop, too sweet to lose? The Indian women had held it in their jars . . . In singing, one made a vessel of one's throat and nostrils and held it on one's breath, caught the stream in a scale of natural intervals.

When Thea holds the ancients' pottery in her hands, her feeling for art is born. When Willa Cather makes her novel one about art, she chooses art not of the word, but of the voice. And not the song, but the voice. She has been able to say everything—it is a dazzling translation—in terms of the human being in a physical world.

The whole work of Willa Cather is an embodiment. The great thing it embodies is, of course, passion. That is its vital principle.

She did not come out of Virginia for nothing, any more than she grew up in Nebraska for nothing. History awed and stirred Willa Cather; and the absence of a history as far as she could see around her, in her growing up, only made her look farther, gave her the clues to discover a deeper past. The scarcity of people, a sense of absence and emptiness, set to work in her mind ideas not of despair but of aspiration, the urgency to make out of whatever was there *something*—a thing of her own. She opened her mind to the past as she would to a wise teacher. When she saw the connections, the natural channels opening, she let the past come flooding into the present.

"To people off alone, as we were, there is something stirring about finding evidences of human labor and care in the soil of an empty country. It comes to you as a sort of message, makes you feel differently about the ground you walk over every day," says Tom Outland in *The Professor's House.*

Willa Cather's story conceptions have their physical bases and their physical counterparts. The shift that took place in her own life when her family moved from its settled home in Virginia to the unbroken prairie of the Divide came about when she was nine years old, so likely to be the most sensitive, most vulnerable year of childhood. Its wrench to the spirit was translated over and over again into the situations in her novels and stories. The shift from one home to another, the shift of feeling, must have become in itself the source of a distinctive fictional pattern which was to fall into place for her; it is the kaleidoscopic wrench to the heart that exposes the deeper feeling there. Not impossibly, the origin of her technique of juxtaposition lay in the Virginia-Nebraska move too. She worked out some of her most significant effects by bringing widely separated lives, times, experiences together—placing them side by side or one within the other, opening out of it almost like a vision—like Tom Outland's story from *The Professor's House*—or existing along with it, waiting in its path, like the mirage.

Personal history may turn into a fictional pattern without closely reproducing it, without needing to reproduce it at all.

Essences are what make patterns. Fictional patterns may well bite deeper than the events of a life will ever of themselves, or by themselves, testify to. The pattern is one of interpretation. There, the connections are as significant as what they join together, or perhaps more so. The meaning comes through the joined and completed structure, out of the worthiness of its accomplishment.

In the novel, relationships, development of acts and their effects, and any number of oblique, *felt* connections, which are as important and as indispensable as the factual ones in composing the plot, form a structure of revelation. The pattern is the plot opened out, disclosing—this was its purpose—some human truth.

Of course, it is a pattern uniquely marked by its author's character; the nature of personal feeling has given it its grain. Willa Cather's revered Flaubert said in a letter, "The secret of masterpieces lies in the concordance between the subject and the temperament of the author." The events of a story may have much or little to do with the writer's own life; but the story *pattern* is the nearest thing to a mirror image of his mind and heart.

The artist needs and seeks distance—his own best distance—in order to learn about his subject. To open up the new, to look back on the old may bring forth like discoveries in the practice of art. Whether their comprehension keeps to the short perimeter around the present or runs far back into the past is secondary to the force, impellment, of human feeling involved: *this* determines its reach.

We need to know only what the work of Willa Cather in its course has to tell us—for it's a great deal—about her independence and courage of mind to guess that Miss Jewett's well-known advice—"You must find a quiet place. You must find your own quiet center of life and write from that"—would not have been the sign to her it was, unless she had arrived at that fact for herself, deep in her own nature. How could she not have? It was central to her life, basic to her conception of character, of situation, in fiction: the writing of one novel had been able to teach her that. When she read that truth of Miss Jewett's, isn't it likely that she simply *recognized* it? As she recognized, in the Dutch masters when she saw them in Paris, her own intention in a book to come:

"Just before I began the book [*The Professor's House*]," runs a well-known letter she wrote, "I had seen, in Paris, an exhibition of old and modern Dutch paintings. In many of them the scene presented was a living-room warmly furnished, or a kitchen full of food and coppers. But in most of the interiors, whether drawing-room or kitchen, there was a square window, open, through which one saw the masts of ships, or a stretch of grey sea. The feeling of the sea that one got through those square windows was remarkable, and gave me a sense of the fleets of Dutch ships that ply quietly on all the waters of the globe."

It is not surprising that the act of recognition is one of the touchstones of her fiction. We see her writing in *The Song of the Lark*: "The faculty of observation was never highly developed in Thea Kronborg. A great deal escaped her eye as she passed through the world. But the things which were for her, she saw; she experienced them physically and remembered them as if they had once been part of herself. The roses she used to see in the florists' shops in Chicago were merely roses. But when she thought of the moonflowers that grew over Mrs. Tellamontez's door, it was as if she had been that vine and had opened up in white flowers every night." And, "Here, in Panther Cañon, there were again things which seemed destined for her."

And before that, ". . . when the English horns gave out the theme of the Largo [this is Thea hearing Dvořák's *New World Symphony* for the first time], she knew that what she wanted was exactly that. Here were the sand hills, the grasshoppers and locusts, all the things that wakened and chirped in the early morning; the reaching and reaching of high plains, the immeasurable yearning of all flat lands. There was home in it, too; first memories, first mornings long ago; the amazement of a new soul in a new world; a soul new and yet old, that had dreamed something despairing, something glorious, in the dark before it was born; a soul obsessed by what it did not know, under the cloud of a past it could not recall."

Recognition, we feel, was for Willa Cather a learning process that didn't stop; and Willa Cather was a born learner. The beautiful early story "The Enchanted Bluff," about the boys whose whole wish was to escape from home and who fail in their lives when they never make the break, turned into a chapter of *My Ántonia* that is more beautiful. Here, as in "The Enchanted Bluff," we have children listening and dreaming as a story is being told to them; Jim tells the children about the coming of Coronado and his search for the Seven Golden Cities in the early days, coming right here to Nebraska, where a sword with the name of its Spanish maker was turned up by a farmer breaking sod. And:

> Presently we saw a curious thing. There were no clouds, the sun was going down in a limpid, gold-washed sky. Just as the lower edge of the red disk rested on the high fields against the horizon, a great black figure suddenly appeared on the face of the sun. We sprang to our feet, straining our eyes toward it. In a moment we realized what it was. On some upland farm, a plough had been left standing in the field. The sun was sinking just behind it. Magnified across the distance by the horizontal light, it stood out against the sun, was exactly contained within the circle of the disk; the handles, the tongue, the share —black against the molten red. There it was, heroic in size, a picture writing on the sun.

> Even while we whispered about it, our vision disappeared; the ball dropped and dropped until the red tip went beneath the earth. The fields below us were dark, the sky was growing pale, and that forgotten plough had sunk back to its own littleness somewhere on the prairie.

The author has come to her quiet center. Nebraska, when she left it, was "Siberia"; now, for her writer's eyes, it is a radiant force of life itself.

. . .

The birth of Willa Cather came, as it happens, in the year Mark Twain began writing *Huckleberry Finn*. The authors' worlds were different, their frontiers were different—the events in *Huck* went back, of course, to the 1830's and '40's— but they worked, in a way that came naturally to them both, to something of the same scale. They stand together in *bigness* —their sense of it, their authority over it. The difference I want to mention is not in scale or in authority over it, but in the fictional uses to which the world is put.

Through each of their lands there flows a river. Mark Twain's Mississippi is the wider and muddier. It is the route and channel of adventure to Huck; around every bend as he takes it, the river is both what he's looking for and what he dreads, and it's got for him what he's not dreamed of till he finds it. It's *experience* he's on raft-level with; it can wash him overboard, he can plunge for it too, and endanger himself and refresh himself and cleanse himself or hide himself, or defy it, or live off it, or dream on it, or show off in it. It is his to live through, and he lives through it—comes out at the other end alive, and ready to take off for a new frontier if they try too hard again to civilize him.

Willa Cather's river is filled with grandeur and power too; it, too, is both danger and rescue, the demander of courage and daring, of sacrifice and reverence and awe; it stirs the heart to a sense of destiny. But the river that waters the plains for Willa Cather is the pure stream of art.

The works of these two are totally unalike except in their very greatest respects, except in being about something big, in the apprehension of the new, and in movement, tireless movement in its direction. And both great writers say: Who can move best but the inspired child of his times? Whose story should better be told than that of the youth who has contrived to cut loose from ties and go flinging himself might and main, in every bit of his daring, in joy of life not to be denied, to vaunt himself in the love of vaunting, in the marvelous curiosity to find out everything, over the preposterous length and breadth of an opening new world, and in so doing to be one with it? The Mississippi River and the unbroken prairie; comedy and tragedy; and indeed all destinies and destinations, all come subordinate to the charge of life itself. The two novelists remain a world apart; and yet both, at their best, celebrate, through the living presence of that world, an undeniable force—the pursuit of truth. They recognize and confront a common evil—the defiling of the proud human spirit.

It is in looking back on her work that we learn how the vast exterior world she shows us novel by novel, a world ever-present and full of weight and substance and stir, visible to us along differing perspectives and in various mutations of time, has been the deliberately fitted form for each novel's own special needs. This world is here to serve her purpose by taking a fictional role, allying itself more or less openly with human destiny. It appears, according to role, a world with the power to crush and suffocate, and the power to give back life; a world to promise everything, and to deny everything; a world to open a way for living, or to close in life's face. It is all her great, expanding, onmoving world; she has made it hers to take at its own beginnings and follow to its slow eclipse; and, in the full circle of it, to bring home the significance of the solitary human spirit which has elected to bring itself there, in its will and its struggle to survive.

She sought for the wholeness of the form—the roundness of the world, the full circle of life. The vital principle, this passion, has of its own a life—a seed, a birth, a growth, a maturing, a decline and sinking into death, back into the earth; it carries within it the pattern of life on earth, and is a part of the same continuity. It is "the old story writing itself over . . . It is we who write it, with the best we have," says Alexandra at the conclusion of *O Pioneers!*

The emotions of her characters, too, have deep roots in the physical world—in that actual physical land to which they were born. In such a land, how clear it is from the start that identity—self-identity—is hard to seize, hard to claim, and hard to hold on to.

Another of the touchstones of Willa Cather's work, I think, is her feeling for the young. "There is no work of art so big or so beautiful," she writes, "that it was not once all contained in some youthful body, like this one [it is Thea's] which lay on the floor in the moonlight, pulsing with ardour and antici- pation." The burning drive of the young, the desire to live, to do, to make, to achieve, no matter what the sacrifice, is the feeling most surpassingly alive to the author, most moving to us. Life had made her terribly certain that being young in the world is not easy. "If youth did not matter so much to itself, it would never have the heart to go on," she says as Thea starts from home. And Dr. Archie, old friend and traveling companion, "knew that the splendid things of life are few, after all, and so very easy to miss." In *O Pioneers!* we read that "There is often a good deal of the child left in people who have had to grow up too soon." Miss Cather has a num- ber of ways to tell us that life is most passionate in the promise, not in the fulfillment.

A strenuous physical life is lived throughout every novel, whether it is the struggle for survival or the keen experience of joy in simple physical well-being; it may reach in some characters the point of total identification with the living world around. It is a form of the passion that is all through Willa Cather's work; her work is written out of it. We see it in many modulations: desire—often exalted as ambition; devotion; loyalty; fidelity; physical nearness and kindness and comfort when it lies at rest. Love? It is affection that warms the life in her stories and hate that chills it. There is reconcile- ment, and there is pity. There is obsession here too, and so is the hunger for something impossible: all of these are forms of love. And there is marriage, though the marriages that occur along the way of the novels are milestones, hardly destinations; as required in the careful building of her plots, they are inclined to be unavailing. Sexual love is not often present in the here and now; we more often learn of it after it is over, or see it in its results. My own feeling is that along with her other superior gifts Willa Cather had a rare sureness as to *her* subject matter, the knowledge of just what to touch and what not to touch in the best interests of her story.

What her characters are most truly meant for, it seems to me, is to rebel. For her heroines in particular, rebelling is much easier than not rebelling, and we may include love, too, in "not rebelling." It is the strong, clear impulse in Willa Cather's stories. It is the real springwater. It is rebelling, we should always add, not for its own sake as much as for the sake of something a great deal bigger—that of integrity, of truth, of art. It is the other face of aspiration. Willa Cather used her own terms; and she left nothing out. What other honorable way is there for an artist to have her say?

The novels have the qualities and the components of love in proportions all their own, then; and I believe this may point again to the thought that they are concerned not with *two* but with *one*, in the number of human beings—not, finally, with relationships but with the desire in one heart and soul to claim what is its own, to achieve its measure of greatness, to overcome any terrible hardship, any terrible odds; and this desire is served by love, rewarded by love (but its absence or failure never compensated for by love); and most of the time, and at its highest moments, the desire is its own drive, its own gratification. One of its forms is indeed pride; and pride is not punished in Willa Cather's novels, it can be deserved:

> Her voice . . . had to do with that confidence, that sense of wholeness and inner well-being that she had felt at moments ever since she could remember . . . It was as if she had an appointment to meet the rest of herself sometime, somewhere. It was moving to meet her and she was moving to meet it. That meeting awaited her, just as surely as, for the poor girl in the [train] seat behind her, there awaited a hole in the earth, already dug.

And then in the city, at the concert, hearing the music that is to change her life, Thea says, "As long as she lived that ecstasy was going to be hers. She would live for it, work for it, die for it; but she was going to have it, time after time, height after height . . . She would have it, what the trumpets were singing! She would have it, have it—it!"

How does Willa Cather make this an emotion for which we have such entire sympathy? Its intensity, I think, is the answer—Thea's intensity partaking of Willa Cather's. Thea's music teacher says of her, "Her secret? It is every artist's secret—passion. That is all. It is an open secret, and perfectly safe. Like heroism, it is inimitable in cheap materials."

This high desire, when merged into other than itself, merges into the whole world. An individuality can be made willing to lose itself only in something as big as the world. It *was* the world, in *O Pioneers!* and in *My Ántonia*. It was not the world itself, except in magnitude and undeniability, in *The Song of the Lark* and, consummately, in *The Professor's House*: it was art.

For this novelist, art, as she saw it and perfected it, always kept the proportions of the great world and the undeniability of the world, and it lived for her as certainly as this world lived. And the strongest *felt* relationship, a reader may come to believe, might be not any of those between the characters, but the one their creator feels for them, for their developing, passionate lives.

In a landscape this wide and pulsing, it seems not at all out of keeping that the greatest passions made real to us are those *for* greatness, and for something larger than life. Men and women do of course fall in love in Willa Cather's novels and their relationship is brought into clear enough focus for us to put good reliance on; but the desire to make a work of art is a stronger one, and more lasting. In the long run, love of art —which is love accomplished without help or need of help from another—is what is deepest and realest in her work.

There is not a trace of disparagement in her treatment of the least of her characters. The irony of her stories is grave, never belittling; it is a showing of sympathy. She *contended* for the life of the individual. Her attack was positive and vigorous and unflinching and proud of winning. This contending was the essence of her stories, formed her plots, gave her room for action. And she did it without preaching. She lacked self-righteousness, and she just as wholly lacked bitterness; what a lesson *A Lost Lady* gives us in doing without bitterness. It is impossible to think of diminishment in anything she thought or wrote. She conceived of character along heroic lines. For her, the heroic life is the artist's as it is the pioneer's. She equated the two.

Set within the land is the dwelling—made by human hands to hold human life. As we know, the intensity of desire for building the house to live in—or worship in—fills the Cather novels. It fills the past for her, it gives the present meaning; it provides for a future: the house is the physical form, the *evidence* that we have lived, are alive now; it will be evidence someday that we were alive once, evidence against the arguments of time and the tricks of history.

In her landscape we learn from both seeing what is there and realizing what is not there; there is always felt the *absence* of habitation. We come to know what degrees there are of the burrow and the roof. "The houses on the Divide were small and were usually tucked away in low places; you did not see them until you came directly upon them," we read of the Bohemian settlement in *O Pioneers!* "Most of them were built of sod itself, and were only the unescapable ground in another form." Mrs. Archie, in *The Song of the Lark*, of whom we are told, "Such little, mean natures are among the darkest and most baffling of created things," liked to "have her house clean, empty, dark, locked, and to be out of it— anywhere."

The Professor's house, shabby and outgrown as it is, is a dated house; but the cliff house, almost older than time, is timeless. "I wish I could tell you what I saw there, just *as* I saw it, on that first morning, through a veil of lightly falling snow," Tom Outland tells him in his story within the story. "Far up above me, a thousand feet or so, set in a great cavern in the

face of the cliff, I saw a little city of stone, asleep . . . It all
hung together, seemed to have a kind of composition . . . The
tower was the fine thing that held all the jumble of houses
together and made them mean something . . . I felt that only
a strong and aspiring people would have built it, and a people
with a feeling for design." "The town hung like a bird's nest
in the cliff, . . . facing an ocean of clear air. A people who had
had the hardihood to build there, and who lived day after day
looking down upon such grandeur, who came and went by
those hazardous trails, must have been . . . a fine people."

"I see them there, isolated, cut off from other tribes, working out their destiny," said Father Duchene, the scholar,
"making their mesa more and more worthy to be a home for
man . . . Like you," he tells Tom Outland, "I feel a reverence
for this place. Wherever humanity has made that hardest of
all starts, and lifted itself out of mere brutality, is a sacred
spot . . . They built themselves into this mesa and humanized
it."

The Professor's House is a novel with unique form, and to
read it is to see it built before our eyes: the making of two
unlike parts into a whole under a sheltering third part which
defines it and is as final as that verse that comes to recite itself
to the Professor's mind. The construction is simple, forthright
and daring. By bringing the Professor's old house and the Cliff
Dwellers' house in combination to the mind, Willa Cather gives
them simultaneous existence, and with the measure of time
taken away, we may see, in the way of the mirage, or a
vision, humanity's dwelling places all brought into one. And it
was there all the time:

> For thee a house was built
> Ere thou wast born;
> For thee a mould was made
> Ere thou of woman camest.

Tom Outland's story, set into *The Professor's House* like
the view from the casement of that Dutch interior, is the

objectively told, factual-seeming counterpart of Thea's experience in the Ancient People's cliff houses in *The Song of the Lark*, which was published ten years earlier. Tom Outland's story has a further difference: the tragic view.

It is the objective chronicler for whom the story comes to a tragic end. For Thea, who has seen in her discovery of the Ancient People something totally and exclusively her own, and her own secret, it remained undamaged as a dream. She apprehended it in her own mind, and her own body, as a message for her. Tom Outland's Cliff City was there in the world, and he wanted the world to discover it as he had, to study it, venerate it, share it; and it was taken away from him, broken and desecrated; it brought about not the self-discovery of Thea, but a crisis and a lasting sorrow in human relationship. In the end, it is more of an interior story than Thea's ever was.

Tom Outland's story is written with a compression and strength that the author had already showed us in *A Lost Lady*, and achieves a simplicity that, as it seems to me, nothing else she wrote ever surpassed. Such simplicity is not what a writer starts with; it is what the writer is able to end with, or hopes to be able.

The Professor's House in whole might show us that the novel, in its excellence as a work of art, stands, itself, as a house finished. Insomuch as it has perfection, perfection has not sealed it, but opened it to us.

A work of art is a *work*: something made, which in the making follows an idea that comes out of human life and leads back into human life. A work of art is the house that is *not* the grave. An achievement of order, passionately conceived and passionately carried out, it is not a thing of darkness. When it is finished, if it is good and sound, somehow all opacity has left it. It stands as clear as candor itself. The fine physical thing has become a transparency through which the idea it was made to embody is thus made totally visible. It could not have been this visible before it was embodied. We see human thought and feeling best and clearest by seeing it through something solid that our hands have made.

"Artistic growth is, more than it is anything else, a refining of the sense of truthfulness." This is said at the end of *The Song of the Lark*. "The stupid believe that to be truthful is easy; only the artist, the great artist, knows how difficult it is." And, Thea's teacher goes on to say, "Every artist makes himself born. It is very much harder than the other time, and longer."

In the Cather novels, there is a setting apart of the artist in value, a setting apart of his life from that of other people's. Artists, in her considered and lifelong view, are perhaps greater, and more deserving to be made way for, than other human beings. This could never have been a popular view, but in trying to understand it, I think she extolled the artist not for what would seem vanity, or for anything less than a function he could perform—the great thing that only an artist would be able, in her eyes, to do. The artist has a role. Thea, meditating on this role, thought, of the people who cared about her singing, "Perhaps each of them concealed another person in himself, just as she did . . . What if one's second self could somehow speak to all those second selves?" At base, I think this is an aspect of the Cather sense of the obligation to give of oneself. "If he achieves anything noble, anything enduring, it must be by giving himself absolutely to his material. And this gift of sympathy is his great gift," Willa Cather said, "is the fine thing in him that alone can make his work fine." The artist is set apart the more entirely, all but symbolically, to give himself away, to fulfill the ultimate role of dedication.

Today neither the artist nor the world holds this idea, and it has faded, along with some of her other strong beliefs (the hero and the heroine, the sanctity of the family), from our own view. Our ideas of history and of art are different from hers, as tomorrow's will be different from today's. We have arrived at new places to stand to obtain our own viewpoint of history. Art, since it grows out of its times, is of itself, and by rights, a changing body. But truth?

Truth is the rock. Willa Cather saw it as unassailable. Today the question is asked if this is indeed so. Many of us align ourselves with Willa Cather—I do—in thinking the truth will hold out; but there are many who feel another way, and indeed, I believe, many who would not feel life was over if there were no truth there.

One of the strangest things about art, nevertheless, is that the rock it is built on is not its real test. Our greatest poem made a mistake about the construction of the universe, but this will never bring the poem down.

Yet plain enough is the structure she built on these rocks she herself believed were eternal. Her work we, today, see entirely on its own, without need of that support. It holds itself independently, as that future church appears to be doing above the dreaming head of Saint Francis of Assisi in Giotto's fresco. Her work has its own firm reason for existence. And here it stands, a monument more unshakable than she might have dreamed, to the independent human spirit she most adored.

She made this work out of her life, her perishable life, which is so much safer a material to build with than convictions, however immutable they seem to the one who so passionately holds them. It is out of our own lives that we, in turn, reach out to it. Because the house of Willa Cather contained, embodied, a spirit, it will always seem to us inhabited. There is life in that house, the spirit she made it for, made it out of; it is all one substance: it is her might and her heart and soul, all together, and it abides.

(1974)

Reality in Chekhov's Stories

&

"How true to life it all is!" the Privy Councilor exclaims when he descends on the country house of his sister. "An idyll!" he says. "They sing and dream in the moonlight! It's charming, I swear to God! May I sit down and dream with you? . . . Upon my soul, that's charming! . . . This is actually life . . . This is what reality is bound to be. Why are you silent? . . . Talk, my friends, sing . . . play! Don't lose time . . . Make all the haste you can to live, my friends . . . Love, marry . . . do silly things." However, he changes the dinner hour to the time they eat in St. Petersburg, causing everything to be ruined, and as time goes on, the child of the family notices he can't tell any of the people in the household apart. And in departing, radiant and happy as ever, blowing kisses, he asks, looking at this little boy himself with astonishment, "What boy is this?" But the little boy, in the course of the same visit, has learned all about the Privy Councilor—even though he'd been prepared for "a gentleman with shoulder-straps, a naked sword, and terrible eyes."

The magistrate in "On Official Business" equates reality and unreality with, respectively, life in Moscow and life in the provinces. In "The Betrothed," a mother and a grandmother have been forced into a realization that "the past was lost and gone . . . and they had now no position in society, no prestige as before . . . So it is when in the midst of an easy careless life the police suddenly burst in at night and make a search, and it turns out that the head of the family has embezzled money or committed forgery—and goodbye then to the easy careless life for ever!"

In "The Steppe," around the campfire, in the course of the long wagon journey across to sell the wool, an old man, who for the most part has sat silent, begins to tell story after story of things that have happened to him in his life. "And in all of them 'long knives' figured, and all alike sounded made up . . . It is strange that whenever he happened to tell a story, he gave unmistakable preference for fiction, and never told what he had really experienced . . . that a man who in his day had travelled all over Russia and seen and known so much, whose wife and children had been burnt to death, so failed to appreciate the wealth of his life that whenever he was sitting by the camp fire he was either silent or talked of what had never been."

Yet—Chekhov goes on to say—"Life is terrible and marvelous, and so, however terrible a story you tell in Russia, however you embroider it with nests of robbers, long knives and such marvels, it always finds an echo of reality in the soul of the listener, and only a man who has been a good deal affected by education looks askance distrustfully . . . The cross by the wayside, the dark bales of wool, the wide expanse of the plain, and the lot of the men gathered by the camp fire— all this was of itself so marvelous and terrible that the fantastic stories of legend and fairy tale were pale and blended with life."

Chekhov's perception of our differing views of reality, with its capacity to understand them all, may have done more than anything else to bring about his revolutionizing of the short story. Surely it lay behind the fact that formal pattern imposed on the story by long tradition gave way to a treatment entirely different—something open to human meaning and answerable to that meaning in all its variety.

The story as Chekhov wrote it was set forth in simple terms of everyday life where it took place. The stuff of life was transmuted into the stuff of his story—the stuff of reality. All the same, "real," as in "the real world," does not, as we know, mean invariable, or static, or ironclad, or consistent, or even trustworthy. What is real in life—and what a Chekhov story was made to reflect with the utmost honesty—may be at the same time what is transient, ephemeral, contradictory, even on the point of vanishing before our eyes. So it isn't just *there*.

In Chekhov's stories, reality always has its origin: it comes to us through the living human being—and not anonymously. It lives, was born, in the particular—not in the general humanity but in this man, that woman, their child. What's real, like them, carries, as they do, the seed of change. It is perishable.

Chekhov shows no fondness for the abstract. Reality—along with good and evil, justice and love, and other subjects of fundamental importance to him—he dealt with in terms of the particular and personal meaning it took on for human beings in the course of their lives.

And so reality is no single, pure ray, no beacon against the dark. It might be thought of as a cluster of lesser lights, visible here on earth like the windows of a village at night, close together but not *one*—some are bright, some dim, some waywardly flickering. All imply people; there are people there for every light.

We can quickly think of a number of kinds of reality Chekhov shows us in his stories. Of course, they all bear some relationship to one another—it is, again, a matter of human connection, a state of kinship or at least of neighborliness. It is what "The Darling" has in common with "A Calamity," "The Name Day Party" with "The Duel"—each presents, or turns upon, its own emerging view of reality.

At a party for a visiting brigade, one of the officers, young, unbearably shy, "whiskered like a lynx," wanders about the rooms alone while the others dance; and suddenly he is kissed in the dark—by a young lady who gives a shriek and runs away. But he is irradiated by happiness. When they are all back in the light, none of the girls he sees quite satisfies his idea of who it was that kissed him, and so, perfectly happily, he composes her from what he sees—one girl's shoulder, another girl's brow.

And from the kiss he goes on to compose his future, too; as the brigade marches away he is imagining bidding her goodbye, "imagining war, and parting, then reunion, the first supper together, children . . ." And from now until the brigade's return, he behaves like a man in love, and "at night, when his comrades talked of love and of women, he drew in his chair, and his face was the face of an old soldier who talks of battles in which he has taken part."

But the present of happiness brought by luck can as easily be taken away when luck changes. Chekhov shows us that fantasy can change a man's life and that living without it will be living with the loss of something real—because the existence of his feelings is real; and they are all he has. Things will not go well for him. The young dreamer kissed by mistake will turn into a man bereaved.

It was not in Chekhov to deny any character in his stories the dignity and purity of singularity. He would have found it not only alien to his art but morally unjust to slur over a man—even a horse thief—as only an example of his class or sex or calling in life.

Human beings are unpredictable and spontaneous, apt to rise up anywhere without announcement, like Moisey Moisevitch's children, away in the middle of the steppe in dead of night, putting their heads up one after another from beneath the patchwork quilt. They also show a power of resilience, a zest even in the face of outrage, like Granny pursuing through the streets the police inspector who is carrying off the family samovar in lieu of unpaid taxes, screaming furiously, "I won't let you have it, I won't let you have it, damn you!" Chekhov's characters, even to the least forceful and least able to speak, nearly always in some measure reflect this human intractability.

The story writer with a temperament to instruct or moralize prefers to do without the fact that people are inconsistent and incalculable; Chekhov, on the other hand, this inspires rather than disturbs. His stories rise to that fact, and suggest it in a thousand details.

A rich old man gets up and dances at his son's wedding. Outside in the yard, peeping in the windows at the celebration, are the peasants. Their lifelong oppressor, the old man has robbed and cheated every one of them, but to see him kick up his heels they "were in raptures, and for the moment forgave him everything—his wealth and the wrongs he had done them." "Well done, Grigory Petrovich!" they cry. "You can still play your part!"

Indeed, Chekhov leads us to discover that what we should have thought the most incongruous detail is in fact the most probable. In "The Murder," the sudden act of violence takes place in a fanatically religious household where ries of devotion are rigorously observed. What nearer to hand for murdering a brother than a bottle of Lenten oil? And since they're all in the kitchen at the time, the sister, over the ironing board, has the flatiron ready to help out with.

And in the same scene there is the still more significant *human* incongruity—a snob. The snob is an accidental witness of the murder—he's only come to the house to borrow money —and found guilty of accepting a bribe to keep silent, receives nearly as harsh a sentence to prison as the others. But he has been the keeper of a refreshment bar in a railway station in a large junction town, before coming down in the world as a waiter in a country tavern. In all their years together on Sakhalin, he never sees the murderer, as he is "ashamed of being acquainted with convicts of the peasant class."

The reality Chekhov sees through his characters' eyes can accommodate the monstrous; and it doesn't rule out even what may be invisible to other eyes.

Kovrin, the young magister, "longed for something vast, infinite, astonishing." One day, speeding to him through the air over the rye fields, the Black Monk appears and holds conversation with him.

Kovrin tells the Monk what joy he has brought. "Yet I know

that when you leave me I shall be tormented by doubt as to your reality. You are a phantom, a hallucination. But that means that I am physically diseased, that I am not in a normal state?"

"What if you are?" says the Monk. "That need not worry you." He tells the magister that the time will come when he will sacrifice not only his health but his life also to the one idea of Eternal Truth. "What more could you desire?"

"How strange that you should repeat what I myself have so often thought!" says Kovrin.

The hallucination of the Black Monk is experienced by a young man of high education, who is not only able to recognize it for what it is—the looming response to the need for it—but also to know the cost of losing it.

"Why have you cured me?" he asks his wife. "I had the mania of greatness. What harm did that cause anyone? I ask you what harm?" And he adds, "How happy were Buddha and Mahomet and Shakespeare that their kind-hearted kinsmen and doctors did not cure them of ecstasy and inspiration! If Mahomet had taken potassium bromide for his nerves, worked only two hours a day, and drunk milk, that astonishing man would have left as little behind him as his dog."

In "Peasants," though theirs is an incredibly hard and thankless life, the three generations of a family we see living crowded together under the roof of one hut spend the long autumn evenings listening to the old father tell them how "Things were better in the old days under the gentry." He describes how they used to live before the Emancipation as if that had been their glorious day: "how in those very parts, where life was now so poor and so dreary, they used to hunt with harriers, greyhounds, retrievers, and when they went out as beaters the peasants were given vodka." After their long day's work the family sits winding silk for twenty kopecks a week, as they listen, and the children are spellbound. "The little girls, sitting and lying on the stove, stared down without blinking; it seemed as though there were a great many of them, like cherubim in the clouds. They liked the stories, they were breathless; they shuddered and turned pale with alternate rapture and terror, and they listened . . . afraid to stir" at the romantic tales of the gentry.

When they lie down to sleep, "the old people, troubled and excited by their reminiscences, thought how precious was youth, of which, whatever it might have been like, nothing was left in the memory but what was living, joyful, touching, and how terribly cold was death, which was not far off, better not to think of it! . . . You turn on the other side: death is forgotten, but old, dreary, sickening thoughts of poverty, of food, of how dear flour is getting, stray through the mind, and a little later again you remember that life is over and you cannot bring it back . . ." The children, too, sleep badly, kept awake by itch and hunger.

All through the story, the talk and the night, we know that young Sasha, whom we meet in the beginning—tender and still innocent, a sensitive child, listening among the cherubim on the stove—brought here from the city by her father, who has come home to live out his last days with his family, will have the same few choices in life her elders had; she is sure to grow up to live no better than they. She may, like Marya, marry a drunkard who will beat her till they must pour cold water over her to revive her, and as a mother, will be glad when her children die; or she will run wild in the night like Fyokla to earn a few tips from the ruffians down by the river, who will send her home naked; or, after the approaching death of her father, she will go back to the city with her then homeless mother—and it is this we see on its way to happen:

"At midday Olga and Sasha reached a big village . . . Stopping near the hut which looked newest and most prosperous, Olga bowed down before the open window, and said in a loud, thin, chanting voice, 'Good Christian folk, give alms, for Christ's sake, that God's blessing may be upon you, and that your parents may be in the Kingdom of Heaven in peace eternal.'

" 'Good Christian folk,' Sasha began chanting, 'give, for Christ's sake, that God's blessing, the Heavenly Kingdom . . .' "

They are on foot to Moscow; and Sasha, on reaching the city, will continue to beg, and as soon as she is old enough, she will live on the streets as a prostitute for the rest of her young days.

The fabrications these peasants make of the truth in order to alleviate the brutal reality of their lives do not alleviate it for us. It comes to us all the more unsparingly. The consistent miracle of Chekhov's realism is that in all its fidelity to its density, its shadings of darkness as in this story, it is not obscuring. Chekhov makes it a transparency; we look through it at the blaze of human truth.

It was his plainest intention that we never should hear him telling us what we should think or feel or believe. He is not trying to teach us, through his characters; he only asks us to understand them.

Religion, government, science, education, the arts are not in themselves either moral or immoral, as he had cause to remark in his letters. Peasants, women, schoolteachers, the military, drunks, Turks, persons over forty or under two, revolutionaries, doctors, the raisers of their own gooseberries— none of them are good or evil in so being but in what they do to each other, the ways they treat their fellow human beings. A character in "A Dreary Story" remarks that "virtue and purity are not very different from vice if they are not free from evil feelings."

Chekhov is also the least self-obtrusive of story writers. It is the story he's written that has gained a self—a clear, unself-conscious identity, vigorous, purposeful, ongoing. This freeing of the form came from the deeps of his temperament, we might suppose. The abhorrence he felt toward coercion in human affairs must have had its own part in clearing away the confines of arbitrary plot, manipulated characters. As the grandson of a serf, who had "squeezed the slave out of himself drop by drop," Chekhov knew all the better what it meant to make himself free as an artist.

Thus he dared to make himself free to enter the body, spirit, mind and heart of a character, and free of any crippling wish to use him as a spokesman for himself, or as a moral example, or as a scapegoat. In the writing of his stories he conscientiously yielded only to the authority of his feeling for human beings as human beings.

And no human being is out of bounds to Chekhov. No state of health or stage of consciousness or time of life could have appeared strange to him. As a storyteller he is within any character he invents—a woman in her seventh month of pregnancy, an aged learned man suffering from insomnia and "strange and inappropriate thoughts," even a little dog being trained for a music-hall act, who "grew so used to the word 'talent,' that every time her master pronounced it, she jumped up as if it had been her name."

Neither did he hesitate to deal with any subject he wished. Chekhov wrote of sex with honesty and lack of fuss, as he wrote of all human experience. As always, it is a character's feelings that give it its meaning. Much ahead of his time, and perhaps of ours, in "The Duel" he treated with candor and seriousness a young woman of compelling sexuality. "The Lady with the Pet Dog" is a compassionate study of a cynical middle-aged man surprised when, almost against his will and against his belief, his sexual worldliness turns into the honesty and difficulty of belated love.

Chekhov's candor, which was natural to him, was more than a revulsion against lying and hypocrisy. It was a tool in his work. His candor was exploratory and painstaking—he might have used it as the doctor in him would know how, treating the need for truth between human beings as an emergency.

"The Duel" here springs foremost to mind—that long, complex, profoundly moving story with a scope that has led some readers to call it a novel. Reality in "The Duel" is very much tied up with its characters' *ideas* of reality.

Laevsky and Nadyezdha, who consider themselves advanced and liberated young people, have run away from Moscow to lead simple lives in Yalta by the Black Sea, where they can live off the land and exercise their freedom. It's what young people of the 1880's did to show their emancipation from the Establishment of their day. But by now Laevsky is tired of Nadyezdha; nothing she does can please him. He is so homesick for Moscow that down here in the lush, warm Caucasus that confronts him daily he sits and dreams of the north, "the dear grey sky, the drizzling rain, the drenched cabmen." "It seemed to him that he had sinned against his own life, . . . against the world of lofty ideas, of learning, and of work, and he conceived that wonderful world as real and possible not on this sea-front with hungry Turks and lazy mountaineers sauntering upon it, but there in the north, where there were operas, theatres, newspapers, and all kinds of intellectual activity. One could only there—not here—be honest, intelligent, lofty, and pure."

Laevsky at the moment, however, can tell himself that his failure is not his fault. It is Turgenev's, who invented the superfluous man, and ought to be responsible for the mess Laevsky's life is fast becoming.

"We really ran away from her husband, but we lied to ourselves and made out that we ran from the emptiness of life of the educated class," Laevsky confides to Samoylenko, the army doctor on the post, who is kind and receptive to everybody's troubles. But it is terrible for Laevsky to realize that the doctor, from whom he now wishes to borrow money, had detected in him the deception which he had so long and carefully concealed from himself: that what he wants to do now is run away to Moscow without Nadyezdha.

Nadyezdha has wearied of Laevsky too, of his lounging about and biting his nails and being always the same. She is already, in secret, unfaithful to him, "with neither the power nor the wish to resist" the burly police captain. Boredom with Laevsky has "led by degrees to her becoming possessed by desire, and as though she were mad, she thought of nothing else day and night. Breathing, looking, walking, she felt nothing but desire. The sound of the sea told her she must love; the darkness of evening—the same; the mountains—the same."

By the time of the picnic—the first of the story's two great scenes—both Laevsky and Nadyezdha are living saturated in feelings of guilt toward each other.

"The Duel" is a story whose conversation, it could be broadly said, is made up of the giving, the asking for, the receiving and the rejection of advice. Everyone can think of and eagerly put forward some excellent plan for other people's lives. The actual duel to which this understandably leads is fought between opponents in ideas.

Von Koren is a young zoologist who has come to the Black Sea to study the embryology of the medusa. Giving Laevsky his scientific scrutiny, he finds him a contamination to society and would feel perfectly willing to drown him. "Otherwise, when the Laevskys multiply, civilization will perish and mankind will degenerate utterly. It will be our fault," he warns the doctor.

And, also into the doctor's ear, Laevsky pours out resentment against Von Koren: "His ideals are despotic too . . . To [him] men are puppets and nonentities . . . He works, will go for his expedition and break his neck there, not for the sake of love for his neighbor, but for the sake of such abstractions as humanity, future generations, an ideal race of men. He exerts himself for the improvement of the human race . . . And what is the human race? Illusion, mirage . . . Despots have always been illusionists."

As for the good army doctor, who deplores the ideas of both young men, he cooks for them, comforts them, gives them beds when they can't face going home, lends them money, tries his best to mediate; and at the picnic, he agrees to cook the fish soup.

The only character in the least susceptible to outside advice is the giggly young deacon, who languishes for his new wife back home. Riding beside him on the way to the picnic, Von Koren suggests that the deacon put his wife in a nunnery, become a monk himself, and after a two-year period of preparation, which Von Koren will supervise himself, join his expedition to the Orient as a priest. And indeed, even before the fish have gone on the fire at the picnic, the deacon is imagining a whole new future for himself, finally as a bishop blessing the masses, while a choir of children sing back to him with their angel voices.

What a perfect setting for this picnic! The towering mountains, the Black River, the bonfire, a little house in view like a fairy-tale hut on hen's legs—this terribly romantic spot, reached by a wild ride along the cliffside, seems not quite real; and Marya Konstantinova, the hostess, implores Laevsky tearfully: "Describe this view!" as though it had another existence in words.

The firelight and its shadows playing over the picnic party add to the mysteriousness; so does the emergence of a second party—quite unknown people—on the opposite side of the river. Even the fish soup, which Samoylenko stirs over the fire, carrying on alone exactly as if he were in his own kitchen, tastes very different to the others from his soup at home. It is a romantically dangerous-looking place, but the danger is real: it comes from the picnickers themselves.

All are attended by their private dreams tonight, accompanied by their secret reflections, pursuing their separate intrigues—Nadyezdha is skimming into the moonlit woods like a nymph, chased by the police captain, who is already by now out of favor. Each one is wrapped in his own image of himself, his own self-deception; their pursuits, all the same, interlock. It is a scene of ambiguity, described with not one ambiguous term, but with shadowless clarity. It is the prelude to the duel.

For the advanced and liberated opponents, Laevsky and Von Koren, are thrown back by the heat of argument into the anachronism of doing physical battle with each other—they will meet at dawn.

But in between the picnic and the duel the most remarkable

night scene takes place, surely one of the most powerful and wrenching in all Chekhov's stories. Laevsky's desperation as he waits sleepless through the long night of terrible storm that sweeps the sea, the town, the mountains, when at last he thinks of his life as "lies, lies, all lies," drives him to implore help from someone. He thinks he will write to his mother . . . But once he brings his mother clearly to mind, he can't write to her. He doesn't believe in God. Yet he has a longing to pray to someone or something, even if it must be the lightning, the clouds: "Dear storm!" "He had an impulse to run to Nadyezdha Fyodorovna, to fall at her feet, to kiss her hands and feet, to beg her forgiveness; but she was his victim, and he was afraid of her as though she were dead."

The night ends, the men return to the picnic scene; storm-washed, it is now where they are to fight the duel. It is with such quietness, one could say tenderness, that Chekhov introduces the many parallels and balances, the repeating themes in contrasting moods and keys of this marvelous story.

Of the duelists and their seconds, no one knows the rules. Everybody is having his first experience—even of the sunrise. There are guilty and embarrassed speeches, awkward moments —somebody's leg goes to sleep. Then they remember duels described in novels—once more Turgenev is called upon: Bazarov had a duel with someone, didn't he?

The faced opponents have never been as widely separated in ideas. In the act of raising his pistol, Laevsky finds he's forgotten to unbutton his overcoat, and "his arm rose as awkwardly as though the sleeve had been cut out of tin." He fires as he'd intended, into the air. Von Koren's pistol, he sees, is truly aimed: Von Koren, who would have drowned Laevsky for the good of humanity, is not going to hesitate to kill him now. "The murder just about to be committed by a decent man in broad daylight, in the presence of decent men, and the stillness and the unknown force that compelled Laevsky to stand still and not to run—how mysterious it all was, how incomprehensible and terrible!"

The comic interruption is just in time: the youthful deacon

—the bishop-to-be—who isn't even supposed to be present at an affair like this, shouts from his hiding place in a bush "He'll kill him!" and spoils Von Koren's aim.

When they all drive home from the spot afterward, it seems to Laevsky "as though they were all coming back from a graveyard in which a wearisome, insufferable man who was a burden to others had just been buried." "Everything is over," he thought of his past.

"The Duel," with its characters joined in the torment of their deceptions, self-deceptions, dreams, illusions and lies, is a story about truth.

"No one knows the real truth," Laevsky thinks at the last. As far as he himself has reached it, it is in what he says to the exhausted, exposed, humiliated Nadyezdha. For he has decided to remain, and she has nowhere else to go.

She has told him everything that had happened to her. "It seemed to her that very likely he scarcely heard and did not understand her, and that if he did know everything he would curse her and kill her, but he listened to her, stroked her face and hair, looked into her eyes and said: 'I have nobody but you . . .'"

The revolution brought about by the gentle Chekhov to the short story was in every sense not destructive but constructive. By removing the formal plot he did not leave the story structureless; he endowed it with another kind of structure—one which embodied the principle of growth. And it was one that had no cause to repeat itself; in each and every story, short or long, it was a structure open to human meaning and answerable to that meaning. It took form from within.

It does so in a way that is endlessly provocative in the story "Gooseberries."

Let us recall what happens when two friends turn aside from a walk in the country to seek shelter from the rain. They chance to be near the house of a friend. They arrive at a working farm, a place of mud and mire; their host is grimy, his house appears dark and forbidding. But everything changes. In their honor the host takes a bath, a whole year's grime is shed like a snakeskin. The guests are invited to bathe too, and Ivan plunges into the river. Swimming and diving and shouting and floating on his back in the river in the rain, among the water lilies, he feels an elation such as he'd felt in youth. A great release is taking place in him. And something with the quality of enchantment begins to surround the party. All now clean, dressed in dry clothing, they move upstairs into the elegant part of the farmhouse; in warm, peaceful, quiet rooms they are attended by a young woman of startling beauty.

Here Ivan tells them a story, and all this seems to have been a preparation for it. It is the story of his brother Nickolay, who had worked all his life for a house and a farm just such as this one. As Ivan talks, the farm, the day, the house with its encrustations of time, the seductive room with its beautiful attendant, its romantic portraits of ladies and generals around the walls, and the rain falling outside, all stand about the story he tells like screens of varying substance of reality and dream.

Nickolay's story is really a terrible story of *getting*, of stinginess and callousness and obsessive greed, costing the woman he married her very life. Above all, he must raise his own gooseberries! When Ivan visited him, after his dream of possessing all this had come true, and was given the first of the gooseberries to taste, and found them hard and sour, Ivan's own life underwent a change.

"What is terrible in life goes on somewhere behind the scenes," he tells his friends now. "Behind the door of every contented, happy man there ought to be someone standing with a little hammer and continually reminding him with a knock that there are unhappy people, that however happy he may be, life will sooner or later show him its claws, and trouble will come to him—illness, poverty, losses, and then no one will see or hear him, just as now he neither sees nor hears others. But there is no man with a hammer . . ."

Quite naturally, his listeners find Ivan's story unsatisfactory.

The host, a man of only forty, is even inattentive. Here in his own beautifully prepared room, he thinks "the story had no direct bearing on his life."

The extraordinary structure of "Gooseberries" is purely subjective. The swing, the breathtaking arc, from the exhilaration of Ivan's swimming in the river to the profound despair into which the telling of his brother's story finally brings him might be a plunge from youth to age, from the rejuvenated swimmer to the old man whose head is ablaze with ideas, who can only cry, "If I were young!" When we recall that, swimming, he kept diving down and touching bottom, we could as easily say he moves from the profundities of joy to the heights of despair. It doesn't matter which we say; in the river, Ivan has experienced happiness of such purity that it is forgetful of self. He can only shout, "By God! By God!" In the end, reaching that same pitch of self-forgetfulness in despair, he changes the cry to "Do good! Do good!"

We are left, the story's swing being brought to rest, the memory of the gooseberries, the smell of Ivan's pipe in the bedroom, and the rain that has never stopped.

"In the Ravine" is in method of telling the antithesis of "Gooseberries." It is a story of a family of Kulaks on their way up, a terrible story of inhumanity set down in almost reportorial objectivity. It is true that we are sometimes close to the mind of Lipa, but this has its own distance from us, for Lipa, as will be remembered, was next to being a saint.

Grigory is the sharp old man whose only soft feeling is the love he has for his three sons. One son, because another woman is needed for the housework, has a peasant girl brought to him as a bride—young, trusting, innocent Lipa who is used to hard work. At the wedding feast he has still not said a single word to her, "so that he did not yet know the sound of her voice."

It is, again, a story full of greed and gluttony; and the greed is second nature to cheating and counterfeiting, to the corruption and spoilation of a village and its people, and it finally allies itself to murder.

The village had been known as "the village where the sexton ate all the caviare at the funeral." The passage of a year has meant that what it will be remembered for now is the cry of Nikifor, Lipa's baby, when another daughter-in-law of the family deliberately splashes a ladle of scalding water over him —for he would have been the heir.

Yet even this unbearable act receives acceptance as only one with the rest of human acts: Lipa, finding her way home alone from the hospital with her dead child in her arms, asks a stranger in the road, "Tell me, grandfather, why a little thing should be tormented before his death? Why?" "Never mind," says the old man, "yours is not the worst of sorrows. Life is long, there will be good and bad to come, there will be everything. Great is Mother Russia!" And after the funeral Lipa, who waits at table for the feast, is spoken to by the priest. "Lifting his fork on which there was a salted mushroom, [he] said to her, 'Don't grieve for the babe. For such is the Kingdom of Heaven.' "

The murderess of the child never alludes to what she has done; she dresses up for the funeral and after the burial proceeds to throw the baby's mother out of the house, and goes ahead to realize her ambitions; her plot is successful. Her own husband, who has cheated everybody and disgraced himself, has indeed been caught and sent to jail, but he is only forgotten about, put out of the family's mind. The old man Grigory, progenitor of the family evils, simply grows old, and soon he, too, is doomed to be forgotten.

There is no justice depicted in this story; instead, at the last, there is a gesture of consummate mercy. The receiver is the old father; the giver, the young mother who was wronged.

We see Lipa coming, after the day's work, along with the other peasants—the old women from the woods where they gather mushrooms, the young from the station where they have been loading bricks. They are singing; it is Lipa leading them all in a high, clear voice. She and her mother meet the old father. Wrapped in his fur collar, as he is in all weathers, the wicked and now betrayed old man has himself been cast out of his house, and is on the street all day; because he is old and forgets to eat, his family is willingly allowing him to starve.

"Lipa bowed low and said:

" 'Good evening, Grigory Petrovich.'

"Her mother, too, bowed. The old man stopped and, saying nothing, looked at the two; his lips were quivering and his eyes full of tears. Lipa took out of her mother's bundle a piece of pie stuffed with buckwheat and gave it to him. He took it and began eating.

"The sun had set by now; its glow died away on the upper part of the road too. It was getting dark and cool. Lipa and Praskovya walked on and for some time kept crossing themselves."

That one act, artless, simple, without premeditation or expectancy, seems to equal, to balance in weight of human meaning, the entire rest of the story—as the girl's clear singing may call up and contain the baby's cry. Lipa doesn't question any longer, only gives. Anguish, unbearable hurt are released into an expression that is purely lyrical—by which the totally objectified reality of the story is transcended.

Chekhov does not condemn his characters. Not to condemn such a one as old Grigory, for instance, not to berate, not even to chide, is in writing fiction no sign of a lack of passion. The depth of Chekhov's feeling for man is the very element out of which his stories spring, out of which they continue to draw their life. The reader who, like the present one, must rely on translations should not venture to speak in close particular about sentences, perhaps. But it seems plain enough to be a fundamental fact of Chekhov's work that the passion is not in the sentence but in the whole.

Passion does not burst from him as a storm, with a storm's threat—driving winds and bolts of lightning, crashes of thunder; it is more like a climate, prevailing, all-enfolding. "The Lady with the Pet Dog" is pervaded with a gentleness that can be ominous as thunder, and a grace that can strike you to the heart; it is a love story concluding with these words: ". . . and it was clear to both of them that the end was still far off, and that what was to be most complicated and difficult for them was only just beginning."

It is a story firmly restrained, whose mood is not broken from first to last; nothing is placed in full direct glare. There is, rather, a quiet shimmering from within, and then the emergence of that last sentence, which is not a summation but a prophecy, and which long after the story ends goes on pulsing light into the mind.

The stories leave no havoc on the surface. Their reach, even their nature, might be reflected on the seismograph; they run close to the nerve of our inner lives.

They don't date. They could not have been written outside the time and place of their origin—they are a living part of both. If there are certain similarities in Chekhov's times and ours that strike us when we read him, the significance is other than historical. Though no two centuries are very much like each other, some hours, perhaps, are; moments are; critical moments nearly always are. Emotions are the same. We are the same. The man, not the day, is the lasting phenomenon.

In the whole population of Chekhov's characters, every single one, the least, the smallest, the youngest, the most obscure, has its clear identity. No life is too brief or too inconsequential for him to be inattentive to its own reality.

Traveling the vast "lilac distances" day after day with the little wagon party, the growing schoolboy in the long story "The Steppe" closely observes that even away off here, people wake up with the same intent in which they lay down, and even their dreams continue to run in character. And one day, just as he himself is about to fall asleep with the others, he sees a very little boy from a nearby encampment slowly draw near; he climbs down over a rock, and simply stares—allured. Asked his name, the tiny child replies with a single sound, like "Tit"—no more, and then, climbing backward over his rock, he withdraws to where he came from. But "Tit" is indelible now. Indeed, after he's been left behind, he returns to our young traveler in a dream. "Tit" emerged, and very briefly, out of vastness and subsided into the mystery of distance and disappearance. But he was "Tit," self-proclaimed, and bringing himself.

Chekhov showed us the implacable facts of existence—the illusions, the deceptions, the mystery, the identity—that reality variously stood for among many characters. How did he, himself, see it? What but the comic vision could accommodate so much, bring it all in? What other frame is generous enough? I think of that vision as an outreach of this artist's compassion —the careful attention to the human scale, a keeping to human proportions. It is the artist's deference, a kind of modesty, a form of ultimate respect, a reverence, for all living things.

The recurring figure in his stories and plays who speaks ardently of his vision of a better future we never do accept as a wholly ironic creation. Chekhov, who saw life as it was, had all the same a quite resilient, a mostly cheerful nature, as he kept reminding his wife in his letters. He hoped for himself, and for us. The comic vision allows for hope too. ("One who desires nothing, hopes for nothing, and fears nothing cannot become an artist," he wrote in an early letter.)

Under crushing oppression from their fellow-men, many characters die in his stories—but just as many do not. Death is by no means Chekhov's pattern. Life is the pattern. The gentle revolutionary in "The Betrothed" succumbs to tuberculosis before his own day comes, but not before he has succeeded in parting Nadya from her smothering bourgeois life and the fiancé she'd been promised to, and has seen her through her escape to St. Petersburg. This escape, it's true, may be unique in Chekhov: it is most famously *not* accomplished in *The Three Sisters*; but what he is showing us is the human need for fighting a way clear to draw free breath. Success and defeat are aspects of the same thing. In the human being, as this great artist spent his short life showing us, anything is possible.

The dying Gusev, lying in fever in the ship's infirmary, is

ridiculed by the sick mate beside him for his uneducated beliefs. Gusev believes, for instance, that a storm at sea means the
wind has broken loose from its chains. But he wonders,
"What is there that is strange or out of the way about . . .
the wind breaking loose from its chains?" When he dies, and is
to be buried at sea, Chekhov writes: "It is strange that a man
should be sewn up in sailcloth and should soon be flying into
the sea. Is it possible that such a thing can happen to anyone?"
And then, when it does happen, deep below the surface of the
sea a shark rips the shroud of Gusev from head to foot, while
above, the sky in which the sun is setting "takes on tender,
joyous, passionate colors for which it is hard to find a name in
the language of man." The story asks what, in life, equally
what in death, is to be called strange? It can only observe: "To
think that this could happen to a human being!"

The very greatest mystery is in unsheathed reality itself. The
realist Chekhov, speaking simply and never otherwise than as
an artist and a humane man, showed us in fullness and plenitude the mystery of our lives.

He was searching for the truth that is inside it, wasn't he,
always?—that real truth which Laevsky in "The Duel" had
doubts that anyone ever knew. Laevsky went on to say that
trying to find it meant going "one step forward and two steps
back." Chekhov knew the odds, too—he lived with the odds.
But what truth this purest of artists found through his stories
is ours forever.

(1977)

II

ON WRITING

Looking at Short Stories

୶ୢ

Looking at short stories as readers and writers together should be a companionable thing. And why not? Stories in their bardic and fairy-tale beginnings were *told*, the listeners—and judgers —all in a circle.

E. M. Forster, in *Aspects of the Novel*, described the great age of the narrative:

> Neanderthal man listened to stories, if one may judge by the shape of his skull. The primitive audience was an audience of shock-heads, gaping around the camp-fire, fatigued with contending against the mammoth or woolly-rhinoceros, and only kept awake by suspense. What would happen next? The novelist droned on, and as soon as the audience guessed what happened next, they either fell asleep or killed him.

That suspense is still with us, but it seems to me that now it exists as something shared. Reader and writer make it a double experience. It is part of the great thing in which they share most—pleasure. And it is certainly part of the strong natural curiosity which readers feel to varying degree and which writers feel to the most compelling degree as to how any one story ever gets told. The only way a writer can satisfy his own curiosity is to write it. And how different this already makes it from telling it! Suspense, pleasure, curiosity, all are bound up in the making of the written story.

Forster went on to distinguish between what Neanderthal man told, the narrative thread, and what the written story has made into an art, the plot. "The king died and then the queen died" is the narrative thread; "The king died and then the queen died of grief" is a plot. We have all come from asking What next? to asking Why? The word which, of course, opened up everything, or as much of everything as the writer is able to handle.

To take a story:

Jack Potter, the town marshal of Yellow Sky, has gone to San Anton' and got married and is bringing his bride back in a Pullman as a dazzling surprise for his hometown. And while the train is on its way, back in Yellow Sky Scratchy Wilson gets drunk and turns loose with both hands. Everybody runs to cover: he has come to shoot up the town. "And his boots had red tops with gilded imprints, of the kind beloved in winter by little sledding boys on the hillsides of New England . . . The only sounds were his terrible invitations . . . He comfortably fusilladed the windows of his most intimate friend. The man was playing with the town; it was a toy for him." The train comes in, Scratchy and the marshal are face to face, and Potter says, "I ain't got a gun on me, Scratchy," and takes only a minute to make up his mind to be shot on his wedding day. "If you ain't got a gun, why ain't you got a gun?" "I ain't got a gun because I've just come from San Anton' with my wife. I'm married." "Married? Married? . . . Is this the lady?" "Yes; this is the lady." " 'Well,' said Wilson at last, slowly, I s'pose it's all off now.' He was not a student of chivalry; it was merely that in the presence of this condition he was a simple child of the earlier plains." He picked up his starboard revolver, and, placing both weapons in their holsters, he went away.

Two predicaments meet here, in Stephen Crane's "The Bride Comes to Yellow Sky." You might say they are magentized toward each other—and collide. One is vanquished with neatness and absurdity; as he goes away, Scratchy's "feet made funnel-shaped tracks in the heavy sand." Here are the plainest equivalents of comedy, two situations in a construction simple as a seesaw, and not without a seesaw's kind of pleasure in reading; like Scratchy Wilson, Crane is playing with us here.

In Katherine Mansfield's "Miss Brill," there is only one character and a single situation; Miss Brill's action consists nearly altogether in sitting down—she goes out to sit in the park, returns to sit on her bed. There is no collision. Rather, the forces meeting in the public gardens have, at the story's end, passed through each other and come out at the other side; there has been not a collision, but a change—something more significant. This is because, although there is one small situation going on, a large, complex one is implied. Life itself corresponds to the part of Scratchy Wilson, so to speak. Not violent life, merely life in a park on Sunday afternoon in Paris. All that it usually does for Miss Brill is promenade, yet, life being life, it does finally threaten. How much more deadly to such a lady than a flourished pistol is a remark overheard about herself. Reality comes to leer at her from a pleasant place, and she has not come prepared to bear it. And so she, who in her innocence could spare even pity for this world—pity, the spectator's emotion—is defeated. A word is spoken and the blow falls and Miss Brill retires, ridiculously easy to mow down, as the man with the pistols was easy to stare down in "Yellow Sky" for comedy's sake. But Miss Brill was from the first defenseless and on the losing side; her defeat is the deeper for it and one feels sure it is for always. So this story, instead of being a simple situation, is an impression of a situation, and tells more for being so.

Looking at these two stories by way of their plots in skeleton, we can't help but notice something: their plots are not unlike. "The Bride Comes to Yellow Sky" is its more unpretentious form, "Miss Brill" shows an interesting variation. It is a plot with two sides, or two halves, or two opposites, or two states of mind or feeling side by side; even one such in repeat would be a form of this. The plot is, of course, life *versus* death, which includes nearly every story in the world.

It could be said equally well that most stories (and novels too) have plots of the errand of search. An idea this pervasive simply pervades life, and the generality that could include in one quick list "The Bear," "The Jolly Corner," "The Short Happy Life of Francis Macomber" and "Araby" doesn't tell us really anything.

And so, plainly, we must distinguish plots not by their skeletons but by their full bodies; for they are embodiments, little worlds. Here is another: let us try to distinguish it as if it were literally a little world, and spinning closely now into our vision.

Now, the first thing we notice about this story is that we can't really see its solid outlines—it seems bathed in something of its own. It is wrapped in an atmosphere. This is what makes it shine, perhaps, as well as what obscures, at first glance, its plain real shape.

We are bearing in mind that the atmosphere in a story may be not the least of its glories, and also the fact that it may give a first impression that will prove contrary to what lies under it. Some action stories fling off the brightest clouds of obscuring and dazzling light, like ours here. Penetrate that atmosphere and the object may show quite dark within, for all its clouds of speed, those primary colors of red and yellow and blue. It looks like one of Ernest Hemingway's stories, and it is.

A story behaves, it goes through motions—that's part of it. Some stories leave a train of light behind them, meteor-like, so that much later than they strike our eyes we may see their meaning like an aftereffect. And Faulkner's seem not meteors but comets; they have a course of their own that brings them around more than once; they reappear in their own time in the sense that they reiterate their meaning and show a whole further story over and beyond their single significance.

If we have thought of Hemingway's stories as being bare and solid as billiard balls, so scrupulously cleaned of adjectives, of every unneeded word, as they are, of being plain throughout as a verb is plain, we may come to think twice about it, from our stargazer distance. The atmosphere that cloaks D. H. Lawrence's stories is of sensation, which is pure but thick cover, a cloak of self-illuminating air, but the atmosphere that surrounds Hemingway's is just as thick and to some readers less illuminating. Action can indeed be inscrutable, more so than sensation can. It can be just as voluptuous, too, just as vaporous, and, as I am able to see it, much more desperately concealing.

In one of Hemingway's early stories, "Indian Camp," Nick goes with his father, a doctor, to see a sick Indian woman. She is suffering in labor and the doctor operates on her without an anaesthetic. In the bunk above her head, her husband lies with a sore foot. After the operation is over and the child successfuly born, the husband is found to have slit his throat because he had not been able to bear his wife's suffering. Nick asks, "Is dying hard, Daddy?" "No, I think it's pretty easy," his father says.

Is this still a red and blue world? I see it as dark as night. Not that it is obscure; rather, it's opaque. Action can be radiant, but in this writer who has action to burn, it is not. The stories are opaque by reason of his intention, which is to moralize. We are to be taught by Hemingway, who is instructive by method, that the world is dangerous and full of fear, and that there is a way we had better be. There is nothing for it but, with bravery, to observe the ritual. And so action can step in front of reality just as surely and with more agility than even sentimentality can. Our belligerent planet Mars has an unknown and unrevealed heart.

Nevertheless, this is not where we stop seeing. For what comes of this, his method? In a painting by Goya, who himself used light, action and morality dramatically, of course, the bullring and the great turbulent wall of spectators are cut in diagonal halves by a great shadow of afternoon (unless you see it as the dark sliced away by the clear, golden light): half the action revealed and half hidden in dense, clotting shade. It's like this in Hemingway's plots. And it seems to be the halving that increases the story.

One power of his, his famous use of dialogue, derives as well from the fact that something is broken in two; language slips, meets a barrier, a shadow is inserted between the speakers. It is an obscuring and at the same time a revealing way to write dialogue, and only great skill can manage it—and make us aware at the same time that communication of a limited kind is now going on as best it can.

As we now see Hemingway's story, not transparent, not radiant, but lit from outside the story, from a moral source, we see that light's true nature: it is a spotlight. And his stories are all taking place as entirely in the present as plays we watch being acted on the stage. Pasts and futures are among the things his characters have not. Outside this light, they are nothing.

Clearly, the fact that stories have plots in common is of no more account than that many people have blue eyes. Plots are, indeed, what the story writer sees with, and so do we as we read. The plot is the Why. Why? is asked and replied to at various depths; the fishes in the sea are bigger the deeper we go. To learn that character is a more awe-inspiring fish and (in a short story, though not, I think, in a novel) one some degrees deeper down than situation, we have only to read Chekhov. What constitutes the reality of his characters is what they reveal to us. And the possibility that they may indeed reveal everything is what makes fictional characters differ so greatly from us in real life; yet isn't it strange that they don't really *seem* to differ? This is one clue to the extraordinary magnitude of character in fiction. Characters in the plot connect us with the vastness of our secret life, which is endlessly explorable. This is their role. What happens to them is what they have been put here to show.

In his story "The Darling," the darling's first husband, the

theatre manager, dies suddenly *because* of the darling's sweet
passivity; this is the causality of fiction. In everyday or real
life he might have held on to his health for years. But under
Chekhov's hand he is living and dying in dependence on, and
in revelation of, Olenka's character. He can only last a page
and a half. Only by force of the story's circumstance is he
here at all; Olenka took him up to begin with because he lived
next door.

> Olenka listened to Kukin with silent gravity, and some-
> times tears came into her eyes. In the end his misfortunes
> touched her; she grew to love him. He was a small thin
> man, with a yellow face; as he talked his mouth worked
> on one side, and there was always an expression of despair
> on his face; yet he aroused a deep and genuine affection
> in her. She was always fond of someone, and could not
> exist without loving. In earlier days she had loved her
> papa, who now sat in a darkened room, breathing with
> difficulty; she had loved her aunt, who used to come every
> other year from Bryansk; and before that, when she was
> at school, she had loved her French master. She was a
> gentle, soft-hearted, compassionate girl, with mild, tender
> eyes and very good health. At the sight of her full rosy
> cheeks, her soft white neck with a little dark mole on it,
> and the kind, naïve smile, which came into her face when
> she listened to anything pleasant, men thought, "Yes, not
> half bad," and smiled too, while lady-visitors could not
> refrain from seizing her hand in the middle of a conver-
> sation, exclaiming in a gush of delight, "You darling!"

Kukin proposes and they are married.

> And when he had a closer view of her neck and her
> plump, fine shoulders, he threw up his hand and said "You
> darling!" . . . And what Kukin said about the theatre
> and the actors she repeated. Like him she despised the

public for their ignorance and indifference to art; she took part in the rehearsals, she corrected the actors, she kept an eye on the behavior of the musicians, and when there was an unfavorable notice in the local paper, she shed tears, and then went to the editor's office to set things right ...

And when Kukin dies, Olenka's cry of heartbreak is this: "Vanitchka, my precious, my darling! Why did I ever meet you! Why did I know you and love you! Your poor broken-hearted Olenka is all alone without you!"

With variations the pattern is repeated, and we are made to feel it as plot, aware of its clear open stress, the variations all springing from Chekhov's boundless and minute perception of character. The timber-merchant, another neighbor, is the one who walks home from the funeral with Olenka. The outcome follows tenderly, is only natural. After three days, he calls. "He did not stay long, only about ten minutes, and he did not say much, but when he left, Olenka loved him—loved him so much that she lay awake all night in a perfect fever."

Olenka and Pustovalov get along very well together when they are married.

> "Timber gets dearer every year; the price rises twenty per cent," she would say to her customers and friends ... "And the freight!" she would add, covering her cheeks with her hands in horror, "the freight!" ... It seemed to her that she had been in the timber trade for ages and ages; and that the most important and necessary thing in life was timber; and there was something intimate and touching to her in the very sound of words such as "post," "beam," "pole," "batten," "lath," "plank," and the like.

Even in her dreams Olenka is in the timber business, dreaming of "perfect mountains of planks and boards," and cries out in her sleep, so that Pustovalov says to her tenderly, "Olenka, what's the matter, darling? Cross yourself!" But the timber merchant inevitably goes out in the timber yard one day without his cap on; he catches cold and dies, to leave Olenka a widow once more. "I've nobody, now you've left me, my darling," she sobs after the funeral. "How can I live without you?"

And the timber merchant is succeeded by a veterinary surgeon—who gets transferred to Siberia. But the plot is not repetition—it is direction. The love which Olenka bears to whatever is nearest her reaches its final and, we discover, its truest mold in maternalism: for there it is most naturally innocent of anything but formless, thoughtless, blameless *embracing*; the true innocence is in never perceiving. Only mother love could endure in a pursuit of such blind regard, caring so little for the reality of either life involved so long as love wraps them together, Chekhov tells us—unpretentiously, as he tells everything, and with the simplest of concluding episodes. Olenka's character is seen purely then for what it is: limpid reflection, mindless and purposeless regard, love that falls like the sun and rain on all alike, vacant when there is nothing to reflect.

We know this because, before her final chance to love, Olenka is shown to us truly alone:

[She] got thinner and plainer; and when people met her in the street they did not look at her as they used to, and did not smile to her; evidently her best years were over and left behind, and now a new sort of life had begun for her, which did not bear thinking about . . . And what was worst of all, she had no opinions of any sort. She saw the objects about her and understood what she saw, but could not form any opinions about them, and did not know what to talk about. And how awful it is not to have any opinions! She wanted a love that would absorb her whole being, her whole soul and reason—that would give her ideas and an object in life, and would warm her old blood.

The answer is Sasha, the ten-year-old son of the veterinary surgeon, an unexpected blessing from Siberia—a schoolchild. The veterinarian has another wife now, but this no longer matters. "Olenka, with arms akimbo, walked about the yard giving directions. Her face was beaming, and she was brisk and alert, as though she had waked from a long sleep . . ." "An island is a piece of land entirely surrounded by water," Sasha reads aloud. " 'An island is a piece of land,' she repeated, and this was the first opinion to which she gave utterance with positive conviction, after so many years of silence and dearth of ideas." She would follow Sasha halfway to school, until he told her to go back. She would go to bed thinking blissfully of Sasha, "who lay sound asleep in the next room, sometimes crying out in his sleep, 'I'll give it to you! Get away! Shut up!' "

The darling herself *is* the story; all else is sacrificed to her; deaths and departures are perfunctory and to be expected. The last words of the story are the child's and a protest, but they are delivered in sleep, as indeed protest to the darlings of this world will always be—out of inward and silent rebellion alone, as this master makes plain.

It is when the plot, whatever it is, is nearest to becoming the same thing on the outside as it is deep inside, that it is purest. When it is identifiable in every motion and progression of its own with the motions and progressions of the story's feeling and its intensity, then this is plot put to its highest use.

This brings us to another story.

One evening, March was standing with her back to the sunset, her gun under her arm, her hair pushed up under her cap. She was half watching, half musing. It was her constant state. Her eyes were keen and observant, but her inner mind took no notice of what she saw. She was always lapsing into this odd, rapt state, her mouth rather screwed up. It was a question whether she was there, actually, consciously present, or not . . . What was she thinking about? Heaven knows. Her consciousness was, as it were, held back.

She lowered her eyes and suddenly saw the fox. He was looking up at her. His chin was pressed down, and his eyes were looking up. They met her eyes. And he knew her. She was spellbound—she knew he knew her. So he looked into her eyes, and her soul failed her. He knew her, he was not daunted.

She struggled, confusedly she came to herself, and saw him making off, with slow leaps over some fallen boughs, slow, impudent jumps. Then he glanced over his shoulder, and ran smoothly away. She saw his brush held smooth like a feather, she saw his white buttocks twinkle. And he was gone, softly, soft as the wind.

In this long story by D. H. Lawrence, "The Fox," March and Banford, two girls, run a chicken farm by themselves in the country. As we see, it has its fox. They struggle against his encroachments, also against poverty and the elements, until a young soldier on leave, Henry, appears in the door one night. He has a vague story about his grandfather's once having lived here. March, the hunter and the man of the place, has not, as you know, shot the fox. But she has been, to use her word to herself, "impressed" by him. And here is Henry:

He had a ruddy, roundish face, with fairish hair, rather long, flattened to his forehead with sweat. His eyes were blue, and very bright and sharp. On his cheeks, on the fresh ruddy skin, were fine fine hairs like a down, but sharper. It gave him a slightly glistening look . . . He stooped, thrusting his head forward . . . He stared brightly, very keenly, from girl to girl, particularly at March, who stood pale, with great dilated eyes. She still had the gun in her hand. Behind her, Banford, clinging to the sofa arm, was shrinking away, with half-averted head.

So Henry, not on any account because of his cock-and-bull story, is taken in to spend his leave here. As expected by all, he proves himself a calculating, willful being, and proposes to marry March.

He scarcely admitted his intention to himself. He kept it as a secret even from himself . . . He would have to go gently . . . It's no good walking out into the forest and saying to the deer: "Please fall to my gun." No, it is a slow, subtle battle . . . It is not so much what you *do*, when you go out hunting, as how you *feel*. You have to be subtle and cunning, and absolutely, fatally ready . . . It is a subtle, profound battle of wills, which takes place in the invisible. And it is a battle never finished till your bullet goes home . . . It is your own *will* which carries the bullet into the heart of your quarry . . . And it was as a young hunter that he wanted to bring down March as his quarry, to make her his wife.

Dreams occur, the fox prowls, March and Banford suffer and argue while Henry, prowling, exerts and practices his will: the farm's fox is disposed of by him.

Here we are at the heart of this story: One night,

March dreamed vividly. She dreamed she heard a sing-ing outside, which she could not understand, singing that roamed round the house, in the fields and in the darkness. It moved her so, that she felt she must weep. She went out, and suddenly she knew it was the fox singing. He was very yellow and bright, like corn. She went nearer to him, but he ran away and ceased singing. He seemed near, and she wanted to touch him. She stretched out her hand, but suddenly he bit her wrist, and at the same instant, as she drew back, the fox, turning round to bound away, whisked his brush across her face, and it seemed his brush was on fire, for it seared and burned her mouth with a great pain. She awoke with the pain of it, and lay trembling as if she were really seared.

Banford, the sensitive one, dies when Henry deliberately fells a tree her way, and Henry and March marry and are to be unhappy and embattled forever after.

And now, in Lawrence's work, what of his extraordinary characters? Are they real, recognizable, neat men and women? Would you know them if you saw them? Not even, I think, if they began to speak on the street as they speak in his stories, in the very words—they would appear as deranged people. And for this there is the most reliable of reasons: Lawrence's characters don't really speak their words, and they're not walking about on the street. They are playing like fountains or radiating like the moon or storming like the sea, or their silence is the silence of wicked rocks. It is borne home to us that Lawrence is writing of human relationships on earth in terms of his own heaven and hell, and on these terms plot and characters are alike sacrificed to something: that which Lawrence passionately believes to transcend both and which is known and found directly through the senses. It is the world of the senses that Lawrence writes in. He almost literally writes from within it. He is first wonderful at making a story world, a place, and then wonderful again when he inhabits it with six characters, the five senses and sex. And the plot is by necessity a symbolic one. We know straight from the start in "The Fox" that every point in the story is to be made *subjectively*. "He knew her. And she knew he knew her." And we know she knew he knew her: this by his almost super-normal appeal to, and approach by way of, what can be seen, felt and heard. What has made this story strange is also what empowers us to understand it. It is hypnotic. Human relationships in his stories are made forces so strong that *what* they are (and what you and I should perhaps find indescribable) is simply, when we read him, accepted without question.

It is characteristic of Lawrence that in describing the relationship between the two women, March and Banford, which is outwardly unconventional, he is stating perfectly clearly within his story's terms the conventional separation at work in the two halves of the personality—the conscious and the unconscious, or the will and the passive susceptibility, what is "ready" and what is submerged. March and Banford may well be the two halves of one woman, of woman herself in the presence of the male will. Lawrence prosecutes his case with the persistence of a lawyer, with the mowing down of any dissent that the prophet is allowed to practice. But what moves, convinces, persuades us, all the same, is, so to speak, the odor of the fox—for the senses, the poetic world that lies far deeper than these shafts of argument or preaching really go, work Lawrence's spell.

For Virginia Woolf in her stories the senses mattered extremely, as we know; toward sex she was a critic. But the beauty and the innovation of her writing are both due to the fact, it seems to this reader, that the imprisonment of life in the word was with her a concern of the intellect as much as it was with the senses. She uses her senses intellectually, while Lawrence, if this is not too easy to say, uses his intellect sensually. While Chekhov patiently builds up character, Lawrence furiously breaks down character. It doesn't need fiction writers to tell us that opposite things are very often done in getting at the truth. But it was Lawrence who was like the True Princess, who felt that beneath forty featherbeds there was a pea. Lawrence was as sensitive to falsity as the True Princess was to the pea, and he was just as sure to proclaim the injury. He quarrels with us terribly, of course, because it matters to him, in getting his story to the way he wants it, to quarrel.

Those who write with cruelty, and Lawrence is one, may not be lacking in compassion but stand in need to write in exorcisement. Chekhov was exorcising nothing, he simply showed it forth. He does not perhaps put his own feelings above life. Lawrence in his stories protests the world, and at the same time he gives the world an almost unbearable wonder and beauty.

His stories may at times remind you of some kind of tropical birds, that are in structure all but awkward—for what is symbolic has a very hard time if it must be at all on the ground; but then when they take wing, as they do, the miracle occurs. For Lawrence is an artist: his birds fly. Outrageousness itself is put to use, along with all that is felicitous. The bird in its flight is in superb command, our eyes are almost put out by iridescence. The phoenix really was his bird.

So much for "The Fox." "The Bear" begins:

There was a man and a dog too this time. Two beasts, counting Old Ben the bear, and two men, counting Boon Hogganbeck, in whom some of the same blood ran which ran in Sam Fathers, even though Boon's was a plebeian strain of it and in only Sam and Old Ben and the mongrel Lion was taintless and incorruptible.

And we're in a different world. There is a world outside, which we're expected to be acquainted with in its several stratifications, to which our inner world communicates and to which it answers. The blood in this story may not be conscious or unconscious, but it can be *tainted*—that is, it can be considered in its relation to action, to opinion, to life going on outside. Blood can be plebeian, mongrel, taintless, incorruptible in one sentence of William Faulkner's, whereas in all of Lawrence it is one thing, the abode of the unconscious.

You will remember that this is a hunting story. A boy has known always of a great bear in the hunting country he was born into; encounters the bear after his initiation into the wilderness, and does not kill him; but at last, years later, with a beast that is trained to be his match (the mongrel, Lion), the fatal encounter takes place, and bear, dog and old pure-blooded Indian all die of it.

We see at once as we read that this narrative has the quality of happening, and the blood of inheriting; the story indeed has signs of having so much to do with the outer world that it can happen, and has happened, more than once. In one respect, this story is a sample of that happening which is continuous, indigenous to the time and the place and the human element in and through which it happens.

Ike McCaslin, in whose experience at various stages we are told the story,

> realized later that it had begun long before that. It had already begun on that day when he first wrote his age in two ciphers and his cousin McCaslin brought him for the first time to the camp, the big woods, to earn for himself from the wilderness the name and state of hunter provided he in his turn were humble and enduring enough.

Humble and enduring—qualities that apply to our relationship with the world.

> He had already inherited then, without ever having seen it, the big old bear with one trap-ruined foot that in an area of almost a hundred square miles had earned for himself a name, a definite designation like a living man— the long legend of corncribs broken down and rifled, of shoats and grown pigs and even calves carried bodily into the woods and devoured, and traps and deadfalls overthrown and dogs mangled and slain, and shotgun and even rifle shots delivered at pointblank range yet with no more effect than so many peas blown through a tube by a child —a corridor of wreckage and destruction beginning back before the boy was born, through which sped, not fast but rather with the ruthless and irresistible deliberation of a locomotive, the shaggy tremendous shape. It ran in his knowledge before he ever saw it. It loomed and towered in his dreams before he ever saw the unaxed woods where it left its crooked print, shaggy, tremendous, red-eyed, not malevolent but just big, too big for the dogs which tried to bay it, for the horses which tried to ride it, for the men and the bullets they fired into it; too big for the very country which was its constricting scope.

See the outer edges of this bear becoming abstract—but this bear is not the fox. "It was as if the boy had already divined what his senses and intellect had not encompassed yet . . ."

For this bear belongs to the world, the world of experience:

> that doomed wilderness whose edges were being constantly and punily gnawed at by men with plows and axes who feared it because it was wilderness, men myriad and nameless even to one another in the land where the old bear earned a name, and through which ran not even a mortal beast but an anachronism indomitable and invincible out of an old, dead time, a phantom, epitome and apotheosis of the old, wild life which the little puny humans swarmed and hacked at in a fury of abhorrence and fear, like pygmies about the ankles of a drowsing elephant;—the old bear, solitary, indomitable, and alone; widowered, childless, and absolved of mortality—old Priam, reft of his old wife, and outliving all his sons.

Experience in the world is the very thread this story is put together with. Here is the footprint:

> Then, standing beside Sam in the thick great gloom of ancient wood and the winter's dying afternoon, he looked quietly down at the rotted log scored and gutted with claw marks and, in the wet earth beside it, the print of the enormous warped two-toed foot . . . For the first time he realized that the bear which had run in his listening and loomed in his dreams since before he could remember, and which therefore must have existed in the listening and the dreams of his cousin and Major de Spain and even old General Compson before they began to remember in their turn, was a mortal animal and that they had departed for the camp each November with no actual intention of slaying it, not because it could not be slain but because so far they had no actual hope of being able to.

Faulkner achieves the startling reality and nearness of the outside world by alternately dilating reality to the reach of abstraction and bringing it home with a footprint. It is reality that not only *is*, but *looms*—and this not just one time to one character, but over and over, with an insistent quality.

There are several encounters between Ike McCaslin and the bear. The final one is a death struggle when the bear is

> on its hind feet, its back against a tree while the bellowing hounds swirled around it and once more Lion [the mongrel dog that is his match] drove in, leaping clear of the ground. This time the bear didn't strike him down. It caught the dog in both arms, almost loverlike, and they both went down.

There is a terrible fight, Lion clings to the bear's throat and the bear tears at Lion's body and wounds him mortally, but Lion will not let go. Boon, Lion's trainer who loves him, when Lion is clawed, runs toward them, a knife in his hand. He flings himself astride the bear and the knife falls.

> It fell just once . . . The bear then surged erect, raising with it the man and the dog too, and turned and still carrying the man and the dog it took two or three steps towards the woods on its hind feet as a man would have walked and crashed down. It didn't collapse, crumple. It fell all of a piece, as a tree falls, so that all three of them, man, dog and bear, seemed to bounce once.

The bear and the dog die of this, and so does Sam Fathers, the Indian, who is found lying motionless face down in the trampled mud when it's all over: not a mark on him, "he just quit." The bodies of the bear and Sam, open-eyed, teeth bared, brown—childless, kinless, peopleless—are stretched out alike.

"The Bear" ends with the death of three and a falling tree, as, you remember, "The Fox" ended—if you count the life-in-death of March and Henry as one death shared. The tree

in Faulkner's story, along with the dying bear and his burden
of victim and killer, is a wilderness falling. The fox is a denizen
of the inner world, purely. The bear is, equally purely, of the
outer world—not simply the material, three-dimensional outer
world, which is good enough, but the measureless outer world
of experience, the knowing and sentient past, the wisdom of
Time and Place. Both bear and fox are vanquished by acts of
the destructive will of man's aggression. But Faulkner's battles,
taking place in an ever-present physical territory which now
and again is also some projected country of the spirit, are conscious battles. Faulkner deals with such aspects of the human
being as dignity and glory and corruptibility and incorrupti-
bility and ridicule and defeat and pride and endurance—especially endurance, a word that might as well be in Cherokee to
Lawrence. Lawrence's battles are won and lost in the "blood
consciousness." It's as if the two worlds of Faulkner and Lawrence were, here, the inside-out of each other.

Faulkner seems to me, rather than an intuitive writer, a
divining one. And his stories seem to race with time, race with
the world, in an indirect ratio, perhaps, to the length of his
sentences. The sixteen-thousand-word sentence in "The Bear"
races like a dinosaur across the early fields of time. It runs along
with a strange quality of seeming all to happen at once. It
makes us realize once again that prose is a structure in its every
part, that the imagination is engineered when we write. A sentence may be in as perfect control as a church or a bridge.

"The Bear" is an apocalyptic story of the end of the wilderness. It ends with the senseless clang on clang of a man idi-
otically pounding pieces of his broken gun together while in
the isolated gum tree over his head forty or fifty squirrels are
running frantically round and round. It signifies, for one thing,
the arrival of the machine age and the squealing treadmill. This
story encompasses past and future, all the past of the land from
Indian times on to now. It has towering heroic figures, wilderness figures, symbolic figures; and through the hunter—whom
we see in the present, in boyhood, the past, the future, in ancestry (in the ledgers and memories and paraphernalia of the

place)—we are aware in every happening of its power to happen again, over and over; we are aware of the whole world of the wilderness, the whole history of Mississippi.

For in "The Bear," the structure of time is constantly in danger of being ripped away, torn down by the author; the *whole* time bulges, tries to get into the present-time of the story. This dilation in time sense and intractability in space sense, the whole surface of the story, has of itself a kind of looming quality, a portentousness. Like the skin of a balloon, time and space are stretched to hold more and more, while the story still holds it as long as it can, and in both form and function it dangerously increases.

And in Part Four of this long story the flimsy partition that keeps the story-time apart from whole time is allowed to fly away entirely. So the entire history of the land and a people crowds into a chapter whose expansion, in sentence and paragraph, is almost outrageous to the eye alone. Time and space have been too well invoked, and they tear through the story running backward and forward, up and down and around, like a pack of beasts themselves out of the world's wilderness. And this is the beauty of the story. Its self-destruction, self-immolation, is the way the story transcends all it might have been had it stayed intact and properly nailed together. There is its wonder.

Of course, such transcending might belong to some subjects and to other subjects it would bring foolishness. In the case of "The Bear" we can assume that to Faulkner the escapement of wild time and place seemed one attribute of the thing he was writing about—the lost attribute, implicit in it, and supplied now, in his story. In letting time and place out of the box he was not, by any standards but our ordinary ones, being reckless. By his own, he was being true, faithful to his composition of the story at hand. There is no other integrity.

We've observed how a story's great emphasis may fall on any of the things that make it up—on character, on plot, on its physical or moral world, in sensory or symbolic form. Now we may venture to say that it's this *ordering* of his story that is closest to the writer behind the writing, and that it's our perception of this ordering that gives us our nearest understanding of him.

And we have observed that the finest story writers seem to be in one sense obstructionists. As if they held back their own best interests—or what would be in another writer their best interests. It's a strange thing. And what is stranger is that if we look for the source of the deepest pleasure we receive from a writer, how often do we not find that it seems to be connected with this very obstruction.

The fact is, apparently, that in pressing to our source of pleasure we have entered into another world. We are speaking of beauty. And beauty is not a blatant or promiscuous or obvious quality; indeed, it is associated with reticence, with stubbornness, of a number of kinds. It arises somehow from a desire not to comply with what may be expected, but to act inevitably, as long as some human truth is in sight, whatever that inevitability may call for. Beauty is not a means, not a way of furthering a thing in the world. It is a result; it belongs to ordering, to form, to aftereffect.

Two qualities that cannot be imitated in this life, beauty and sensitivity, may in fiction's making be related to each other. But, reading and writing, we can only strive for one. Sensitivity in ourselves. And then beauty we may know, when we see it.

I think it ought to be said that a fiction writer can try anything. He has tried a great deal, but presumably not everything. The possibilities are endless because the stirring of the imagination never rests, and because we can never stop trying to make feeling felt.

So we know what will most pertinently describe the writing of our future too. Not rules, not esthetics, not problems and their solutions: not rules so long as there is imagination; not esthetics until after there is passion; not even problems that will always rise again and again for the honest writer. For at the other end of the writing is the reader. There is sure to be somewhere the reader, who is a user himself of imagination and thought, who knows, perhaps, as much about the need of communication as the writer.

Reader and writer, we wish each other well. Don't we want and don't we understand the same thing? A story of beauty and passion, some fresh approximation of human truth?

(1949)

Writing and Analyzing a Story

~§

Writers are often asked to give their own analysis of some story they have published. I never saw, as reader or writer, that a finished story stood in need of any more from the author: for better or worse, there the story is. There is also the question of whether or not the author could provide the sort of analysis asked for. Story writing and critical analysis are indeed separate gifts, like spelling and playing the flute, and the same writer proficient in both has been doubly endowed. But even he can't rise and do both at the same time.

To me as a story writer, generalizations about writing come tardily and uneasily, and I would limit them, if I were wise, by saying that any conclusions I feel confidence in are stuck to the particular story, part of the animal. The most trustworthy lesson I've learned from work so far is the simple one that the writing of each story is sure to open up a different prospect and pose a new problem; and that no past story bears recognizably on a new one or gives any promise of help, even if the writing mind had room for help and the wish that it would come. Help offered from outside the frame of the story would be itself an intrusion.

It's hard for me to believe that a writer's stories, taken in their whole, are written in any typical, predictable, systematically developing, or even chronological way—for all that a serious writer's stories are ultimately, to any reader, so clearly identifiable as his. Each story, it seems to me, thrives in the course of being written only as long as it seems to have a life of its own.

Yet it may become clear to a writer in retrospect (or so it did to me, although I may have been simply tardy to see it) that his stories have repeated themselves in shadowy ways, that they have returned and may return in future too—in variations—to certain themes. They may be following, in their own development, some pattern that's been very early laid down. Of course, such a pattern is subjective in nature; it may lie too deep to be consciously recognized until a cycle of stories and the actions of time have raised it to view. All the same, it is a pattern of which a new story is not another copy but a fresh attempt made in its own full-bodied right and out of its own impulse, with its own pressure, and its own needs of fulfillment.

It seems likely that all of one writer's stories do tend to spring from the same source within him. However they differ in theme or approach, however they vary in mood or fluctuate in their strength, their power to reach the mind or heart, all of one writer's stories carry their signature because of the one impulse most characteristic of his own gift—to praise, to love, to call up into view. But then, what countless stories by what countless authors share a common source! For the source of the short story is usually lyrical. And all writers speak from, and speak to, emotions eternally the same in all of us: love, pity, terror do not show favorites or leave any of us out.

The tracking down of a story might do well to start not in the subjective country but in the world itself. What in this world leads back most directly, makes the clearest connection to these emotions? What is the pull on the line? For some outside signal has startled or moved the story-writing mind to complicity: some certain irresistible, alarming (pleasurable or disturbing), magnetic person, place or thing. The outside world and the writer's response to it, the story's quotients, are always different, always differing in the combining; they are always—or so it seems to me—most intimately connected with each other.

This living connection is one that by its nature is not very open to generalization or discoverable by the ordinary scrutinies of analysis. Never mind; for its existence is, for any purpose but that of the working writer, of little importance to the story itself. It is of merely personal importance. But it is of extraordinary, if temporary, use to the writer for the particular story. Keeping this connection close is a writer's testing device along the way, flexible, delicate, precise, a means of guidance. I would rather submit a story to the test of its outside world, to show what it was doing and how it went about it, than to the method of critical analysis which would pick the story up by its heels (as if it had swallowed a button) to examine the writing process as analysis in reverse, as though a story—or any system of feeling—could be more accessible to understanding for being hung upside down.

It is not from criticism but from this world that stories come in the beginning; their origins are living reference plain to the writer's eye, even though to his eye alone. The writer's mind and heart, where all this exterior is continually *becoming* something—the moral, the passionate, the poetic, hence the *shaping* idea—can't be mapped and plotted. (Would this help—any more than a map hung on the wall changes the world?) It's the form it takes when it comes out the other side, of course, that gives a story something unique—its life. The story, in the way it has arrived at what it is on the page, has been something learned, by dint of the story's challenge and the work that rises to meet it—a process as uncharted for the writer as if it had never been attempted before.

Since analysis has to travel backward, the path it goes is an ever-narrowing one, whose goal is the vanishing point, beyond which only "influences" lie. But the writer of the story, bound in the opposite direction, works into the open. The choices multiply, become more complicated and with more hanging on them, as with everything else that has a life and moves. "This story promises me fear and joy and so I write it" has been the writer's beginning. The critic, coming to the end of his trail, may call out the starting point he's found, but the writer knew his starting point first and for what it was—the jumping-off place. And all along, the character of the choices—the critic's decisions and the writer's—is wholly different. I think that the writer's out-bound choices were to him the *believable* ones, not necessarily defensible on other grounds; impelled, not subject to scheme but to feeling; that they came with an arrow inside them. They have been *fiction's* choices: one-way and fateful; strict as art, obliged as feeling, powerful in their authenticity.

The story and its analysis are not mirror-opposites of each other. They are not reflections, either one. Criticism indeed is an art, as a story is, but only the story is to some degree a vision; there is no explanation outside fiction for what its writer is learning to do. The simplest-appearing work may have been brought off (when it does not fail) on the sharp edge of experiment, and it was for this its writer was happy to leave behind him all he knew before, and the safety of that, when he began the new story.

I feel that our ever-changing outside world and some learnable lessons about writing fiction are always waiting side by side for us to put into connection, if we can. A writer should say this only of himself and offer an example. In a story I wrote recently called "No Place for You, My Love," the outside world—a definite place in it, of course—not only suggested how to write it but repudiated a way I had already tried. What follows has no claim to be critical analysis; it can be called a piece of hindsight from a working point of view.

What changed my story was a trip. I was invited to drive with an acquaintance, one summer day, down south of New Orleans to see that country for the first (and so far, only) time; and when I got back home, full of the landscape I'd seen,

I realized that without being aware of it at the time, I had treated the story to my ride, and it had come into my head in an altogether new form. I set to work and wrote the new version from scratch.

As first written, the story told, in subjective terms, of a girl in a claustrophobic predicament: she was caught fast in the over-familiar, monotonous life of her small town, and immobilized further by a prolonged and hopeless love affair; she could see no way out. As a result of my ride, I extricated—not the girl, but the story.

This character had been well sealed inside her world, by nature and circumstance, just where I'd put her. But she was sealed in to the detriment of the story, because I'd made hers the point of view. The primary step now was getting outside her mind; on that instant I made her a girl from the Middle West. (She'd been before what I knew best, a Southerner.) I kept outside her by taking glimpses of her through the eyes of a total stranger: casting off the half-dozen familiars the first girl had around her, I invented a single new character, a man whom I brought into the story *to be* a stranger, and I was to keep out of his mind, too. I had double-locked the doors behind me.

It would have been for nothing had the original impulse behind the story not proved itself alive; it now took on new energy. That country—that once-submerged, strange land of "south from South"—which had so stamped itself upon my imagination put in an unmistakable claim now as the very image of the story's predicament. It pointed out to me at the same time where the real point of view belonged. Once I'd escaped those characters' minds, I saw it was outside them—suspended, hung in the air between two people, fished alive from the surrounding scene. As I wrote further into the story, something more real, more essential, than the characters were on their own was revealing itself. In effect, though the characters numbered only two, there had come to be a sort of third character along on the ride—the presence of a relationship between the two. It was what grew up between them meeting as strangers, went on the excursion with them, nodded back and forth from one to the other—listening, watching, persuading or denying them, enlarging or diminishing them, forgetful sometimes of who they were or what they were doing here—in its domain—and helping or betraying them along.

(Here I think it perhaps should be remembered that characters in a short story have not the size and importance and capacity for development they have in a novel, but are subservient altogether to the story as a whole.)

This third character's role was that of hypnosis—it was what a relationship *can do*, be it however brief, tentative, potential, happy or sinister, ordinary or extraordinary. I wanted to suggest that its being took shape as the strange, compulsive journey itself, was palpable as its climate and mood, the heat of the day—but was its spirit too, a spirit that held territory, that which is seen fleeting past by two vulnerable people who might seize hands on the run. There are moments in the story when I say neither "she felt" nor "he felt" but "they felt."

This is to grant that I rode out of the old story on the back of the girl and then threw away the girl; but I saved my story, for, entirely different as the second version was, it was what I wanted to tell. Now my subject was out in the open, provided at the same time with a place to happen and a way to say it was happening. All I had to do was recognize it, which I did a little late.

Anyone who has visited the actual scene of this story will possibly recognize it when he meets it here, for the story is visual and the place is out of the ordinary. The connection between a story and its setting may not always be so plain. For no matter whether the "likeness" is there for all to see or not, the place, once entered into the writer's mind in a story, is, in the course of writing the story, *functional*.

Thus I wanted to make seen and believed what was to me, in my story's grip, literally apparent—that secret and shadow are taken away in this country by the merciless light that prevails there, by the river that is like an exposed vein of ore, the road that descends as one with the heat—its nerve (these are all terms in the story), and that the heat is also a visual illusion, shimmering and dancing over the waste that stretches ahead. I was writing of a real place, but doing so in order to write about my subject. I was writing of exposure, and the shock of the world; in the end I tried to make the story's inside outside and then leave the shell behind.

The vain courting of imperviousness in the face of exposure is this little story's plot. Deliver us all from the naked in heart, the girl thinks (this is what I kept of her). "So strangeness gently steels us," I read today in a poem of Richard Wilbur's. Riding down together into strange country is danger, a play at danger, secretly poetic, and the characters, in attempting it as a mutual feat, admit nothing to each other except the wicked heat and its comical inconvenience. The only time they will yield or touch is while they are dancing in the crowd that to them is comically unlikely (hence insulating, non-conducting) or taking a kiss outside time. Nevertheless it happens that they go along aware, from moment to moment, as one: as my third character, the straining, hallucinatory eyes and ears, the roused-up sentient being of that place. Exposure begins in intuition; and the intuition comes to its end in showing the heart that has expected, while it dreads, that exposure. Writing it as I'd done before, as a story of concealment, in terms of the hermetic and the familiar, had somehow resulted in my own effective concealment of what I meant to show.

Now, the place had suggested to me that something demonaic was called for—the speed of the ride pitted against the danger of an easy or conventionally tempting sympathy, the heat that in itself drives on the driver in the face of an inimical world. Something wilder than ordinary communication between well-disposed strangers, and more ruthless and more tender, more pressing and acute, than their automatic, saving ironies and graces, I felt, and do so often feel, has to come up against a world like that.

I did my best to merge, or even to identify, the abstract

with the concrete as it became possible in this story—where setting, characters, mood, and method of writing all worked as parts of the same thing and subject to related laws and conditionings. The story *had* to be self-evident, and to hold its speed to the end—a speed I think of as racing, though it may not seem so to the reader.

Above all, I had no wish to sound mystical, but I admit that I did expect to sound mysterious now and then, if I could: this was a circumstantial, realistic story in which the reality *was* mystery. The cry that rose up at the story's end was, I hope unmistakably, the cry of that doomed relationship—personal, mortal, psychic—admitted in order to be denied, a cry that the characters were first able (and prone) to listen to, and then able in part to ignore. The cry was authentic to my story: the end of a journey *can* set up a cry, the shallowest provocation to sympathy and love does hate to give up the ghost. A relationship of the most fleeting kind has the power inherent to loom like a genie—to become vocative at the last, as it has already become present and taken up room; as it has spread out as a destination however unlikely; as it has glimmered and rushed by in the dark and dust outside, showing occasional points of fire. Relationship *is* a pervading and changing mystery; it is not words that make it so in life, but words have to make it so in a story. Brutal or lovely, the mystery waits for people wherever they go, whatever extreme they run to.

I had got back at the end of the new story to suggesting what I had taken as the point of departure in the old, but there was no question in my mind which story was nearer the mark of my intention. This may not reflect very well on the brightness of the author at work; it may cause a reader to wonder how often a story has to rescue itself. I think it goes to show, all the same, that subject, method, form, style, all wait upon— indeed hang upon—a sort of double thunderclap at the author's ears: the break of the living world upon what is already stirring inside the mind, and the answering impulse that in a moment of high consciousness fuses impact and image and fires them off together. There never really was a sound, but the impact is always recognizable, granting the author's sensitivity and sense; and if the impulse so projected is to some degree fulfilled, it may give some pleasure in its course to the writer and reader. The living world itself remains just the same as it always was, and luckily enough for the story, among other things, for it can test and talk back to the story any day in the week. Between the writer and the story he writes, *there* is the undying third character.

(1955)

Place in Fiction

Place is one of the lesser angels that watch over the racing hand of fiction, perhaps the one that gazes benignly enough from off to one side, while others, like character, plot, symbolic meaning, and so on, are doing a good deal of wing-beating about her chair, and feeling, who in my eyes carries the crown, soars highest of them all and rightly relegates place into the shade. Nevertheless, it is this lowlier angel that concerns us here. There have been signs that she has been rather neglected of late; maybe she could do with a little petitioning.

What place has place in fiction? It might be thought so modest a one that it can be taken for granted: the location of a novel; to use a term of the day, it may make the novel "regional." The term, like most terms used to pin down a novel, means little; and Henry James said there isn't any difference between "the English novel" and "the American novel," since there are only two kinds of novels at all, the good and the bad. Of course Henry James didn't stop there, and we all hate generalities, and so does place. Yet as soon as we step down from the general view to the close and particular, as writers must and readers may and teachers well know how to, and consider what good writing may be, place can be seen, in her own way, to have a great deal to do with that goodness, if not to be responsible for it. How so?

First, with the goodness—validity—in the raw material of writing. Second, with the goodness in the writing itself—the achieved world of appearance, through which the novelist has his whole say and puts his whole case. There will still be the lady, always, who dismissed *The Ancient Mariner* on grounds of implausibility. Third, with the goodness—the worth—in the writer himself: place is where he has his roots, place is where he stands; in his experience out of which he writes, it provides the base of reference; in his work, the point of view. Let us consider place in fiction in these three wide aspects.

Wide, but of course connected—vitally so. And if in some present-day novels the connection has apparently slipped, that makes a fresh reason for us to ponder the subject of place. For novels, besides being the pleasantest things imaginable, are powerful forces on the side. Mutual understanding in the world being nearly always, as now, at low ebb, it is comforting to remember that it is through art that one country can nearly always speak reliably to another, if the other can hear at all. Art, though, is never the voice of a country; it is an even more precious thing, the voice of the individual, doing its best to speak, not comfort of any sort, indeed, but truth. And the art that speaks it most unmistakably, most directly, most variously, most fully, is fiction; in particular, the novel.

Why? Because the novel from the start has been bound up in the local, the "real," the present, the ordinary day-to-day of human experience. Where the imagination comes in is in directing the use of all this. That use is endless, and there are only four words, of all the millions we've hatched, that a novel rules out: "Once upon a time." They make a story a fairy tale by the simple sweep of the remove—by abolishing the present and the place where we are instead of conveying them to us. Of course we shall have some sort of fairy tale with us always— just now it is the historical novel. Fiction is properly at work on the here and now, or the past made here and now; for in novels *we* have to be there. Fiction provides the ideal texture through which the feeling and meaning that permeate our own personal, present lives will best show through. For in his theme

—the most vital and important part of the work at hand—the novelist has the blessing of the inexhaustible subject: you and me. You and me, here. Inside that generous scope and circumference—who could ask for anything more?—the novel can accommodate practically anything on earth; and has abundantly done so. The novel so long as it be *alive* gives pleasure, and must always give pleasure, enough to stave off the departure of the Wedding Guest forever, except for that one lady.

It is by the nature of itself that fiction is all bound up in the local. The internal reason for that is surely that *feelings* are bound up in place. The human mind is a mass of associations—associations more poetic even than actual. I say, "The Yorkshire Moors," and you will say, "*Wuthering Heights*," and I have only to murmur, "If Father were only alive—" for you to come back with "We could go to Moscow," which certainly is not even so. The truth is, fiction depends for its life on place. Location is the crossroads of circumstance, the proving ground of "What happened? Who's here? Who's coming?"—and that is the heart's field.

Unpredictable as the future of any art must be, one condition we may hazard about writing: of all the arts, it is the one least likely to cut the cord that binds it to its source. Music and dancing, while originating out of place—groves!—and perhaps invoking it still to minds pure or childlike, are no longer bound to dwell there. Sculpture exists out in empty space: that is what it commands and replies to. Toward painting, place, to be so highly visible, has had a curious and changing relationship. Indeed, wasn't it when landscape invaded painting, and painting was given, with the profane content, a narrative content, that this worked to bring on a revolution to the art? Impressionism brought not the likeness-to-life but the mystery of place onto canvas; it was the method, not the subject, that told this. Painting and writing, always the closest two of the sister arts (and in ancient Chinese days only the blink of an eye seems to have separated them), have each a still closer connection with place than they have with each other; but a difference lies in their respective requirements of it, and even further in the way they use it—the written word being ultimately as different from the pigment as the note of the scale is from the chisel.

One element, which has just been mentioned, is surely the underlying bond that connects all the arts with place. All of them celebrate its mystery. Where does this mystery lie? Is it in the fact that place has a more lasting identity than we have, and we unswervingly tend to attach ourselves to identity? Might the magic lie partly, too, in the *name* of the place—since that is what *we* gave it? Surely, once we have it named, we have put a kind of poetic claim on its existence; the claim works even out of sight—may work forever sight unseen. The Seven Wonders of the World still give us this poetic kind of gratification. And notice we do not say simply "The Hanging Gardens"—that would leave them dangling out of reach and dubious in nature; we say "The Hanging Gardens of Babylon," and there they are, before our eyes, shimmering and garlanded and exactly elevated to the Babylonian measurement.

Edward Lear tapped his unerring finger on the magic of place in the limerick. There's something unutterably convincing about that Old Person of Sparta who had twenty-five sons and one darta, and it is surely beyond question that he fed them on snails and weighed them in scales, because we know where that Old Person is *from*—Sparta! We certainly do not need further to be told his *name*. "Consider the source." Experience has ever advised us to base validity on point of origin.

Being shown how to locate, to place, any account is what does most toward *making* us believe it, not merely allowing us to, may the account be the facts or a lie; and that is where place in fiction comes in. Fiction is a lie. Never in its inside thoughts, always in its outside dress.

Some of us grew up with the china night-light, the little lamp whose lighting showed its secret and with that spread enchantment. The outside is painted with a scene, which is one thing; then, when the lamp is lighted, through the porcelain sides a new picture comes out through the old, and they are seen as one. A lamp I knew of was a view of London till it was lit; but then it was the Great Fire of London, and you could go beautifully to sleep by it. The lamp alight is the combination of internal and external, glowing at the imagination as one; and so is the good novel. Seeing that these inner and outer surfaces do lie so close together and so implicit in each other, the wonder is that human life so often separates them, or appears to, and it takes a good novel to put them back together.

The good novel should be steadily alight, revealing. Before it can hope to be that, it must of course be steadily visible from its outside, presenting a continuous, shapely, pleasing and finished surface to the eye.

The sense of a story when the visibility is only partial or intermittent is as endangered as Eliza crossing the ice. Forty hounds of confusion are after it, the black waters of disbelief open up between its steps, and no matter which way it jumps it is bound to slip. Even if it has a little baby moral in its arms, it is more than likely a goner.

The novel must get Eliza across the ice; what it means—the way it proceeds—is always in jeopardy. It must be given a surface that is continuous and unbroken, never too thin to trust, always in touch with the senses. Its world of experience must be at every step, through every moment, within reach as the world of appearance.

This makes it the business of writing, and the responsibility of the writer, to disentangle the significant—in character, incident, setting, mood, everything—from the random and meaningless and irrelevant that in real life surround and beset it. It is a matter of his selecting and, by all that implies, of changing "real" life as he goes. With each word he writes, he acts—as literally and methodically as if he hacked his way through a forest and blazed it for the word that follows. He makes choices at the explicit demand of this one present story; each choice implies, explains, limits the next, and illuminates the one before. No two stories ever go the same way, although in different hands one story might possibly go any one of a thousand ways; and though the woods may look the same from outside, it is a new and different labyrinth every time. What tells the author his way? Nothing at all but what he knows inside himself: the same thing that hints to him afterward how far he has missed it, how near he may have come to the heart of it. In a working sense, the novel and its place have become one: work has made them, for the time being, the same thing, like the explorer's tentative map of the known world.

The reason why every word you write in a good novel is a lie, then, is that it is written expressly to serve the purpose; if it does not apply, it is fancy and frivolous, however specially dear to the writer's heart. Actuality, it is true, is an even bigger risk to the novel than fancy writing is, being frequently even more confusing, irrelevant, diluted and generally far-fetched than ill-chosen words can make it. Yet somehow, the world of appearance in the novel has got to *seem* actuality. Is there a reliable solution to the problem? Place being brought to life in the round before the reader's eye is the readiest and gentlest and most honest and natural way this can be brought about, I think; every instinct advises it. The moment the place in which the novel happens is accepted as true, through it will begin to glow, in a kind of recognizable glory, the feeling and thought that inhabited the novel in the author's head and animated the whole of his work.

Besides furnishing a plausible abode for the novel's world of feeling, place has a good deal to do with making the characters real, that is, themselves, and keeping them so. The reason is simply that, as Tristram Shandy observed, "We are not made of glass, as characters on Mercury might be." Place *can* be transparent, or translucent: not people. In real life we have to express the things plainest and closest to our minds by the clumsy word and the half-finished gesture; the chances are our most usual behavior makes sense only in a kind of daily way, because it has become familiar to our nearest and dearest, and still demands their constant indulgence and understanding. It is our describable outside that defines us, willy-nilly, to others, that may save us, or destroy us, in the world; it may be our shield against chaos, our mask against exposure; but whatever it is, the move we make in the place we live has to signify our intent and meaning.

Then think how unprotected the poor character in a novel is, into whose mind the author is inviting us to look—unprotected and hence surely unbelievable! But no, the author has expressly seen to believability. Though he must know all, again he works with illusion. Just as the world of a novel is more highly selective than that of real life, so character in a novel is much more definite, less shadowy than our own, in order that we may believe in it. This is not to say that the character's scope must be limited; it is our vision of it that is guided. It is a kind of phenomenon of writing that the likeliest character has first to be enclosed inside the bounds of even greater likelihood, or he will fly to pieces. Paradoxically, the more narrowly we can examine a fictional character, the greater he is likely to loom up. We must see him set to scale in his proper world to know his size. Place, then, has the most delicate control over character too: by confining character, it defines it.

Place in fiction is the named, identified, concrete, exact and exacting, and therefore credible, gathering spot of all that has been felt, is about to be experienced, in the novel's progress. Location pertains to feeling; feeling profoundly pertains to place; place in history partakes of feeling, as feeling about history partakes of place. Every story would be another story, and unrecognizable as art, if it took up its characters and plot and happened somewhere else. Imagine *Swann's Way* laid in London, or *The Magic Mountain* in Spain, or *Green Mansions* in the Black Forest. The very notion of moving a novel brings ruder havoc to the mind and affections than would a century's alteration in its time. It is only too easy to conceive that a bomb that could destroy all trace of places as we know them, in life and through books, could also destroy all feelings as we know them, so irretrievably and so happily are recognition, memory, history, valor, love, all the instincts of poetry and praise, worship and endeavor, bound up in place. From the dawn of man's imagination, place has enshrined the spirit; as soon as man stopped wandering and stood still and looked about him, he found a god in that place; and from then on, that was where the god abided and spoke from if ever he spoke.

Feelings are bound up in place, and in art, from time to time, place undoubtedly works upon genius. Can anyone well explain otherwise what makes a given dot on the map come passionately alive, for good and all, in a novel—like one of those novae that suddenly blaze with inexplicable fire in the heavens? What brought a *Wuthering Heights* out of Yorkshire, or a *Sound and the Fury* out of Mississippi?

If place does work upon genius, how does it? It may be that place can focus the gigantic, voracious eye of genius and bring its gaze to point. Focus then means awareness, discernment, order, clarity, insight—they are like the attributes of love. The act of focusing itself has beauty and meaning; it is the act that, continued in, turns into mediation, into poetry. Indeed, as soon as the least of us stands still, that is the moment something extraordinary is seen to be going on in the world. The drama, old beyond count as it is, is no older than the first stage. Without the amphitheatre around it to persuade the ear and bend the eye upon a point, how could poetry ever have been spoken, how have been heard? Man is articulate and intelligible only when he begins to communicate inside the strict terms of poetry and reason. Symbols in the end, both are permanent forms of the act of focusing.

Surely place induces poetry, and when the poet is extremely attentive to what is there, a meaning may even attach to his poem out of the spot on earth where it is spoken, and the poem signify the more because it does spring so wholly out of its place, and the sap has run up into it as into a tree.

But we had better confine ourselves here to prose. And then, to take the most absolutely unfanciful novelist of them all, it is to hear him saying, "*Madame Bovary—c'est moi.*" And we see focusing become so intent and aware and conscious in this most "realistic" novel of them all as to amount to fusion. Flaubert's work is indeed of the kind that is embedded immovably as rock in the country of its birth. If, with the slicers of any old (or new) criticism at all, you were to cut down through *Madame Bovary*, its cross section would still be the same as the cross section of that living earth, in texture, color, composition, all; which would be no surprise to Flaubert. For such fusion always means accomplishment no less conscious than it is gigantic—effort that must exist entirely as its own reward. We all know the letter Flaubert wrote when he had just found, in the morning paper, in an account of a minister's visit to Rouen, a phrase in the Mayor's speech of welcome

which I had written the day before, textually, in my *Bovary* . . . Not only were the idea and the words the same, but even the rhythm of the style. It's things like this that give me pleasure . . . Everything one invents is true, you may be perfectly sure of that! Poetry is as precise as geometry . . . And besides, after reaching a certain point, one no longer makes any mistakes about the things of the soul. My poor Bovary, without a doubt, is suffering and weeping this very instant in twenty villages of France.

And now that we have come to the writer himself, the question of place resolves itself into the point of view. In this changeover from the objective to the subjective, wonderful and unexpected variations may occur.

Place, to the writer at work, is seen in a frame. Not an empty frame, a brimming one. Point of view is a sort of burning-glass, a product of personal experience and time; it is burnished with feelings and sensibilities, charged from moment to moment with the sun-points of imagination. It is an instrument—one of intensification; it acts, it behaves, it is temperamental. We have seen that the writer must accurately choose, combine, superimpose

upon, blot out, shake up, alter the outside world for one absolute purpose, the good of his story. To do this, he is always
seeing double, two pictures at once in his frame, his and the
world's, a fact that he constantly comprehends; and he works
best in a state of constant and subtle and unfooled reference
between the two. It is his clear intention—his passion, I should
say—to make the reader see only one of the pictures—the author's—under the pleasing illusion that it is the world's; this
enormity is the accomplishment of a good story. I think it
likely that at the moment of the writer's highest awareness of,
and responsiveness to, the "real" world, his imagination's
choice (and miles away it may be from actuality) comes closest to being infallible for his purpose. For the spirit of things
is what is sought. No blur of inexactness, no cloud of vague-
ness, is allowable in good writing; from the first seeing to the
last putting down, there must be steady lucidity and uncom-
promise of purpose. I speak, of course, of the ideal.

One of the most important things the young writer comes to
see for himself is that point of view *is* an instrument, not an
end in itself, that is useful as a glass, and not as a mirror to reflect a dear and pensive face. Conscientiously used, point of
view will discover, explore, see through—it may sometimes
divine and prophesy. Misused, it turns opaque almost at once
and gets in the way of the book. And when the good novel is
finished, its cooled outside shape, what Sean O'Faolàin has
called "the veil of reality," has all the burden of communicating that initial, spontaneous, overwhelming, driving charge
of personal inner feeling that was the novel's reason for being.
The measure of this representation of life corresponds most
tellingly with the novel's life expectancy: whenever its world
of outside appearance grows dim or false to the eye, the novel
has expired.

Establishing a chink-proof world of appearance is not only
the first responsibility of the writer; it is the primary step in
the technique of every sort of fiction: lyric and romantic, of
course; the "realistic," it goes without saying; and other sorts

as well. Fantasy itself must touch ground with at least one toe, and ghost stories must have one foot, so to speak, in the grave. The black, squat, hairy ghosts of M. R. James come right out of Cambridge. Only fantasy's stepchild, poor science-fiction, does not touch earth anywhere; and it is doubtful already if happenings entirely confined to outer space are ever going to move us, or even divert us for long. Satire, engaged in its most intellectual of exercises, must first of all establish an impeccable *locus operandi*; its premise is the kingdom where certain rules apply. The countries Gulliver visits are the systems of thought and learning Swift satirizes made visible one after the other and set in operation. But while place in satire is a purely artificial construction, set up to be knocked down, in humor place becomes its most revealing and at the same time is itself the most revealed. This is because humor, it seems to me, of all forms of fiction, entirely accepts place for what it is.

"Spotted Horses," by William Faulkner, is a good case in point. At the same time that this is just about Mr. Faulkner's funniest story, it is the most thorough and faithful picture of a Mississippi crossroads hamlet that you could ever hope to see. True in spirit, it is also true to everyday fact. Faulkner's art, which often lets him shoot the moon, tells him when to be literal too. In all its specification of detail, both mundane and poetic, in its complete adherence to social fact (which nobody knows better than Faulkner, surely, in writing today), by its unerring aim of observation as true as the sights of a gun would give, but Faulkner has no malice, only compassion; and even and also in the joy of those elements of harlequinade-fantasy that the spotted horses of the title bring in—in all that shining fidelity to place lies the heart and secret of this tale's comic glory.

Faulkner is, of course, the triumphant example in America today of the mastery of place in fiction. Yoknapatawpha County, so supremely and exclusively and majestically and totally itself, is an everywhere, but only because Faulkner's first concern is for what comes first—Yoknapatawpha, his own created world. I am not sure, as a Mississippian myself, how widely it is realized and appreciated that these works of such marvelous imaginative power can also stand as works of the carefulest and purest representation. Heightened, of course: their specialty is they are twice as true as life, and that is why it takes a genius to write them. "Spotted Horses" may not have happened yet; if it had, some others might have tried to make a story of it; but "Spotted Horses" could happen tomorrow—that is one of its glories. It could happen today or tomorrow at any little crossroads hamlet in Mississippi; the whole combination of irresistibility is there. We have the Snopses ready, the Mrs. Littlejohns ready, nice Ratliff and the Judge ready and sighing, the clowns, sober and merry, settled for the evening retrospection of it in the cool dusk of the porch; and the Henry Armstids armed with their obsessions, the little periwinkle-eyed boys armed with their indestructibility; the beautiful, overweening spring, too, the moonlight on the pear trees from which the mockingbird's song keeps returning; and the little store and the fat boy to steal and steal away at its candy. There are undoubtedly spotted horses too, in the offing —somewhere in Texas this minute, straining toward the day. After Faulkner has told it, it is easy for one and all to look back and see it.

Faulkner, simply, knew it already; it is a different kind of knowledge from Flaubert's, and proof could not add much to it. He was born knowing, or rather learning, or rather prophesying, all that and more; and having it all together at one time available while he writes is one of the marks of his mind. If there *is* any more in Mississippi than is engaged and dilated upon, and made twice as real as it used to be and applies now to the world, in the one story "Spotted Horses," then we would almost rather not know it—but I don't bet a piece of store candy that there is. In Faulkner's humor, even more measurably than in his tragedy, it is all there.

It may be going too far to say that the exactness and concreteness and solidity of the real world achieved in a story correspond to the intensity of feeling in the author's mind and to the very turn of his heart; but there lies the secret of our confidence in him.

Making reality real is art's responsibility. It is a practical assignment, then, a self-assignment: to achieve, by a cultivated sensitivity for observing life, a capacity for receiving its impressions, a lonely, unremitting, unaided, unaidable vision, and transferring this vision without distortion to it onto the pages of a novel, where, if the reader is so persuaded, it will turn into the reader's illusion. How bent on this peculiar joy we are, reader and writer, willingly to practice, willingly to undergo, this alchemy for it!

What is there, then, about place that is transferable to the pages of a novel? The best things—the explicit things: physical texture. And as place has functioned between the writer and his material, so it functions between the writer and reader. Location is the ground conductor of all the currents of emotion and belief and moral conviction that charge out from the story in its course. These charges need the warm hard earth underfoot, the light and lift of air, the stir and play of mood, the softening bath of atmosphere that give the likeness-to-life that life needs. Through the story's translation and ordering of life, the unconvincing raw material becomes the very heart's familiar. Life *is* strange. Stories hardly make it more so; with all they are able to tell and surmise, they make it more believably, more inevitably so.

I think the sense of place is as essential to good and honest writing as a logical mind; surely they are somewhere related. It is by knowing where you stand that you grow able to judge where you are. Place absorbs our earliest notice and attention, it bestows on us our original awareness; and our critical powers spring up from the study of it and the growth of experience inside it. It perseveres in bringing us back to earth when we fly too high. It never really stops informing us, for it is forever astir, alive, changing, reflecting, like the mind of man itself. One place comprehended can make us understand other places better. Sense of place gives equilibrium; extended, it is sense of direction too. Carried off we might be in spirit, and should be, when we are reading or writing something good; but it is the sense of place going with us still that is the ball of golden thread to carry us there and back and in every sense of the word to bring us home.

What can place *not* give? Theme. It can present theme, show it to the last detail—but place is forever illustrative: it is a picture of what man has done and imagined, it is his visible past, result. Human life is fiction's only theme.

Should the writer, then, write about home? It is both natural and sensible that the place where we have our roots should become the setting, the first and primary proving ground, of our fiction. Location, however, is not simply to be used by the writer—it is to be discovered, as each novel itself, in the act of writing, is discovery. Discovery does not imply that the place is new, only that we are. Place is as old as the hills. Kilroy at least has been there, and left his name. Discovery, not being a matter of writing our name on a wall, but of seeing what that wall is, and what is over it, is a matter of vision.

One can no more say, "To write stay home," than one can say, "To write leave home." It is the writing that makes its own rules and conditions for each person. And though place is home, it is for the writer writing simply *locus*. It is where the particular story he writes can be pinned down, the circle it can spin through and keep the state of grace, so that for the story's duration the rest of the world suspends its claim upon it and lies low as the story in peaceful extension, the *locus* fading off into the blue.

Naturally, it is the very breath of life, whether one writes a word of fiction or not, to go out and see what is to be seen of the world. For the artist to be unwilling to move, mentally or spiritually or physically, out of the familiar is a sign that spiritual timidity or poverty or decay has come upon him; for what is familiar will then have turned into all that is tyrannical.

One can only say: writers must always write best of what

they know, and sometimes they do it by staying where they know it. But not for safety's sake. Although it is in the words of a witch—or all the more because of that—a comment of Hecate's in *Macbeth* is worth our heed: "Security/ Is mortal's chiefest enemy." In fact, when we think in terms of the spirit, which are the terms of writing, is there a conception more stupefying than that of security? Yet writing of what you know has nothing to do with security: what is more dangerous? How can you go out on a limb if you do not know your own tree? No art ever came out of not risking your neck. And risk—experiment—is a considerable part of the joy of doing, which is the lone, simple reason all writers of serious fiction are willing to work as hard as they do.

The open mind and the receptive heart—which are at last and with fortune's smile the informed mind and the experienced heart—are to be gained anywhere, any time, without necessarily moving an inch from any present address. There must surely be as many ways of seeing a place as there are pairs of eyes to see it. The impact happens in so many different ways.

It may be the stranger within the gates whose eye is smitten by the crucial thing, the essence of life, the moment or act in our long-familiar midst that will forever define it. The inhabitant who has taken his fill of a place and gone away may look back and see it for good, from afar, still there in his mind's eye like a city over the hill. It was in the New Zealand stories, written eleven thousand miles from home and out of homesickness, that Katherine Mansfield came into her own. Joyce transplanted not his subject but himself while writing about it, and it was as though he had never left it at all: there it was, still in his eye, exactly the way he had last seen it. From the Continent he wrote the life of Dublin as it was then into a book of the future, for he went translating his own language of it on and on into a country of its own, where it set up a kingdom as renowned as Prester John's. Sometimes two places, two countries, are brought to bear on each other, as in E. M. Forster's work, and the heart of the novel is heard beating most plainly, most passionately, most personally when two places are at meeting point.

There may come to be new places in our lives that are second spiritual homes—closer to us in some ways, perhaps, than our original homes. But the home tie is the blood tie. And had it meant nothing to us, any other place thereafter would have meant less, and we would carry no compass inside ourselves to find home ever, anywhere at all. We would not even guess what we had missed.

It is noticeable that those writers who for their own good reasons push out against their backgrounds nearly always passionately adopt the new one in their work. Revolt itself is a reference and tribute to the potency of what is left behind. The substitute place, the adopted country, is sometimes a very much stricter, bolder, or harsher one than the original, seldom more lax or undemanding—showing that what was wanted was structure, definition, rigidity—perhaps these were wanted, and understanding was not.

Hemingway in our time has sought out the formal and ruthless territories of the world, archaic ones often, where there are bullfight arenas, theatres of hunting and war, places with a primitive, or formidable, stripped-down character, with implacable codes, with inscrutable justices and inevitable retributions. But whatever the scene of his work, it is the *places* that never are hostile. People give pain, are callous and insensitive, empty and cruel, carrying with them no pasts as they promise no futures. But place heals the hurt, soothes the outrage, fills the terrible vacuum that these human beings make. It heals actively, and the response is given consciously, with the ardent care and explicitness, respect and delight of a lover, when fishing streams or naming over streets becomes almost something of the lover's secret language—as the careful conversations between characters in Hemingway bear hints of the secret language of hate. The response to place has the added intensity that comes with the place's not being native or taken for granted, but found, chosen; thereby is the rest more heavily repudiated. It is the response of the aficionado; the response, too, is adopted. The title "A Clean Well Lighted Place" is just what the human being is not, for Hemingway, and perhaps it is the epitome of what man would like to find in his fellow-man but never has yet, says the author, and never is going to.

We see that point of view is hardly a single, unalterable vision, but a profound and developing one of great complexity. The vision itself may move in and out of its material, shuttle-fashion, instead of being simply turned on it, like a telescope on the moon. Writing is an expression of the writer's own peculiar personality, could not help being so. Yet in reading great works one feels that the finished piece transcends the personal. All writers great and small must sometimes have felt that they have become part of what they wrote even more than it still remains a part of them.

When I speak of writing from where you have put down roots, it may be said that what I urge is "regional" writing. "Regional," I think, is a careless term, as well as a condescending one, because what it does is fail to differentiate between the localized raw material of life and its outcome as art. "Regional" is an outsider's term; it has no meaning for the insider who is doing the writing, because as far as he knows he is simply writing about life. Jane Austen, Emily Brontë, Thomas Hardy, Cervantes, Turgenev, the authors of the books of the Old Testament, all confined themselves to regions, great or small— but are they regional? Then who from the start of time has not been so?

It may well be said that all work springing out of such vital impulse from its native soil has certain things in common. But what signifies is that these are not the little things that it takes a fine-tooth critic to search out, but the great things, that could not be missed or mistaken, for they are the beacon lights of literature.

It seems plain that the art that speaks most clearly, explicitly, directly and passionately from its place of origin will remain the longest understood. It is through place that we put out roots, wherever birth, chance, fate or our traveling selves set us down; but where those roots reach toward—whether in America, England or Timbuktu—is the deep and running vein, eternal and consistent and everywhere purely itself, that feeds and is fed by the human understanding. The challenge to writers today, I think, is not to disown any part of our heritage. Whatever our theme in writing, it is old and tried. Whatever our place, it has been visited by the stranger, it will never be new again. It is only the vision that can be new; but that is enough.

(1956)

Words into Fiction

We start from scratch, and words don't; which is the thing that matters—matters over and over again. For though we grow up in the language, when we begin using words to make a piece of fiction, that is of course as different from using even the same words to say hello on the telephone as putting paint on canvas is. This very leap in the dark is exactly what writers write fiction in order to try. And surely they discovered that daring, and developed that wish, from reading. My feeling is that it's when reading begins to impress on us what degrees and degrees and degrees of communication are possible between novelists and ourselves as readers that we surmise what it has meant, can mean, to write novels.

Indeed, learning to write may be a part of learning to read. For all I know, writing comes out of a superior devotion to reading. I feel sure that serious writing does come, must come, out of devotion to the thing itself, to fiction as an art. Both reading and writing are experiences—lifelong—in the course of which we who encounter words used in certain ways are persuaded by them to be brought mind and heart within the presence, the power, of the imagination. This we find to be above all the power to reveal, with nothing barred.

But of course writing fiction, which comes out of life and

has the object of showing it, can't be learned from copying out of books. Imitation, or what is in any respect secondhand, is precisely what writing is not. How it is learned can only remain in general—like all else that is personal—an open question; and if ever it's called settled, or solved, the day of fiction is already over. The solution will be the last rites at the funeral. Only the writing of fiction keeps fiction alive. Regardless of whether or not it is reading that gives writing birth, a society that no longer writes novels is not very likely to read any novels at all.

Since we must and do write each our own way, we may during actual writing get more lasting instruction not from another's work, whatever its blessings, however better it is than ours, but from our own poor scratched-over pages. For these we can hold up to life. That is, we are born with a mind and heart to hold each page up to, and to ask: is it valid?

Reading the work of other writers and in the whole, and our long thoughts in retrospect, can tell us all we are able to know of fiction and at firsthand, but this is about *reading*.

The writer himself studies intensely how to do it while he is in the thick of doing it; then when the particular novel or story is done, he is likely to forget how; he does well to. Each work is new. Mercifully, the question of *how* abides less in the abstract, and less in the past, than in the specific, in the work at hand; I chance saying this is so with most writers. Maybe some particular problems, with their confusions and might-have-beens, could be seen into with profit just at the windup, but more likely it's already too late. Already the *working* insight, which is what counts, is gone—along with the story it made, that made it.

And rightly. Fiction finished has to bear the responsibility of its own meaning, it is its own memory. It is now a thing apart from the writer; like a letter mailed, it is nearer by now to its reader. If the writer has had luck, it has something of its own to travel on, something that can make it persist for a while, an identity, before it must fade.

How can I express outside fiction what I think this reality of fiction is?

As a child I was led, an unwilling sightseer, into Mammoth Cave in Kentucky, and after our party had been halted in the blackest hole yet and our guide had let us wait guessing in cold dark what would happen to us, suddenly a light was struck. And we stood in a prism. The chamber was bathed in color, and there was nothing else, we and our guide alike were blotted out by radiance. As I remember, nobody said boo. Gradually we could make out that there was a river in the floor, black as night, which appeared to come out of a closet in the wall; and then, on it, a common rowboat, with ordinary countrified people like ourselves sitting in it, mute, wearing hats, came floating out and on by, and exited into the closet in the opposite wall. I suppose they were simply a party taking the more expensive tour. As we tourists mutually and silently stared, our guide treated us to a recitation on bats, how they lived in uncounted numbers down here and reached light by shooting up winding mile-high chimneys through rock, never touching by so much as the crook of a wing. He had memorized the speech, and we didn't see a bat. Then the light was put out—just as it is after you've had your two cents' worth in the Baptistry of Florence, where of course more happens: the thing I'm trying here to leave out. As again we stood damp and cold and not able to see our feet, while we each now had something of our own out of it, presumably, what I for one remember is how right I had been in telling my parents it would be a bore. For I was too ignorant to know there might be more, or even less, in there than I could see unaided.

Fiction is not the cave; and human life, fiction's territory, merely contains caves. I am only trying to express what I think the so-called raw material is *without its interpretation*; without its artist. Without the act of human understanding— and it is a double act through which we make sense to each other—experience is the worst kind of emptiness; it is obliteration, black or prismatic, as meaningless as was indeed that loveless cave. Before there is meaning, there has to occur some personal act of vision. And it is this that is continuously projected as the novelist writes, and again as we, each to ourselves, read.

If this makes fiction sound full of mystery, I think it's fuller than I know how to say. Plot, characters, setting, and so forth, are not what I'm referring to now; we all deal with those as best we can. The mystery lies in the use of language to express human life.

In writing, do we try to solve this mystery? No, I think we take hold of the other end of the stick. In very practical ways, we rediscover the mystery. We even, I might say, take advantage of it.

As we know, a body of criticism stands ready to provide its solution, which is a kind of translation of fiction into another language. It offers us close analysis, like a headphone we can clamp on at the U.N. when they are speaking the Arabian tongue. I feel that we can accept this but only with distinct reservations—not about its brilliance or its worth, but about its time and place of application. While we are in the middle of reading some novel, the possibility of the critical phrase "in other words" is one to destroy, rather than make for, a real—that is, imaginative—understanding of the author. Indeed, it is one sure way to break off his carefully laid connection.

Fiction is made to show forth human life, in some chosen part and aspect. A year or so of one writer's life has gone into the writing of a novel, and then to the reader—so long at least as he is reading it—it may be something in his life. There is a remarkable chance of give-and-take. Does this not suggest that, in the novel at least, words have been found for which there may be no other words? If fiction matters—and many lives are at stake that it does—there can be, for the duration of the book, *no* other words.

The point for us if we write is that nearly everything we can learn about writing can be set down only in fiction's terms. What we know about writing the novel *is* the novel.

Try to tear it down, take it back to its beginning, and you

are not so much lost as simply nowhere. Some things once done you can't undo, and I hope and believe fiction is one of them. What its own author knows about a novel is flexible till the end; it changes as it goes, and more than that, it will not be the same knowledge he has by the time the work ends as he had when it began. There is a difference not so much in measure of knowledge, which you would take for granted, as in kind of knowledge. The idea is now the object. The idea is something that you or I might just conceivably have had in common with the author, in the vague free air of the everyday. But not by the wildest chance should we be able to duplicate by one sentence what happened to the idea; neither could the author himself write the same novel again. As he works, his own revision, even though he throws away his changes, can never be wholly undone. The novel has passed through that station on its track. And as readers, we too proceed by the author's arbitrary direction to his one-time-only destination: a journey rather strange, hardly in a straight line, altogether personal.

There has occurred the experience of the writer in writing the novel, and now there occurs the experience of the reader in reading it. More than one mind and heart go into this. We may even hope to follow into a kind of future with a novel that to us seems good, drawn forward by what the long unfolding has promised and so far revealed. By yielding to what has been, by all his available means, *suggested*, we are able to see for ourselves a certain distance beyond what is possible for him simply to *say*. So that, although nobody else ought to say this, the novelist *has* said, "In other words . . ."

Thus all fiction may be seen as a symbol, if this is desired—and how often it is, so it seems. But surely the novel exists within the big symbol of fiction itself—not the other way round, as a conglomeration of little symbols. I think that fiction is the hen, not the egg, and that the good live hen came first.

Certainly symbols fill our daily lives, our busily communicative, if not always communicating, world; and any number of them come with perfect naturalness into our daily conversation and our behavior. And they are a legitimate part of fiction, as they have always been of every art—desirable as any device is, so long as it serves art. Symbols have to spring from the work direct, and stay alive. Symbols for the sake of symbols are counterfeit, and were they all stamped on the page in red they couldn't any more quickly give themselves away. So are symbols failing their purpose when they don't keep to proportion in the book. However alive they are, they should never call for an emphasis greater than the emotional reality they serve, in their moment, to illuminate. One way of looking at Moby Dick is that his task as a symbol was so big and strenuous that he *had* to be a whale.

Most symbols that a fiction writer uses, however carefully, today are apt to be as swiftly spotted by his reader as the smoke signals that once crossed our plains from Indian to Indian. Using symbols and—still worse—finding symbols is such a habit. It follows that too little comes to be suggested, and this, as can never be affirmed often enough, is the purpose of every word that goes into a piece of fiction. The imagination has to be involved, and more—ignited.

How much brighter than the symbol can be the explicit observation that springs firsthand from deep and present feeling in one breast. Indeed, it is something like this, spontaneous in effect, pure in effect, that takes on the emotional value of a symbol when it was first minted, but which as time passes shrinks to become only a counter.

When Chekhov says there were so many stars out that one could not have put a finger between them, he gives us more than night, he gives us *that* night. For symbols can only grow to be the same when the same experiences on which fiction is based are more and more partaken of by us all. But Chekhov's stars, some as large as a goose's egg and some as small as hempseed, are still exactly where they were, in the sky of his story

"Easter Eve." And from them to us that night still travels—for so much more than symbols, they are Chekhov looking at his sky.

Communication through fiction frequently happens, I believe, in ways that are small—a word is not too small; that are unannounced; that are less direct than we might first suppose on seeing how important they are. It isn't communication happening when you as the reader follow or predict the novel's plot or agree with, or anticipate, or could even quote the characters; when you hail the symbols; even when its whole landscape and climate have picked you up and transported you where it happens. But communication is going on, and regardless of all the rest, when you believe the writer.

Then is plausibility at the bottom of it? When we can read and say, "Oh, how right, I think so too," has the writer come through? Only stop to think how often simple plausibility, if put to measure a good story, falls down, while the story stands up, never wavers. And agreement isn't always, by any means, a mark of having been reached.

As a reader who never held a gun, I risk saying that it isn't exactly plausible that Old Ben, the bear in Faulkner's story, when he was finally brought down by a knife-thrust, had already in him fifty-two little hard lumps which were old bullets that had had no effect on him. Yet as a reader caught in the story, I think I qualify to bear witness that nothing less than fifty-two bullets could have been embedded in Old Ben or Old Ben he would not be. Old Ben and every one of his bullets along with him are parts of the truth in this story, William Faulkner's particular truth.

Belief doesn't depend on plausibility, but it seems to be a fact that validity of a kind, and this is of course a subjective kind, gained in whatever way that had to be, is the quality that makes a work reliable as art. This reliability comes straight out of the writer himself. In the end, it is another personal quotient in writing fiction; it is something inimitable. It is that by which each writer *lets us believe*—doesn't ask us to, can't make us, simply lets us.

To a large extent a writer cannot help the material of his fiction. That is, he cannot help where and when he happened to be born; then he has to live somewhere and somehow and with others, and survive through some history or other if he is here to write at all. But it is not to escape his life but more to pin it down that he writes fiction (though by pinning it down he no doubt does escape it a little). And so certainly he does choose his subject. It's not really quibbling to say that a writer's subject, in due time, chooses the writer—not of course *as* a writer, but as the man or woman who comes across it by living and has it to struggle with. That person may come on it by seeming accident, like falling over a chair in a dark room. But he may invite it with wide-open arms, so that it eventually walks in. Or his subject may accrue, build up and build up inside him until it's intolerable to him not to try to write it in terms he can understand: he submits it to the imagination, he finds names, sets something down. "In other words . . ."

So he does choose his subject, though not without compulsion, and now not too much stands in the way of the writer's learning something for himself about his own writing. For he has taken the fatal step when he put himself into his subject's hands. He might even do well to feel some misgivings: he and his fiction were never strangers, but at moments he may wonder at the ruthlessness of the relationship, which is honesty, between it and himself.

His inspiration, so-called, may very easily, then, be personal desperation—painful or pleasurable. All kinds of desperation get to be one in the work. But it will be the particular desperation that the particular writer is heir to, subject to, out of which he learns in daily life, by which, in that year, he is driven, on which he can feel, think, construct something, write out in as many drafts as he likes and then not get to much of an end. What he checks his work against remains, all the way, not books, not lore, neither another's writing nor in the large his own, but life that breathes in his face. Still, he may get to *his* end, have *his* say.

It really is his say. We have the writer's own vision of

everything in the world when we place his novel in the center. Then so much is clear: how he sees life and death, how much he thinks people matter to each other and to themselves, how much he would like you to know what he finds beautiful or strange or awful or absurd, what he can do without, how well he has learned to see, hear, touch, smell—all as his sentences go by and in their time and sequence mount up. It grows clear how he imposes order and structure on his fictional world; and it is terribly clear, in the end, whether, when he calls for understanding, he gets any.

And of course he knew this would be so: he has been, and he is, a *reader*. Furthermore, all his past is in his point of view; his novel, whatever its subject, is the history itself of his life's experience in feeling. He has invited us, while we are his readers, to see with his point of view. Can we see? And what does he feel passionately about? Is it honest passion? The answer to that we know from the opening page. For some reason, honesty is one thing that it's almost impossible to make a mistake about in reading fiction.

Let us not think, however, that we ever plumb it all—not one whole novel; and I am not speaking of the great ones exclusively. It is for quite other reasons that we never know all of a single person. But the finished novel transcends the personal in art. Indeed, that has been its end in view.

For fiction, ideally, is highly personal but objective. It is something which only you can write but which is not, necessarily, *about* you. Style, I think, is whatever it is in the prose which has constantly pressed to give the writing its objectivity. Style does not obtrude but exists as the sum total of all the ways that have been taken to make the work stand on its own, apart. Born subjective, we learn what our own idea of the objective is as we go along.

Style is a product of highly conscious effort but is not self-conscious. Even with esthetic reasons aside, the self-consciousness would not be justified. For if you have worked in any serious way, you *have* your style—like the smoke from a fired cannon, like the ring in the water after the fish is pulled out or jumps back in. I can't see that a writer deserves praise in particular for his style, however good: in order for him to have written what he must have very much wanted to write, a way had to be found. A reader's understanding of his style—as the picture, or the reflection, or the proof of a way in which communication tried to happen—is more to be wished for than any praise; and when communication does happen, the style is in effect beyond praise.

What you write about is in the public domain. Subject you can choose, but your mind and heart compel you. Point of view you develop in order to transcend it. Style you acquire in the pursuit of something else which may turn out to be the impossible. Now let me mention shape.

In fiction, as we know, the shapes the work takes are marvelous, and vary most marvelously in our minds. It is hard to speak further about them. Specific in the work, in the mind, but not describable anywhere else—or not by me; shape is something felt. It is the form of the work that you feel to be under way as you write and as you read. At the end, instead of farewell, it tells over the whole, as a whole, to the reader's memory.

In sculpture, this shape is left in rock itself and stands self-identifying and self-announcing. Fiction is made of words to travel under the reading eye, and made to go in one sequence and one direction, slowly, accumulating; time is an element. The words follow the contours of some continuous relationship between what can be told and what cannot be told, to be in the silence of reading the lightest of the hammers that tap their way along this side of chaos.

Fiction's progress is of course not tactile, though at once you might rejoin by saying that some of Lawrence's stories, for instance, *are*—as much as a stroke of the hand down a horse's neck. Neither is shape necessarily, or even often, formal, though James, for example, was so fond of making it so. There is no more limit to the kinds of shape a fictional work may take than there appears to be to the range and character of our minds.

The novel or story ended, shape must have made its own impression on the reader, so that he feels that some design in life (by which I mean esthetic pattern, not purpose) has just been discovered there. And this pattern, shape, form that emerges for you then, a reader at the end of the book, may do the greatest thing that fiction does: it may move you. And however you have been moved by the parts, this still has to happen from the whole before you know what indeed you have met with in that book.

From the writer's view, we might say that shape is most closely connected with the work itself, is the course it ran. From the reader's view, we might say that shape is connected with recognition; it is what allows us to know and remember what in the world of feeling we have been living through in that novel. The part of the mind in both reader and writer that form speaks to may be the deep-seated perception we all carry in us of the beauty of order imposed, of structure rising and building upon itself, and finally of this coming to rest.

It is through the shaping of the work in the hands of the artist that you most nearly come to know what can be known, on the page, of his mind and heart, and his as apart from the others. No other saw life in an ordering exactly like this. So shape begins and ends subjectively. And that the two concepts, writer's and reader's, may differ, since all of us differ, is neither so strange nor so important as the vital fact that a connection has been made between them. Our whole reading lives testify to the astonishing degree to which this can happen.

This ordering, or shape, a felt thing that emerges whole for us at the very last, as we close the novel to think back, was to the writer, I think, known first thing of all. It was surmised. And this is above all what nobody else knew or could have taught or told him. Besides, at that point he was not their listener. He could not, it seems, have cast his work except in the mold it's in, which was there in his mind all the hard way through. And this notwithstanding thousands of other things that life crowded into his head, parts of the characters that we shall never meet, flashes of action that yielded to other flashes, conversations drowned out, pieces of days and nights, all to be given up, and rightly.

For we have to remember what the novel is. Made by the imagination for the imagination, it is an illusion come full circle —a very exclusive thing, for all it seems to include a good deal of the world. It was wholly for the sake of illusion, made by art out of, and in order to show, and to be, some human truth, that the novelist took all he knew with him and made that leap in the dark.

For he must already have apprehended and come to his own jumping-off place before he could put down on paper that ever-miraculous thing, the opening sentence.

(1965)

Must the
Novelist Crusade?

Not too long ago I read in some respectable press that Faulkner would have to be reassessed because he was "after all, only a white Mississippian." For this reason, it was felt, readers could no longer rely on him for knowing what he was writing about in his life's work of novels and stories, laid in what he called "my country."

Remembering how Faulkner for most of his life wrote in all but isolation from critical understanding, ignored impartially by North and South, with only a handful of critics in forty years who were able to "assess" him, we might smile at this journalist as at a boy let out of school. Or there may have been an instinct to smash the superior, the good, that is endurable enough to go on offering itself. But I feel in these words and others like them the agonizing of our times. I think they come of an honest and understandable zeal to allot every writer his chance to better the world or go to his grave reproached for the mess it is in. And here, it seems to me, the heart of fiction's real reliability has been struck at—and not for the first time by the noble hand of the crusader.

It would not be surprising if the critic I quote had gained his knowledge of the South from the books of the author he repudiates. At any rate, a reply to him exists there. Full evidence as to whether any writer, alive or dead, can be believed is always at hand in one place: any page of his work. The color of his skin would modify it just about as much as would the binding of his book. Integrity can be neither lost nor concealed nor faked nor quenched nor artificially come by nor outlived, nor, I believe, in the long run denied. Integrity is no greater and no less today than it was yesterday and will be tomorrow. It stands outside time.

The novelist and the crusader who writes both have their own place—in the novel and the editorial respectively, equally valid whether or not the two happen to be in agreement. In my own view, writing fiction places the novelist and the crusader on opposite sides. But they are not the sides of right and wrong. Honesty is not at stake here and is not questioned; the only thing at stake is the proper use of words for the proper ends. And a mighty thing it is.

Because the printed page is where the writer's work is to be seen, it may be natural for people who do not normally read fiction to confuse novels with journalism or speeches. The very using of words has these well-intentioned people confused about the novelist's purpose.

The writing of a novel is taking life as it already exists, not to report it but to make an object, toward the end that the finished work might contain this life inside it, and offer it to the reader. The essence will not be, of course, the same thing as the raw material; it is not even of the same family of things. The novel is something that never was before and will not be again. For the mind of one person, its writer, is in it too. What distinguishes it above all from the raw material, and what distinguishes it from journalism, is that inherent in the novel is the possibility of a shared act of the imagination between its writer and its reader.

"All right, Eudora Welty, what are you going to do about it? Sit down there with your mouth shut?" asked a stranger over long distance in one of the midnight calls that I suppose have waked most writers in the South from time to time. It is part of the same question: Are fiction writers on call to be crusaders? For us in the South who are fiction writers, is writing a novel *something we can do about it?*

It can be said at once, I should think, that we are all agreed upon the most important point: that morality as shown through human relationships is the whole heart of fiction, and the serious writer has never lived who dealt with anything else.

And yet, the zeal to reform, which quite properly inspires the editorial, has never done fiction much good. The exception occurs when it can rise to the intensity of satire, where it finds a better home in the poem or the drama. Large helpings of naïveté and self-esteem, which serve to refresh the crusader, only encumber the novelist. How unfair it is that when a novel is to be written, it is never enough to have our hearts in the right place! But good will all by itself can no more get a good novel written than it can paint in watercolor or sing Mozart.

Nevertheless, let us suppose that we feel we might help if we were to write a crusading novel. What will our problems be?

Before anything else, speed. The crusader's message is prompted by crisis; it has to be delivered on time. Suppose John Steinbeck had only now finished *The Grapes of Wrath?* The ordinary novelist has only one message: "I submit that this is one way we are." This can wait. When we think of Ibsen, we see that causes themselves may in time be forgotten, their championship no longer needed; it is Ibsen's passion that keeps the plays alive.

Next, we as the crusader-novelist shall find awkward to use the very weapon we count on most: the generality. On fiction's pages, generalities clank when wielded, and hit with equal force at the little and the big, at the merely suspect and the really dangerous. They make too much noise for us to hear what people might be trying to say. They are fatal to tenderness and are in themselves non-conductors of any real, however modest, discovery of the writer's own heart. This discovery is the best hope of the ordinary novelist, and to make it he begins not with the generality but with the particular in front of his eyes, which he is able to examine.

Taking a particular situation existing in his world, and what he feels about it in his own breast and what he can make of it in his own head, he constructs on paper, little by little, an equivalent of it. Literally it may correspond to a high degree or to none at all; emotionally it corresponds as closely as he can make it. Observation and the inner truth of that observation as he perceives it, the two being tested one against the other: to him this is what the writing of a novel is.

We, the crusader-novelist, having started with our generality, must end with a generality; they had better be the same. In the place of climax, we can deliver a judgment. How can the plot seem disappointing when it is a lovely argument spread out? It is because fiction is stone-deaf to argument.

The ordinary novelist does not argue; he hopes to show, to disclose. His persuasions are all toward allowing his reader to see and hear something for himself. He knows another bad thing about arguments: they carry the menace of neatness into fiction. Indeed, what we as the crusader-novelist are scared of most is confusion.

Great fiction, we very much fear, abounds in what makes for confusion; it generates it, being on a scale which copies life, which it confronts. It is very seldom neat, is given to sprawling and escaping from bounds, is capable of contradicting itself, and is not impervious to humor. There is absolutely everything in great fiction but a clear answer. Humanity itself seems to matter more to the novelist than what humanity thinks it can prove.

When a novelist writes of man's experience, what else is he to draw on but the life around him? And yet the life around him, on the surface, can be used to show anything, absolutely anything, as readers know. The novelist's real task and real responsibility lie in the way he uses it.

Situation itself always exists; it is whatever life is up to here and now, it is the living and present moment. It is transient, and it fluctuates. Using the situation, the writer populates his novel with characters invented to express it in their terms.

It is important that it be in their terms. We cannot in fiction set people to acting mechanically or carrying placards to make their sentiments plain. People are not Right and Wrong, Good and Bad, Black and White personified; flesh and blood and the sense of comedy object. Fiction writers cannot be tempted to make the mistake of looking at people in the generality— that is to say, of seeing people as not at all *like us*. If human beings are to be comprehended as real, then they have to be treated as real, with minds, hearts, memories, habits, hopes, with passions and capacities like ours. This is why novelists begin the study of people from within.

The first act of insight is throw away the labels. In fiction, while we do not necessarily write about ourselves, we write out of ourselves, using ourselves; what we learn from, what we are sensitive to, what we feel strongly about—these become our characters and go to make our plots. Characters in fiction are conceived from within, and they have, accordingly, their own interior life; they are individuals every time. The character we care about in a novel we may not approve of or agree with—that's beside the point. But he has got to seem alive. Then and only then, when we read, we experience or surmise things about life itself that are deeper and more lasting and less destructive to understanding than approval or disapproval.

The novelist's work is highly organized, but I should say it is organized around anything but logic. Just as characters are not labels but are made from the inside out and grow into their own life, so does a plot have a living principle on which it hangs together and gradually earns its shape. A plot is a thousand times more unsettling than an argument, which may be answered. It is not a pattern imposed; it is inward emotion acted out. It is arbitrary, indeed, but not artificial. It is possibly so odd that it might be called a vision, but it is organic to its material: it is a working vision, then.

A writer works *through* what is around him if he wishes to get to what he is after—no kind of proof, but simply an essence. In practice he will do anything at all with his material: shape it, strain it to the breaking point, double it up, or use it backward; he will balk at nothing—see *The Sound and the Fury*—to reach that heart and core. But even in a good cause he does not falsify it. The material itself receives deep ultimate respect: it has given rise to the vision of it, which in turn has determined what the novel shall be.

The ordinary novelist, who can never make a perfect thing, can with every novel try again. But if we write a novel to prove something, one novel will settle it, for why prove a thing more than once? And what, then, is to keep all novels by all right-thinking persons from being pretty much alike? Or exactly alike? There would be little reason for present writers to keep on, no reason for the new writers to start. There's no way to know, but we might guess that the reason the young write no fiction behind the Iron Curtain is the obvious fact that to be acceptable there, all novels must conform, and so must be alike, hence valueless. If the personal vision can be made to order, then we should lose, writer and reader alike, our own gift for perceiving, seeing through the fabric of everyday to what to each pair of eyes on earth is a unique thing. We'd accept life exactly like everybody else, and so, of course, be content with it. We should not even miss our vanished novelists. And if life ever became not worth writing fiction about, that, I believe, would be the first sign that it wasn't worth living.

With a blueprint to work with instead of a vision, there is a good deal that we as the crusader-novelist must be at pains to leave out. Unavoidably, I think, we shall leave out one of the greatest things. This is the mystery in life. Our blueprint for sanity and of solution for trouble leaves out the dark. (This is odd, because surely it was the dark that first troubled us.)

We leave out the wonder because with wonder it is impossible to argue, much less to settle. The ordinary novelist thinks it had better be recognized. Reckless as this may make him, he believes the insoluble is part of his material too.

The novelist works neither to correct nor to condone, not at all to comfort, but to make what's told alive. He assumes at the start an enlightenment in his reader equal to his own, for they are hopefully on the point of taking off together from that base into the rather different world of the imagination.

It's not only the fact that this world is bigger and that fewer constrictions apply that may daunt us as crusaders. But the imagination itself is the problem. It is capable of saying everything but no. In our literature, what has traveled the longest way through time is the great affirmative soul of Chaucer. The novel itself always affirms, it seems to me, by the nature of itself. It says what people are like. It doesn't, and doesn't know how to, describe what they are *not* like, and it would waste its time if it told us what we ought to be like, since we already know that, don't we? But we may not know nearly so well what we are as when a novel of power reveals this to us. For the first time we may, as we read, see ourselves in our own situation, in some curious way reflected. By whatever way the novelist accomplishes it—there are many ways—truth is borne in on us in all its great weight and angelic lightness, and accepted as home truth.

Passing judgment on his fellows, which is trying enough for anybody, is frustrating for an author. It is hardly the way to make the discoveries about living that he must have hoped for when he began to write. If he does not pass judgment, does this mean he has no conscience? Of course he has a conscience; it is, like his temperament, his own, and he is one hundred per-cent answerable to it, whether it is convenient or not. What matters is that a writer is committed to his own moral prin-ciples. If he is, when we read him we cannot help but be aware of what these are. Certainly the characters of his novel and the plot they move in are their ultimate reflections. But these convictions are implicit; they are deep down; they are the rock on which the whole structure of more than that novel rests.

Indeed, we are more aware of his moral convictions through a novel than any flat statement of belief from him could make us. We are aware in that part of our mind that tells us truths about ourselves. Yet it is only by way of the imagination—the novelist's to ours—that such private neighborhoods are reached.

There is still to mention what I think will give us, as the crusader-novelist, the hardest time: our voice will not be our own. The crusader's voice is the voice of the crowd and must rise louder all the time, for there is, of course, the other side to be drowned out. Worse, the voices of most crowds sound alike. Worse still, the voice that seeks to do other than communicate when it makes a noise has something brutal about it; it is no longer using words as words but as something to brandish, with which to threaten, brag or condemn. The noise is the simple assertion of self, the great, mindless, general self. And for all its volume it is ephemeral. Only meaning lasts. Nothing was ever learned in a crowd, from a crowd, or by addressing or trying to please a crowd. Even to deplore, yelling is out of place. To deplore a thing as hideous as the murder of the three civil rights workers demands the quiet in which to absorb it. Enormities can be lessened, cheapened, just as good and delicate things can be. We can and will cheapen all feeling by letting it go savage or parading in it.

Writing fiction is an interior affair. Novels and stories always will be put down little by little out of personal feeling and personal beliefs arrived at alone and at firsthand over a period of time as time is needed. To go outside and beat the drum is only to interrupt, interrupt, and so finally to forget and to lose. Fiction has, and must keep, a private address. For life is *lived* in a private place; where it means anything is inside the mind and heart. Fiction has always shown life where it is lived, and good fiction, or so I have faith, will continue to do this.

A Passage to India is an old novel now. It is an intensely moral novel. It deals with race prejudice. Mr. Forster, not by preaching at us, while being passionately concerned, makes us know his points unforgettably as often as we read it. And does he not bring in the dark! The points are good forty years after their day *because of the splendor of the novel.* What a lesser novelist's harangues would have buried by now, his imagination still reveals. Revelation of even the strongest forces is delicate work.

Indeed, great fiction shows us not how to conduct our behavior but how to feel. Eventually, it may show us how to face our feelings and face our actions and to have new inklings about what they mean. A good novel of any year can initiate us into our own new experience.

From the working point of view of the serious writer of fiction, nothing has changed today but the externals. They are important externals; we may have developed an increased awareness of them, which is certainly to the good; we have at least the same capacity as ever for understanding, the same eyes and ears, same hearts to feel, same minds to agonize or remember or to try to put things together, see things in proportion with. While the raw material of our fiction is changing dramatically—as indeed it is changing everywhere—we are the same instruments of perceiving that we ever were. I should not trust us if we were not. And we do not know what is to be made out of experience at any time until the personal quotient has been added. To convey what we see around us, whatever it is, so as to let it speak for itself according to our lights is the same challenge it ever was, not a different one, not a greater one, only perhaps made harder by the times. Now as ever we must keep writing from what we know; and we must really know it.

No matter how fast society around us changes, what remains is that there is a relationship in progress between ourselves and other people; this was the case when the world seemed stable, too. There are relationships of the blood, of the passions and the affections, of thought and spirit and deed. There is the relationship between the races. How can one kind of relationship be set apart from the others? Like the great root system of an old and long-established growing plant, they are all tangled up together; to separate them you would have to cleave the plant itself from top to bottom.

What must the Southern writer of fiction do today? Shall he do anything different from what he has always done?

There have already been giant events, some of them wrenchingly painful and humiliating. And now there is added the atmosphere of hate. We in the South are a hated people these days; we were hated first for actual and particular reasons, and now we may be hated still more in some vast unparticularized way. I believe there must be such a thing as sentimental hate. Our people hate back.

I think the worst of it is we are getting stuck in it. We are like trapped flies with our feet not in honey but in venom. It's not love that is the gluey emotion; it's hate. As far as writing goes, which is as far as living goes, this is a devastating emotion. It could kill us. This hate seems in part shame for self, in part self-justification, in part panic that life is really changing.

Fury at ourselves and hurt pride, anger aroused too often, outrage at being hated need not obscure forever the sore spots we Southerners know better than our detractors. For some of us have shown bad hearts. As in the case of our better qualities, we are locally blessed with an understanding and intimate knowledge of our faults that our worst detractors cannot match, and have been in a less relentless day far more relentless, more eloquent, too, than they have yet learned to be.

I do not presume to speak for my fellow Southern writers, a group of individuals if there ever was one. Yet I would like to point something out: in the rest of the country people seem suddenly aware now of what Southern fiction writers have been writing about in various ways for a great long time. We do not need reminding of what our subject is. It is human-kind, and we are all part of it. When we write about people, black or white, in the South or anywhere, if our stories are worth the reading, we are writing about everybody.

In the South, we who are now at work may not learn to write it before we learn, or learn again, to live it—our full life in the South within its context, in its relation to the rest of the world. "Only connect," Forster's ever wise and gentle and daring words, could be said to us in our homeland quite literally at this moment. And while the Southern writer goes on portraying his South, which I think nobody else can do and which I believe he must do, then if his work is done well enough, it will reflect a larger mankind as it has done before.

And so finally I think we need to write with love. Not in self-defense, not in hate, not in the mood of instruction, not in rebuttal, in any kind of militance, or in apology, but with love. Not in exorcisement, either, for this is to make the reader bear a thing for you.

Neither do I speak of writing forgivingly; out of love you can write with straight fury. It is the *source* of the under-standing that I speak of; it's this that determines its nature and its reach.

We are told that Turgenev's nostalgic, profoundly reflec-tive, sensuously alive stories that grew out of his memories of early years reached the Czar and were given some credit by him when he felt moved to free the serfs in Russia. Had Turgenev set out to write inflammatory tracts instead of the sum of all he knew, could express, of life learned at firsthand, how much less of his mind and heart with their commitments, all implicit, would have filled his stories! But he might be one of us now, so directly are we touched with a hundred and thirteen years gone by since they were first published.

Indifference would indeed be corrupting to the fiction writer, indifference to any part of man's plight. Passion is the chief ingredient of good fiction. It flames right out of sympathy for the human condition and goes into all great writing. (And of course passion and the temper are different things; writing in the heat of passion can be done with extremely good temper.) But to distort a work of passion for the sake of a cause is to cheat, and the end, far from justifying the means, is fairly sure to be lost with it. Then the novel will have been not the work of imagination, at once passionate and objective, made by a man struggling in solitude with something of his own to say, but a piece of catering.

To cater to is not to love and not to serve well either. We do need to bring to our writing, over and over again, all the abundance we possess. To be able, to be ready, to enter into the minds and hearts of our own people, all of them, to comprehend them (us) and then to make characters and plots in stories that in honesty and with honesty reveal them (ourselves) to us, in whatever situation we live through in our own times: this is the continuing job, and it's no harder now than it ever was, I suppose. Every writer, like everybody else, thinks he's living through the crisis of the ages. To write honestly and with all our powers is the least we can do, and the most.

Time, though it can make happenings and trappings out of date, cannot do much to change the realities apprehended by the imagination. History will change in Mississippi, and the hope is that it will change in a beneficial direction and with a merciful speed, and above all bring insight, understanding. But when William Faulkner's novels come to be pictures of a society that is no more, they will still be good and still be authentic because of what went into them from the man himself. Mankind still tries the same things and suffers the same falls, climbs up to try again, and novels are as true at one time as at another. Love and hate, hope and despair, justice and injustice, compassion and prejudice, truth-telling and lying work in all men; their story can be told in whatever skin they are wearing and in whatever year the writer can put them down.

Faulkner is not receding from us. Indeed, his work, though it can't increase in itself, increases us. His work throws light on the past and on today as it becomes the past—the day in its journey. This being so, it informs the future too.

What is written in the South from now on is going to be taken into account by Faulkner's work; I mean the remark literally. Once Faulkner had written, we could never unknow what he told us and showed us. And his work will do the same thing tomorrow. We inherit from him, while we can get fresh and firsthand news of ourselves from his work at any time.

A source of illumination is not dated by what passes along under its ray, is not qualified or disqualified by the nature of the traffic. When the light of Faulkner's work will be discovering things to us no more, it will be discovering *us*. Even we shall lie enfolded in perspective one day: what we hoped along with what we did, what we didn't do, and not only what we were but what we missed being, what others yet to come might dare to be. For we *are* our own crusade. Before ever we write, we are. Instead of our judging Faulkner, he will be revealing us in books to later minds.

(1965)

"Is Phoenix Jackson's Grandson Really Dead?"

A story writer is more than happy to be read by students; the fact that these serious readers think and feel something in response to his work he finds life-giving. At the same time he may not always be able to reply to their specific questions in kind. I wondered if it might clarify something, for both the questioners and myself, if I set down a general reply to the question that comes to me most often in the mail, from both students and their teachers, after some classroom discussion. The unrivaled favorite is this: "Is Phoenix Jackson's grandson really *dead*?"

It refers to a short story I wrote years ago called "A Worn Path," which tells of a day's journey an old woman makes on foot from deep in the country into town and into a doctor's office on behalf of her little grandson; he is at home, periodically ill, and periodically she comes for his medicine; they give it to her as usual, she receives it and starts the journey back.

I had not meant to mystify readers by withholding any fact; it is not a writer's business to tease. The story is told through Phoenix's mind as she undertakes her errand. As the author at one with the character as I tell it, I must assume that the boy is alive. As the reader, you are free to think as you like, of course: the story invites you to believe that no matter what happens, Phoenix for as long as she is able to walk and can hold to her purpose will make her journey. The *possibility* that she would keep on even if he were dead is there in her devotion and its single-minded, single-track errand. Certainly the *artistic* truth, which should be good enough for the fact, lies in Phoenix's own answer to that question. When the nurse asks, "He isn't dead, is he?" she speaks for herself: "He still the same. He going to last."

The grandchild is the incentive. But it is the journey, the going of the errand, that is the story, and the question is not whether the grandchild is in reality alive or dead. It doesn't affect the outcome of the story or its meaning from start to finish. But it is not the question itself that has struck me as much as the idea, almost without exception implied in the asking, that for Phoenix's grandson to be dead would some-how make the story "better."

It's *all right*, I want to say to the students who write to me, for things to be what they appear to be, and for words to mean what they say. It's all right, too, for words and appearances to mean more than one thing—ambiguity is a fact of life. A fiction writer's responsibility covers not only what he presents as the facts of a given story but what he chooses to stir up as their implications; in the end, these implications, too, become facts, in the larger, fictional sense. But it is not all right, not in good faith, for things *not* to mean what they say.

The grandson's plight was real and it made the truth of the story, which is the story of an errand of love carried out. If the child no longer lived, the truth would persist in the "worn-ness" of the path. But his being dead can't increase the truth of the story, can't affect it one way or the other. I think I signal this, because the end of the story has been reached before old Phoenix gets home again: she simply starts back. To the question "Is the grandson really dead?" I could reply that it doesn't make any difference. I could also say that I did not make him up in order to let him play a trick on Phoenix. But my best answer would be: "*Phoenix is alive.*"

The origin of a story is sometimes a trustworthy clue to the author—or can provide him with the clue—to its key image; maybe in this case it will do the same for the reader. One day I saw a solitary old woman like Phoenix. She was walking; I saw her, at middle distance, in a winter country landscape, and watched her slowly make her way across my line of vision. That sight of her made me write the story. I invented an errand for her, but that only seemed a living part of the figure she was herself: what errand other than for someone else could be making her go? And her going was the first thing, her persisting in her landscape was the real thing, and the first and the real were what I wanted and worked to keep. I brought her up close enough, by imagination, to describe her face, make her present to the eyes, but the full-length figure moving across the winter fields was the indelible one and the image to keep, and the perspective extending into the vanishing distance the true one to hold in mind.

I invented for my character, as I wrote, some passing adventures—some dreams and harassments and a small triumph or two, some jolts to her pride, some flights of fancy to console her, one or two encounters to scare her, a moment that gave her cause to feel ashamed, a moment to dance and preen—for it had to be a *journey*, and all these things belonged to that, parts of life's uncertainty.

A narrative line is in its deeper sense, of course, the tracing out of a meaning, and the real continuity of a story lies in this probing forward. The real dramatic force of a story depends on the strength of the emotion that has set it going. The emotional value is the measure of the reach of the story. What gives any such content to "A Worn Path" is not its circumstances but its *subject*: the deep-grained habit of love.

What I hoped would come clear was that in the whole surround of this story, the world it threads through, the only certain thing at all is the worn path. The habit of love cuts through confusion and stumbles or contrives its way out of difficulty, it remembers the way even when it forgets, for a dumbfounded moment, its reason for being. The path is the thing that matters.

Her victory—old Phoenix's—is when she sees the diploma in the doctor's office, when she finds "nailed up on the wall the document that had been stamped with the gold seal and framed in the gold frame, which matched the dream that was hung up in her head." The return with the medicine is just a matter of retracing her own footsteps. It is the part of the journey, and of the story, that can now go without saying.

In the matter of function, old Phoenix's way might even do as a sort of parallel to your way of work if you are a writer of stories. The way to get there is the all-important, all-absorbing problem, and this problem is your reason for undertaking the story. Your only guide, too, is your sureness about your subject, about what this subject is. Like Phoenix, you work all your life to find your way, through all the obstructions and the false appearances and the upsets you may have brought on yourself, to reach a meaning—using inventions of your imagination, perhaps helped out by your dreams and bits of good luck. And finally too, like Phoenix, you have to assume that what you are working in aid of is life, not death.

But you would make the trip anyway—wouldn't you?—just on hope.

(1974)

Some Notes on Time in Fiction

Time and place, the two bases of reference upon which the novel, in seeking to come to grips with human experience, must depend for its validity, operate together, of course. They might be taken for granted as ordinary factors, until the novelist at his work comes to scrutinize them apart.

Place, the accessible one, the inhabited one, has blessed identity—a proper name, a human history, a visible character. Time is anonymous; when we give it a face, it's the same face the world over. While place is in itself as informing as an old gossip, time tells us nothing about itself except by the signals that it is passing. It has never given anything away.

Unlike time, place has surface, which will take the imprint of man—his hand, his foot, his mind; it can be tamed, domesticized. It has shape, size, boundaries; man can measure himself against them. It has atmosphere and temperature, change of light and show of season, qualities to which man spontaneously responds. Place has always nursed, nourished and instructed man; he in turn can rule it and ruin it, take it and lose it, suffer if he is exiled from it, and after living on it he goes to it in his grave. It is the stuff of fiction, as close to our living lives as the earth we can pick up and rub between our fingers, something we can feel and smell. But time is like the wind of the abstract. Beyond its all-pervasiveness, it has no quality that we apprehend but rate of speed, and our own acts and thoughts are said to give it that. Man can feel love for place; he is prone to regard time as something of an enemy.

Yet the novelist lives on closer terms with time than he does with place. The reasons for this are much older than any novel; they reach back into our oldest lore. How many of our proverbs are little nutshells to pack the meat of time in! ("He that diggeth a pit shall fall into it." "Pride goeth before destruction, and a haughty spirit before a fall.") The all-withstanding devices of myth and legend (the riddle of the Sphinx, Penelope's web, the Thousand and One Nights) are constructed of time. And time goes to make that most central device of all, the plot itself—as Scheherazade showed us in her own telling.

Indeed, these little ingots of time are ingots of plot too. Not only do they contain stories, they convey the stories—they speak of life-in-the-movement, with a beginning and an end. All that needed to be added was the middle; then the novel came along and saw to that.

Only the nursery fairy tale is not answerable to time, and time has no effect upon it; time winds up like a toy, and toy it is: when set to "Once upon a time" it spins till it runs down at "Happy ever after." Fairy tales don't come from old wisdom, they come from old foolishness—just as potent. They follow rules of their own that are quite as strict as time's (the magic of number and repetition, the governing of the spell); their fairy perfection forbids the existence of choices, and the telling always has to be the same. Their listener is the child, whose gratification comes of the fairy tale's having no suspense. The tale is about wishes, and thus grants a wish itself.

Real life is not wished, it is lived; stories and novels, whose subject is human beings in relationship with experience to undergo, make their own difficult way, struggle toward their own resolutions. Instead of fairy immunity to change, there is the vulnerability of human imperfection caught up in human emotion, and so there is growth, there is crisis, there is fulfillment, there is decay. Life moves toward death. The novel's progress is one of causality, and with that comes suspense. Suspense is a necessity in a novel because it is a main condition of our existence. Suspense is known only to mortals, and its agent and messenger is time.

The novel is time's child—"I could a tale *unfold*"—and bears all the earmarks, and all the consequences.

The novelist can never do otherwise than work with time, and nothing in his novel can escape it. The novel cannot begin without his starting of the clock; the characters then, and not until then, are seen to be alive, in motion; their situation can declare itself only by its unfolding. While place lies passive, time moves and is a mover. Time is the bringer-on of action, the instrument of change. If time should break down, the novel itself would lie in collapse, its meaning gone. For time has the closest possible connection with the novel's meaning, in being the chief conductor of the plot.

Thus time is not a simple length, on which to string beadlike the novel's episodes. Though it does join acts and events in a row, it's truer to say that it leads them in a direction, it induces each one out of the one before and into the one next. It is not only the story's "then—and then," it may also be a "but" or a "nevertheless"; and it is always a "thus" and a "therefore."

Why does a man do a certain thing now, what in the past has brought him to it, what in the future will come of it, and into what sequence will he set things moving now? Time, in which the characters behave and perform, alone and with others, through the changes rung by their situation, uncovers motive and develops the consequences. Time carries out a role of resolver. ("As a man soweth, so shall he reap.")

Clock time has an arbitrary, bullying power over daily affairs that of course can't be got around (the Mad Hatter's tea party). But it has not the same power in fiction that it has in life. Time is plot's right arm, indeed, but is always answerable to it. It can act only in accordance with the plot, lead only toward the plot's development and fulfillment.

Fiction does not hesitate to accelerate time, slow it down, project it forward or run it backward, cause it to skip over itself or repeat itself. It may require time to travel in a circle, to meet itself in coincidence. It can freeze an action in the middle of its performance. It can expand a single moment like the skin of a balloon or bite off a life like a thread. It can put time through the hoop of a dream, trap it inside an obsession. It can set a fragment of the past within a frame of the present and cause them to exist simultaneously. In Katherine Anne Porter's perfect short story "The Grave," a forgotten incident from her country-Texas childhood abruptly projects itself upon a woman's present; its meaning—too deep for the child's understanding—travels twenty years through time and strikes her full force on a city street in another country. In this story, time moves by metamorphosis, and in the flash it discloses another, earlier metamorphosis—the real one, which had lain there all the while in the past that the young woman had left behind her.

In going in the direction of meaning, time has to move through a mind. What it will bring about is an awakening there. Through whatever motions it goes through, it will call forth, in a mind or heart, some crucial recognition. ("I imagined that I bore my chalice safely through a throng of foes.")

What can a character come to know, of himself and others, by working through a given situation? This is what fiction asks, with an emotional urgency driving it all the way; and can he know it in time? Thus time becomes, as sharply as needed, an instrument of pressure. Any novel's situation must constitute some version of a matter of life or death. In the face of time, life is always at stake. This may or may not be the case in a literal sense; but it does need to be always the case as a matter of spiritual or moral survival. It may lie not so much in being rescued as in having learned what constitutes one's own danger, and one's own salvation. With the refinements of the danger involved, suspense is increased. Suspense has exactly the value of its own meaning.

In fiction, then, time can throb like a pulse, tick like a bomb, beat like the waves of a rising tide against the shore; it can be made out as the whisper of attrition, or come to an end with the explosion of a gun. For time is of course subjective, too. ("It tolls for thee.")

Time appears to do all these things in novels, but they are *effects*, necessary illusions performed by the novelist; and they make no alteration in the pace of the novel, which is one of a uniform steadiness and imperturbability. The novel might be told episodically, hovering over one section of time and skipping over the next; or by some eccentric method—Henry Green spoke of his as going crabwise; but however its style of moving, its own advance must remain smooth and unbroken, its own time all of a piece. The plot goes forward at the pace of its own necessity, its own heartbeat. Its way ahead, its line of meaning, is kept clear and unsnarled, stretched tight as a tuned string.

Time in a novel is the course through which, and by which, all things in their turn are brought forth in their significance—events, emotions, relationships in their changes, in their synchronized move toward resolution. It provides the order for the dramatic unfolding of the plot: revelation is not revelation until it is dramatically conceived and carried out.

The close three-way alliance of time, plot and significance can be seen clearly demonstrated in the well-written detective novel. We can learn from it that plot, by the very strength, spareness and boldness of its construction-in-motion, forms a kind of metaphor. I believe every well-made plot does, and needs to do so. But a living metaphor. From the simplest to the most awesomely complicated, a plot is a device organic to human struggle designed for the searching out of human truth. It is from inception highly sensitive to time, it acts within time, and it is in its time that we ourselves see it and follow it.

As readers, we accept more or less without blinking the novel's playing-free with time. Don't we by familiar practice accept discrepancies much like them in daily living? Fictional time bears a not too curious resemblance to our own interior clock; it is so by design. Fiction penetrates chronological time to reach our deeper version of time that's given to us by the way we think and feel. This is one of the reasons why even the first "stream-of-consciousness" novels, difficult as they must have been for their authors breaking new ground, were rather contrarily easy for the reader to follow.

Fictional time may be more congenial to us than clock time, precisely for human reasons. An awareness of time goes with us all our lives. Watch or no watch, we carry the awareness with us. It lies so deep, in the very grain of our characters, that who knows if it isn't as singular to each of us as our thumbprints. In the sense of our own transience may lie the one irreducible urgency telling us to do, to understand, to love.

We are mortal: this is time's deepest meaning in the novel as it is to us alive. Fiction shows us the past as well as the present moment in mortal light; it is an art served by the indelibility of our memory, and one empowered by a sharp and prophetic awareness of what is ephemeral. It is by the ephemeral that our feeling is so strongly aroused for what endures, or strives to endure. One time compellingly calls up the other. Thus the ephemeral, being alive only in the present moment, must be made to live in the novel as *now*, while it transpires, in the transpiring.

Fiction's concern is with the ephemeral—that is, the human —effects of time, these alone. In action, scene and metaphor, these are set how unforgettably before our eyes! I believe the images of time may be the most indelible that fiction's art can produce. Miss Havisham's table in its spiderwebs still laid for her wedding feast; the "certain airs" in *To the Lighthouse* that "fumbled the petals of roses"—they come instantaneously to mind. And do you not see the movement of Gusev's body in the sea, after his burial from the hospital ship: see it go below the surface of the sea, moving on down and swaying rhythmically with the current, and then being met by the shark: "After playing a little with the body the shark nonchalantly puts its jaws under it, cautiously touches it with its teeth, and the sailcloth is rent its full length from head to foot." "Was it possible that such a thing might happen to anyone?" is the question Chekhov has asked as Gusev was slid into the sea, and in this chilling moment we look upon the story's answer, and we see not simply an act taking place in time; we are made, as witnesses, to see time happen. We look upon its answer as it occurs in time. This moment, this *rending*, is what might happen to anyone.

When passion comes into the telling, with a quickening of human meaning, changes take place in fictional time. Some of them are formidable.

I was recently lent a book by a student which had set itself to clear up *The Sound and the Fury* by means of a timetable; the characters' arrivals and departures, including births and deaths, were listed in schedule, with connections to and from the main points of action in the novel. What has defeated the compiler is that *The Sound and the Fury* remains, after his work as before it, approachable only as a novel. He was right, of course, in seeing time to be at the bottom of it. Time, though—not chronology.

Think of the timepieces alone. Think of only one timepiece: Dilsey has to use the Compson clock; it has only one hand. "The clock tick-tocked, solemn and profound. It might have been the dry pulse of the decaying house itself; after a while it whirred and cleared its throat and struck." It strikes five times. "Eight o'clock," says Dilsey. Even while the clock is striking, chronology is in the act of yielding to another sort of time.

Through the telling of the story three times in succession by three different Compsons in the first-person and then once again in the third-person, we are exposed to three different worlds of memory, each moving in its own orbit. "He thirty-three," Luster says of Benjy, "thirty-three this morning," and the reply comes, "You mean he been three years old thirty years." Benjy's memory is involuntary and not conscious of sequence or connections: a stick run along the palings of a fence. But time of whatever nature leaves a residue in passing, and out of Benjy comes a wail "hopeless and prolonged. It was nothing. Just sound. It might have been all time and injustice and sorrow become vocal for an instant by a conjunction of planets."

Time to Quentin is visible—his shadow; is audible—his grandfather's watch; and it is the heavy load that has to be carried inside him—his memory. Excruciatingly conscious, possessing him in torture, that memory works in spite of him and of all he can do, anywhere he can go, this last day of his life. The particular moment in time that links him forever to the past—his world—conditions *all* time. The future may be an extension of the past *where possible*; the future can include memory *if bearable*. But time will repeatedly assault what has been intact; which may be as frail as the virginity of Caddy. If experience is now, at every stage, a tragedy of association in the memory, how is the rememberer to survive? Quentin spends his last day, as he's spent his life, answering that he is already dead. He has willed the past some quality, some power, by which it can arrest the present, try to stop it from happening; can stop it.

Who, in the swirling time of this novel, knows the actual time, and can tell the story by it? Jason, of course. He keeps track of time to the second as he keeps track of money to the penny. Time is money, says Jason. And he cheats on both and is in turn cheated by both; we see him at the end a man "sitting quietly behind the wheel of a small car, with his invisible life ravelled out about him like a worn-out sock."

By all the interior evidence, we will come nearest to an understanding of this novel through the ways it speaks to us out of its total saturation with time. We read not in spite of the eccentric handling of time, but as well as we can by the aid of it. If a point is reached in fiction where chronology has to be torn down, it must be in order to admit and make room for what matters overwhelmingly more to the human beings who are its characters.

Faulkner has crowded chronology out of the way many times to make way for memory and the life of the past, as we know, and we know for what reason. "Memory believes before knowing remembers," he says (in *Light in August*). Remembering is so basic and vital a part of staying alive that it takes on the strength of an instinct of survival, and acquires the power of an art. Remembering is done through the blood, it is a bequeathment, it takes account of what happens before a man is born as if he were there taking part. It is a physical absorption through the living body, it is a spiritual heritage. It is also a life's work.

"There is no such thing as was," Faulkner remarked in answer to a student's question as to why he wrote long sentences. "To me, no man is himself, he is the sum of his past. There is no such thing really as was, because the past is. It is a part of every man, every woman, and every moment. All of his and her ancestry, background, is all a part of himself and herself at any moment. And so a man, a character in a story at any moment in action, is not just himself as he is then, he is all that made him; and the long sentence," he adds, "is an attempt to get his past and possibly his future into the instant in which he does something . . ."

Distortion of time is a deeply conscious part of any novel's conception, is an organic part of its dramatic procedure, and throughout the novel's course it matters continuously and increasingly, and exactly as the author gives it to us. The dilations, the freezing of moments, the persistent recurrences and proliferations, all the extraordinary tamperings with time in *The Sound and the Fury*, are answers to the meaning's questions, evolving on demand. For all Faulkner does to chronological time here—he explodes it—he does nothing that does not increase the dramatic power of his story. The distortions to time give the novel its deepest seriousness of meaning, and charge it with an intense emotional power that could come from nowhere else. Time, in the result, is the living essence of *The Sound and the Fury*. It appears to stand so extremely close to the plot that, in a most extraordinary way, it almost becomes the plot itself. It *is* the portentous part; it is the plot's long reverberation. Time has taken us through every degree of the long down-spiral to the novel's meaning—into the meaning; it has penetrated its way. It has searched out every convolution of a human predicament and brought us to the findings of tragedy.

Faulkner's work is, we know, magnetized to a core of time, to his conception of it as the continuing and continuousness of man. Faulknerian time is in the most profound and irrefutable sense *human* time. (*Corruption* is that which time brings to the Compsons' lives. *Progress* is the notion of those who are going to make something out of it: "What's in it for me?" ask the Snopeses.) His deepest felt and most often repeated convictions—"They endured." "Man will prevail"—are the long-reached and never-to-be-relinquished resolutions of his passionate idea of human time. And they contain, burned into them, all the plots of Faulkner's novels and stories.

Time, in a novel, may become the subject itself. Mann, attacking the subjectivity of man's knowledge of time, and Proust, discovering a way to make time give back all it has taken, through turning life by way of the memory into art, left masterpieces that are like clocks themselves, giant clocks stationed for always out in the world, sounding for us the high hours of our literature. But from greatest to least, don't most novels reflect that personal subjective time that lived for their writers throughout the writing?

There is the constant evidence of it in a writer's tempo, harmony, the inflections of his work, the symmetry and proportions of the parts in the whole; in the felt rhythms of his prose, his emotion is given its truest and most spontaneous voice; the cadence which is his alone tells us—it would almost do so in spite of him—his belief or disbelief in the story he intends us to hear. But I have in mind something more than this governing of a writer's style.

Faulkner has spoken for the record of his difficulties in writing *The Sound and the Fury*, the novel he loved best and considered his most imperfect; he spoke of its four parts as four attempts, and four failures, to tell his story. In their own degree, many other novels give evidence in themselves of what this difficulty suggests: the novel's duration is in part the measurable amount of time the novelist needs to apprehend and harness what is before him; time is part of the writing too. The novel finished and standing free of him is not the mirror-reflection of that writing-time, but is its equivalent. A novel's duration is, in some respect, exactly how long it takes the particular author of a particular novel to explore its emotional resources, and to give his full powers to learning their scope and meeting their demands, and finding out their truest procedure.

In the very imperfections of *The Sound and the Fury*, which come of a giant effort pushed to its limit and still trying, lies a strength we may set above perfection. They are the human quotient, and honorable as the marks left by the hand-held chisel in bringing the figure out of recalcitrant stone—which is another way of looking at time.

(1973)

III

REVIEWS

The Western Journals of Washington Irving

Edited and Annotated by John Francis McDermott

Delightful mode of life—exercise on horseback all the fore part of the day—diversified by hunting incidents—then about 3 o'clock encamping in some beautiful place with full appetite for repose, lying on the grass under green trees—in genial weather with a blue, cloudless sky —then so sweet sleeping at night in the open air, & when awake seeing the moon and stars through the tree tops—such zest for the hardy, simple, but savory meats, the product of the chase—venison roasted on spits or broiled on the coals—turkeys just from the thicket—honey from the tree—coffee—or delightful prarie tea. The weather is in its perfection—golden sunshine—not oppressive but animating—skies without a cloud—or if there be clouds, of feathery texture and lovely tints—air pure, bland, exhilarating—an atmosphere of perfect transparency—and the whole country having the mellow tint of autumn. How exciting to think that we are breaking thro a country hitherto untrodden by white man, except perchance the solitary trapper—a glorious world spread around us without an inhabitant.

Thus Washington Irving in the Wild West of America in 1832, and though it is dubious if he himself had made the camp, ridden the chase, rounded up the turkeys or stirred the brew, assuredly he was under a green tree, and writing it down momentarily in a journal.

That the original New Yorker ever had the experience of washing his own clothes and eating stewed polecat for breakfast was more or less a happy chance. It was just after his return from seventeen years abroad; at the time he was probably weary of the lavish welcoming fetes accorded him in New York, and certainly highly curious about the new world opening up at home. An opportunity came for him to join Bean's Rangers on a minor military expedition—one gathers, as a kind of combination guest artist and responsibility. He rode horseback and sat on rafts, met the Indians and lived the life for three months—covering land and river from St. Louis across to Independence, down through the present states of Missouri and Kansas to Fort Gibson, then a big loop over the Oklahoma prairies and back.

The five extant Journals kept by Irving were copied by Mr. McDermott, who provides also an interesting introduction. The book is charmingly put together; Mr. McDermott makes excellent correlation of this and contemporary material into some amusing counterplay. There are maps and reproductions of Irving's casual and fluent pencil sketches, and a sample chapter from the "Tour on the Praries" resulting from the notes, for comparison's sake, rounding out the book in a satisfying and scholarly manner.

That Irving spent his days in delight is evident everywhere. He seemed to meet new things, new people, the excitements and pleasures of a strange life with an emotion somewhere justly between intoxication and amusement, between curiosity and pleasant objectivity. The notes are set down with an unselfconsciousness that is still elegant. Their directness and spontaneity have the charm which Irving himself would probably shrink to consider achieved until his writing was "finished"—and prevaricated on and romanticized, says Mr. McDermott—as in the "Tour."

Chances are, such delicacy seldom went West. The writing that was to spring out of the West would never be like this; and Irving's work is unique in Western annals because it is not robust nor rambunctious nor raw; there is not any smartness or swaggering in any word of Irving's writing any more than there was in any bone of his body.

Perhaps the most appealing thing about Irving here is his marvelous eye for detail—that dateless quality. He takes time to note: "Intense curiosity with which an Indian watches Dr. ODwyer while he shaves," and "Little dog looking on at shoeing horse as if studying the art or waiting for his turn." The notes are generally pictorial, often beautiful—he remarks ahead the "blue lines of untrodden country." He is swift to compose a whole little landscape; then fill it with action.

Aground near natives house—show boat on the Illinois shore with flag—groups assembled there—rifle shooting— horse race along shore—negro laugh—sunset—party breaks up—some in boat across glassy river singing ballad —others on horseback through the woods—some on foot—some loiter on shore—beautiful, clear evening sky— moon nearly full—rising over the Kentucky shore above tufted forest—night hawks.

Camp—fire—meat roasted on sticks—savory—our salon of trees lighted up by fire—sky and stars in center—bat flitting across—faces of men & black boy roasting meat— greyhound with spectral face—we sit on bear skins & the meat put on spits before us—cut it off with knife & eat— coffee.

These word-pictures, set down in their immediacy, make valuable records of their time. They prove that Irving was a good reporter. Especially, he was fascinated by Indians, as he always was by the romantic and legendary in American life which related it to the Old World. He seems never to have caught sight of a new Indian without noting it.

Pass several Creeks—one with scarlet turban and plume of black feathers like a cock's tail—one with white turban with red feathers—Oriental look—like Sultans on the stage—some have raquet with which they have been playing ball—some with jacket and shirts but legs and thighs bare—middle sized, well made and vigorous. Yesterday one had brilliant bunch of sumach. They look like fine birds on the Prarie.

He was equally meticulous to enter little bits of Indian legends when he ran across them: "An old squaw left alone when her party had gone hunting prayed the Great Spirit to make something to amuse her—he made the mosquito." But there is marked absence of any of our own Western tall tales in this book, samples of our wild humor or ways of talking. One single bit of laconic speech is set down, "Old Genl Nix used to say God made him two drinks scant."

It is apparent that Irving never identified himself with all this. He remained ever the detached gentleman and observer, seeing the pageant through urban eyes. When the Western scene threatened vulgarity, he suddenly saw it romantically, instead. Thugs heightened to gypsies, and Mason and his gang, Irving understood, gave back money to poor people, like Robin Hood.

Before daybreak howling of wolves—at daybreak imitations of cocks crowing, hens cackling, among youngsters of the camp—horses driven in—breakfast—Whistling—singing—dancing—hallooing after horses—joking, laughing, scampering after horses—Bugle sounds. . . . Cries of "Who has seen my horse? & c."

There are like stage directions for a spectacle. They are not a participator's words. Irving does not consciously condescend —and is a great defender, of course, of the Indians—but he does refer to the guides and such in the party as "servants" and the Frenchman Antoine as "the half-breed," and there is a quiet impression that everybody else waited on Mr. Irving. There is appraisal without rapport.

The West was a curiosity; Irving was the visiting New Yorker. He rather expected to find things romantic, and he did: "Fires lit in dell—looks like a robbers' retreat." He enjoyed himself. He never did learn to spell "prairie," though.

(1944)

GEORGE R. STEWART'S

Names on the Land

_&_

Outlaws X-roads, Shiloh, Schenectady, Santa Fe—how did we get these names? And when?

The record of our place-names is of course the skeleton story of our nation; in that array the intrinsic and underlying structure shows. Exploration and claiming—Cape Fear, Louisiana; colonization—Jamestown; immigration—New Rochelle; Revolution—Lafayette; expansion—Deadman's Gulch. Our names tell us everything if we can read them. But every name has a name behind that—one more story, a sea-change. The ambition of this book is staggering—like a demonstration of our national character in itself. Mr. Stewart uses the x-ray method on his material, but he has the zest of a forty-niner, and what he makes is not a case, but a strike, and his book is a beauty. Only a passionate lover of facts, of facts rooted in the country and the people and the history of the land, could have written it. Mr. Stewart has written a meteorological novel (_Storm_) and a factual account of the Donner party. But what facts are closer to people, more revealing of people's hearts, than the names they bestow?

The scope here is so large, and the details so minute—taking in the whole country from the beginning on (with a nod at the Ice Age) and from one end to the other—that the story would collapse under its own weight in the hands of a man less deft at organizing it—a problem which was only one to tempt Mr. Stewart, one imagines, and lead him on. The lay reader such as the present reviewer has no way of knowing what degree of accuracy the work reaches, but will bet that it is good and high. Mr. Stewart has a reputation for getting data. In dealing with this material there must be guesswork and deduction in addition to the mountainous research; indeed, part of the fascination of the book lies in its ingenuity. A knowledge of languages, including the Algonquian, a familiarity with American history from the earliest times on, a clear geographical grasp of the country from all four corners, a knowledge of law and land grants, miner's slang, Indian beliefs, agricultural developments, Mormon saints and weather—a sizable background appears behind this book.

In the United States (Mr. Stewart does deplore that makeshift name for our country) are places named for battles, for a lost comrade, for the day of a saint, for a homesick moment, for a lure to bring neighbors, for kings and queens; places named for the namer, for a dead pony, for Lafayette, for a tavern sign, for a future wife, for a murder, for a deer in the creek, for a night of bad cards, for a rock that looked like the bosom of a lady, for a cockfight, for a poem in Scotland. Tradition, hope, love, pride, delight in the romantic, the bawdy, the beautiful, hope of gain, a keen and seeing eye, and likely a strutting fancy—these went into the naming of places in America. All Europe and Asia gave us names—and Puritans, Huguenots, Mormons and Quakers, miners, missionaries, outlaws, fishermen, scholars, traders, trappers, surveyors, priests, and planters' wives.

The astonishing variety of our names is to be expected, Mr. Stewart holds—after all, four centuries of changing peoples and changing aspirations went into the naming. Variety comes too, because in giving names to places, we cherished their strong link with actual persons and events and gave names "which seem to have stories of life and death behind them." Variety also sprang from democracy—that stubborn local pride in the local name, and the feeling that I have just as much right to give and keep a name as you have. Chicken Bristle, or die. So we have Lexington and Union and also Sweetwater, Marked Tree, Gunsight Hills, Cape Disappointment, Broken Bow, Roaring Run, Massacre Lake. And we have always loved a revolutionary, Mr. Stewart points out, and honored him, no further questions asked, with a town name—Kossuth, Kosciusko, even Ypsilanti did not stop us.

In the beginning the French were hunting a passage to the South Sea; the Spanish were looking for treasure in a fabulous kingdom and the elixir of life; the British were nosing for present holdings; the Dutch seeking trade. In all these pursuits, naming a place was an important point, a gain on the rivals. The differences in naming were clear-cut from the start. The Spanish always named places after the saint's day on which they found them, so that their maps are really calendars on which voyages can be read like diaries. The Dutch gave a practical name to each little kill and hook of the river they settled on, but they never did name the Hudson—it was simply "the river"—the English reproached them. The English, of course, drew upon courts and houses in England, gained favors or obeyed the king.

Ranging over four centuries, with pages packed with names and events, the book remains clear in trend, felicitous in pictures of the times which build along the way. We see the whole complexity and confusion of that early time when Joliet and Père Marquette with their boatmen, in two birchbark canoes, set off down the Mississippi:

At last, near the middle of June in 1673, they came to the great river, which was already known by name. They wrote the word as Mississippi. But Marquette, it would seem, called it also Conception, and Joliet called it Buade, after the family name of Count Frontenac, the Governor. Thus all at once the river had three names—an Indian name for the boatmen, a religious name for the priest, and a political name for the officer.

In all the conglomeration of detail, the major design is not lost sight of, and we are shown panoramas of the nation as a whole at a given time, as

. . . in the reign of Charles II, new great names arose, until twelve colonies and the Province of Maine were well established. In addition some cities and all the great rivers and capes and bays and islands of that coast had their names. Inland, the French had scattered names as far as Lake Superior and Kansas and Arkansas, and the Spaniards even further to the southwest. Since 1607 almost every year had seen the establishment of some new great name. In 1681 La Salle first used Louisiana; within a year Pennsylvania and Philadelphia were established; about the same time the Spaniards were beginning to use Texas. But the next two generations of men were to give few great names; instead they would fill in with thousands of little names, and establish new habits.

As he proceeds, the author shows how habit of life determined the kind of name. In the Virginia colonies, towns took the names of plantations, of little private chapels and churches, which were often named with Elizabethan fancy (Orphan's Gift, Chapel Hill, Chaplin's Choice, Jordan's Journey, Flower dieu Hundred). In the middle colonies, especially in Pennsylvania, towns took the names of the tavern signs, whose pictures survived as village names (Bird-in-Hand, Broad Axe, King of Prussia, Red Lion). When the Mormons went West they had a whole private holy book to draw names from and their own population of saints, and needed no dim-memoried dragon-killer to name a town St. George after. When the forty-niners went West they were in such a hurry that big things like mountains and rivers got names that were simple pinning-down affairs, the explicit "West Fork of the South Fork of the North Fork of the San Joaquin," so they could be found again. It was in the naming of their mining camps that they gave vent to their real enthusiasm and high spirits, for "No censorship restrained them; society was of men only. Most of them looked upon their sojourn in California . . . as temporary and riotous adventure . . . Doubtless the more sophisticated often invented the most outlandish names; two Harvard men named Shirt-tail Canyon."

Mr. Stewart pays close attention to the change of temper and mood of the country as reflected in its styles of names. In the eighteenth century the Yankee name ascended over the Puritan. A town in Vermont was named by honest combat, fought out on the hemlock plank floor of a new barn, the winner rising full of splinters to shout, "There, the name is Barre, by God!" Canton, Massachusetts, was named "at the instance of a prominent citizen, who maintained that his Massachusetts town was antipodal to the Chinese city," and all around, other prominent Yankee citizens came to the conclusion that they were antipodal to Canton, too, and Cantons sprang up thickly. "Actually, such an opinion was startlingly wrong . . . The very perversity of the story is almost an argument for it. It seems just what a crotchety Yankee of 1798 would be likely to maintain." He points out how "Illogically, as the religious fervor of the Puritans declined, biblical names grew more numerous. Perhaps they began to seem less holy." A town in Connecticut could be named Borzah in spite of Jeremiah 49:13. ("I have sworn to myself, saith the Lord, that Borzah shall become a desolation, a reproach, a waste, and a curse.") And he points out also, in defending, for example, an Alabama schoolmaster who named a muddy little river in his neck of the woods the Styx:

> The classical interests of the later eighteenth century are as much part of the history of the United States as the existence of the Indian tribes or the Revolution. To maintain, as many have done, that Rome and Troy are mere

excrescences on our map is to commit the fallacy of denying one part of history in favor of another part—or else
to be ignorant of history. The ideals and aspirations of the
Americans of that period deserve their perpetuation.

There are accounts given of all the great expeditions, full of
flavor and detail, always contributing to the general picture of
growth, of changing habits of thought, of the great surge
westward. The Lewis and Clark expedition flowered with the
indulgence of proud and extravagant fancy, heralding the
great day of the West ahead, as when Captain Lewis com-
memorated his lady love:

> I determined to give it the name, and in honour of Miss
> Maria W——d, called it Maria's River. It is true that the
> hue of the waters of this turbulent and troubled stream
> but illy comport with the pure celestial virtue and amiable
> qualifications of that lovely fair one; but on the other hand
> it is a noble river.

At the same time Captain Clark was writing down: "This rock
which I shall cal Popy's Tower is 200 feet high and 400 paces
in secumpherance." This grandiose spirit led straight to the
times when a camping party, sitting around a fire at night,
would get up a hilarious game to name some mountain range.
And they named mountains differently from the mountains of
the east: instead of Sugar Loaf and Haystack were Saddle
Mountain, Two Top, Rabbit's Ears, Nipple Butte and Coffin.

The book deals constantly with the Indians, of course, and
manages to correct many an error about Indian names. Trans-
ference, translation and false etymology are the three ways in
which a place name can be passed from language to language,
Mr. Stewart points out. So the Indian names enduring as such
are not the actual, original Indian names—they are what the
French priests wrote down, what the Spanish thought they
sounded like, what the English thought they undoubtedly
meant, what the Dutch made sound as nearly Dutch as they

could. Schenectady, for instance, is an anglicized form of the Dutch conception of a New York State Indian word.

Mr. Stewart points out the important difference in the ways an Indian and a white man named a river. The European conception of a river was of a stream with a source, to which it and all its branches could and should be traced, and it had a single name. "What is the name of this river?" excited explorers would ask the Indians. "Big Rock," the Indians would answer, pointing to a big rock in front of them. "Big Rock" was the name of the river *there*. At the bend it would be named "Little Bend." Mississippi, a French version of an Algonquian word, probably means "big river," but could never mean "Father of Waters" as the geography books told us—an abstract term no clear-headed Indian would ever give a river for a name. In the same way, the Indians running out to greet the white man in the southwest yelled "Techas! Techas!" This meant simply "Friends!" The Spaniards immediately thought the Indians were referring to some wonderful kingdom lying just back of them—Texas. But the Indians were hardly ever referring to anything except what was up at the moment.

The book abounds in the modest tale along with the mighty, telling how places were named:

Once a surveyor named Strange became separated from his comrades and hopelessly lost in the forest. Years later, forty miles from where he last was seen, men found his bones beneath a great beech tree. Against it leaned his rifle, the shotgun pouch still dangling. In the smooth bark could still be read the carved words in plaintive doggerel:

Strange is my name, and
I'm on strange ground,
And strange it is I can't be
found.

So the stream once known as Turkey Run became Strange Creek.

Mr. Stewart deals with the great namers, John Smith, Penn
—perhaps the greatest, Colonel William Byrd (who decried
the first Lover's Leap, naming the Blue Ridge) and many more.
He enumerates the towns named after Washington, Lafayette,
Lincoln, Jackson. He writes also:

Of all Americans to have their names preserved in large
cities, John Young is the most obscure. He came as an
early settler in 1798. Untroubled by modesty, he named
the place Youngstown; then, according to tradition, he
traded a deerskin for a quart of whisky, and celebrated
his immortality.

He was a man of no importance. But why should not
John Young stand as a symbol? If he was a man of little
note, so also were nearly all his fellow frontiersmen. They
died; their wooden grave-markers (if they had any)
rotted into dust, and they were forgotten. But if we believe in democracy, why should not John Young, whisky
and all, stand as their symbol, with the blast-furnaces of
Youngstown flaming to their memory?

This book is a labor of love, such as few people would have
had the energies, much less the abilities, or the pure courage,
to undertake—and finish. The whole is written with a grace
and engaging humor belying the work behind it. The nation
from Seldom Seen to Possum Glory, Hog Eye to Bug Tustle,
does owe Mr. Stewart a debt of gratitude for getting the tre-
mendous material here between the covers of a book. "As the
train announcer calls out the stations for a Philadelphia local,
half the past of the nation unfolds." "It is a rich and poetic
heritage," indeed.

(1945)

VIRGINIA WOOLF'S

Granite and Rainbow

᪐

Of course, an editor who sent out a new book called *Men Without Women* to Virginia Woolf knew what he was doing. The *New York Herald Tribune* received a very far-sighted review. (The title she decided merely "to stare out of countenance.") She thought Hemingway's characters talked too much, but she would, "if life were longer," care to read the stories again. Hemingway "lets his dexterity, like the bullfighter's cloak, get between him and the fact . . . But the true writer stands close up to the bull and lets the horns—call them life, truth, reality, whatever you like—pass him close each time."

This is published today in *Granite and Rainbow*. It seems there were still pieces that were left out by Virginia Woolf herself when she put together both series of *The Common Reader*, and that eluded her husband when he published three books of her papers after she was dead. Two lady scholars from America—a country she always thought showed signs of being restless—found them, and are thanked for this collection by Mr. Woolf in a foreword. Seventeen years after her death appear twenty-five essays and book reviews—eleven written before 1920, twelve written during the twenties, one in 1930, one in 1940. Writing them earned her the time to write her novels, and the least of them is a graceful and imperturbable monument to Interruption, though it saddens us to see her "whipping the heads off poppies," as she called it to Lytton Strachey—and Marie Corelli was surely a poppy—with *The Waves* waiting in manuscript on her table.

The essays are the heart of the book. For one thing, she is back in invited company—Sterne, Defoe, Jane Austen, Peacock, the old cronies. The finest and longest piece, "Phases of Fiction," was written for the old *Bookman*, which published it in three parts in 1929. "There is . . . some design that has been traced upon our minds which reading brings to light," she says, and brings it to light.

That beautiful mind! That was the thing. Lucid, passionate, independent, acute, proudly and incessantly nourished, eccentric for honorable reasons, sensitive for every reason, it has marked us forever. Hers was a sensitivity beside which a Geiger counter is a child's toy made of a couple of tin cans and a rather common piece of string. Allow it its blind spots, for it could detect pure gold. In the presence of poetic fire, it sent out showers of sparks of its own. It was a mind like some marvelous enchanter's instrument that her beloved Elizabethans might have got rumor of and written poems about.

She has told how, after the enormous pressure under which she wrote her fiction, the intensity of feeling she lived through, the exacerbations she suffered, writing criticism was, for her, release. Critics, she once observed, are persons who have "done their work as a good housemaid does hers; they have tidied up after the party was over." The reading and rereading she set herself to do for *The Common Reader*, for instance—"to go through English literature like a string through cheese"—would, she said, be good for her mind—"rest it anyhow," for "one day, all of a sudden, fiction will burst in."

In the early pieces there are no early sentences. "Far be it from us to hazard any theory as to the nature of art" is, so far as I can see, the only slip she ever made. Her early recognitions range from fine ("No one felt more seriously the importance of writing than she did," of Katherine Mansfield) to finest: once she saw that streak of vulgarity in Henry James, she was incapable of being scared by his ghost stories, until she got to *The Turn of the Screw*; a masterpiece made her afraid of the dark. She scatters treasure everywhere she reads. "The novelist (of all those practicing the arts) . . . is terribly exposed to life . . . He can no more cease to receive impressions than a fish in mid-ocean can cease to let the water run through his gills." This aside comes in the course of reviewing a second-rate novel about which she presently observes that "a hundred pages have flashed by like a hedge seen from an express train."

And now what we can do—for no farewell glimpse is ever satisfactory—is what Virginia Woolf herself loved to do in her own reading: let the work as a whole swim up into the mind. "Breaking the mold" she called the task she set herself. The novel, of course, was never to be the same after the day she started work on it. As novel succeeded novel she proceeded to break, in turn, each mold of her own. It is a perilous life. The innovators of fiction, like the Jumblies of Mr. Lear, come from lands that are far and few, and they go to sea in a sieve.

"Every moment is the centre and meeting-place of an extraordinary number of perceptions which have not yet been expressed," she wrote in one of these essays. It was 1927. She was forming her prophecy of what the novel of the future would deal with. She was just in time: *To the Lighthouse* was about to burst in.

(1958)

The Letters of
Virginia Woolf, Volume II

Edited by Nigel Nicolson and Joann Trautmann

"Life would split asunder without letters," Virginia Woolf wrote in *Jacob's Room*, the high point in this period of her working life. During it—between 1912 and 1922—she wrote six hundred of those saving letters. They are published now as Volume II in the projected six being edited by Nigel Nicolson and Joanne Trautmann.

By now, the traumas of her growing up—all those family deaths—are behind her (though never to be forgotten). So is the casting about for the kind of friends she can share her life with—now she knows. She has just married Leonard Woolf.

She writes Lytton Strachey from their honeymoon in Spain; they are walking, talking, and: "My God! You can't think with what fury we fall on printed matter, so long denied us by our own writing! I read 3 new novels in two days: Leonard waltzed through the Old Wives Tale like a kitten after its tail."

They come home to Asheham, the house in Sussex—"the best in the world for reading Shakespeare"—where "All the morning we write in two separate rooms. Leonard is in the middle of a new novel; but as the clock strikes twelve, he begins to write an article upon Labour for some pale sheet, or a review of French literature for the Times, or a history of

Co-operation ... We sew [sic] articles all over the world—I'm writing a lot for the Times too, reviews and articles and biographies of dead women—so we hope to make enough to keep our horse."

Two milestones were shortly passed in Virginia's life without her awareness, the publication of her first novel, *The Voyage Out*, and the move to Hogarth House. It was to aid in her recovery from this most severe period of insanity that Leonard cast about for a plaything "sufficiently absorbing to take her mind off her work."

"Have you heard about our Printing Press?" Virginia writes to Margaret Llewelyn Davies. "We're both so excited that we can talk and think of nothing else, and I think there's a chance of damaging the Webb influence irretrievably (which is my ambition in life)."

The hand-press, bought in a shop off the street, fitted onto the Woolf's dining-room table, and they were teaching themselves how to work it from a sixteen-page pamphlet that came with it. (A school of printing in Fleet Street had turned them down: they were the wrong age and the wrong class—middle in both, as Leonard has told in *Beginning Again*.)

"We want to start on something very short and very sublime," Virginia writes Lady Robert Cecil. This is exactly the way we want the story of the Hogarth Press told. "I see that real printing will devour one's life," she writes Vanessa, and later goes on: "After 2 hours work at the press, Leonard heaved a terrific sigh and said, 'I wish to God we'd never bought the cursed thing!' To my relief, though not surprise, he added, 'Because I shall never do anything else.' You can't think how exciting, soothing, ennobling and satisfying it is. And so far we've only done the dullest and most difficult part —setting up notice."

"We find we have only 50 friends in the world—and most of them stingy," she writes Lady Ottoline Morrell. "Could you think of any generous people?" She enlists Vanessa's help with the covers. The binding equipment turns up from Cousin

Emma Vaughn, though she, with her obsessive concern for German prisoners, naturally had to offer it to a camp of these first.

"Two Stories"—Leonard's "Three Jews," Virginia's "The Mark on the Wall," with woodcuts by Carrington—was printed in an edition of 150 copies, of which the stingy friends bought only 135. In 1918 "Prelude" was printed on a bigger machine, borrowed, and bound with their own hands in an edition of 300 copies. It had been rejected by all publishers up to now, but Virginia thought Katherine Mansfield "had a much better idea of writing than most." In May, 1919, the Hogarth Press was to issue three bound books together: Virginia's "Kew Gardens," John Middleton Murry's "The Critic in Judgment," and Eliot's "Poems"; and Virginia was breaking off a letter with "I must go now and boil some glue."

The Hogarth Press, Asheham, and the circle of Bloomsbury form the real background of the letters. World War I was going on, but we are grateful, knowing that she was to be lacerated by the second, to find Virginia now comparatively immune. She was spared the great personal losses so many of the English suffered: Leonard was exempt for physical reasons, as were a number of their friends; others were conscientious objectors—two of them, not by chance being Duncan Grant and David Garnett, were farmed out with Vanessa at Charleston. When air raids over London and Sussex got to be a habit, so did the Woolfs' sitting in the cellar; mainly this was boring, with only the servants to talk to. The pinch was noticed when it came to butter and tea and the importing of good paper for the Press.

We are in Bloomsbury when it was young, when the creative juices were running high and there was a heady current of daring in the air. Seen through the eyes of one who helped make it, it is restored to us briefly here, a society every bit its own, brightly conscious of itself, civilized, unsentimental, liberally disposed, not only led by, but thrilled by, the intelligence, young artists and writers wandering in and out of one another's houses in a sort of homemade state of grace. We see the Bloomsberries themselves in their own earliness, before they take on the blur of time and reminiscence: "Nessa left the room and reappeared with a small parcel about the size of a large slab of chocolate. On one side are painted six apples by Cézanne. Roger [Fry] very nearly lost his senses. I've never seen such a sight of intoxication. He was like a bee on a sunflower."

Mr. Nicolson's policy of editing the letters is to include everything. There is no order but the chronological. The effect is one of profusion, like a spacious Edwardian flower bowl being constantly added to out of the advancing garden, useful little zinnias stuck in with the great peonies, spires of delphinium and the night stock, as they come into bloom. The method is appropriate to Virginia Woolf. Side by side may be letters helping Vanessa find a cook, paying her respects to Thomas Hardy for his whole lifetime, sharing whatever she's reading with Lytton ("I read the book of Job last night—I don't think God comes well out of it"), supplying Vanessa with a new list of names for her coming child ("I like a name that has the look of a clear green wave"), asking money for a fund for Eliot so he can get out of the bank, reassuring a young man she's never met, David Garnett, who's apologized for his escapade of breaking into Asheham with a few of his friends, while the Woolfs were away, and making away with the food: "As a matter of fact, we are not at all annoyed—It seems a very sensible thing to do ... It's a relief to find it was you. Leonard is reading your poems, and says they are the best return you could make for the raid."

Mr. Nicolson in his introduction remarks, "She gives only part of herself to anybody." Moved primarily by natural courtesy, one imagines, she used her gift of the light touch more often than not. But these beautiful, spontaneous letters never underestimate the seriousness of experience, or betray her sense of its magnitude. What she gives in her letters comes from her awareness of the other person, the part of herself, it seems to me, that matters in the other's circumstances. This sensitivity in giving is Virginia Woolf's particular mark: it can guide her to speak from an extraordinary depth of candor. To Saxon Sydney-Turner, friend of her brother Thoby who had died young, she can write: "I've a feeling that I want somehow to give you back or that some one else should give you back what you lost in Thoby. For I've often thought that you were the one person who understood about him—I mean that his death meant almost more to you and me than to anyone, and I think we shared together some of the worst things. I know anyhow that you helped me then—and often I've known that we both kept him with us, though we did not talk of him."

Just before a violent period of her illness was coming on, she wrote to Margaret Llewelyn Davies about being ill before in a letter that seems to all but lay bare the very mystery of what she suffered: "And I wanted to say that all through that terrible time I thought of you, and wanted to look at a picture of you, but was afraid to ask! You saved Leonard, I think, for which I shall always bless you, by giving him things to do. It seems odd, for I saw you little, but I felt you had a grasp on me, and I could not utterly sink. I write this because I do not want to say it, and yet I think you will like to know it."

Mr. Nicolson relates that Virginia and Leonard, after the first months, did not often sleep together. He sounds confident, if one wants to stop there. The tenderest letter in the book, the most directly declaring, is a brief one written to Leonard after they had been married for four years, on one of the rare occasions when they were separated.

Be that as it may, what her readers have always known from her writings is that a need for intimacy lies at the very core of Virginia Woolf's life. Besides the physical, there are other orders of intimacy, other ways to keep life from splitting asunder. Lightly as it may touch on the moment, almost any letter she writes is to some degree an expression of this passion, of which the eventual work of art was *The Waves*.

So richly present is Vanessa Bell in these letters written to her and about her (Vanessa's outnumber the rest) that it seems odd to realize we never hear her speak in her own voice (obviously, not at all like Virginia's), never read her side of the correspondence, when even her handwriting is brought close to our eyes—with "the quality of a great sheep dog paw—a sheep dog which has been trotting sagaciously through the mud after its lambs all day long." This painter sister was closer even than a sister; Virginia would now and then speak of herself as Vanessa's child, "your first-born." It is possible that Virginia was seeking the maternal in everyone she loved, Leonard included; but in Vanessa she found it.

There's a touching corollary. "I like myself as a child," she writes Vanessa; the letter comes from Cornwall, scene of their childhood visits, where the lighthouse, of *To the Lighthouse*, stands. She writes Saxon, too: "I think how I was a nice little girl here, and ran along the top of the stone walls, and told Mr. Gibbs after tea that I was full to the chin . . . Do you like yourself as a child? I like myself, before the age of 10, that is— before consciousness sets in." (Compare this with Mrs. Vallance's thoughts in the starlit garden in *Mrs. Dalloway's Party*, the little sequence recently published, but written in these days.)

Vanessa really wanted to hear nothing from her but the latest gossip, Virginia was fond of telling her. "Let me see what I have in my bag for you." Samples:

"I got her (Violet Dickinson) to tell me a series of death bed scenes of the Lyttleton family—the poor old Bishop Arthur L. was pestered to death by them. 'Now you're practically dead, Arthur, you *must* collect yourself and tell us what you see. Don't you feel anything like immortality coming on?' "

"Janet Case still more or less bedridden . . . though she was writing an article upon illegitimacy in Sweden for a newspaper. Downstairs, Emphie was playing very badly on the violin to a party of wounded soldiers. The house is crowded with photo-

graphs of old pupils, deceased parents and the Elgin Marbles . . .
Does this convey any of the spirit of Hampstead to you?"

"I think there is a good deal of the priest, it may be of the
eunoch, in [Logan Pearsall Smith] . . . He thought it very
delightful to extract the flower of Urn Burial, 6 words long,
and print it by itself in an exquisite little volume, to carry in
the breast pocket, like a scent bottle. He has several of these
sentences always on his person, and reads them aloud in a high
nasal chant . . ."

It is most often when she shoots darts at the aristocracy that
malice appears; and springing from a rather exceptional insight,
it still has a quiver to it. "The other day," she tells Vanessa,
"we went to tea with Nelly Cecil, and met old Beatrice Thyme,
who is more like a sunburnt tinker who has just had a mug of
beer than ever, notwithstanding the death of her mother and
nephew. She was as black as a rook, with one very large
Bumble Bee, carried out in pearls and saphires, attached to her
throat. She is going to live in lodgings over St. Johns Wood
post office, in order to economise; she uses margarine instead
of butter, and wears no underclothes. She spends all her time
reading family letters, and tying them up in bundles, as they
are too many to burn, and all perfectly dull. Nelly is going to
economise by living in Henry James' flat. It is wonderful how
entirely detached from sanity the aristocracy are; one feels
like a fly on a ceiling when one talks to them."

Vanessa sometimes provided the subject herself of gossip
around London, but criticism of her is not to be tolerated
from holier-than-thou Cousin Dorothea Stephen. Virginia sent
her this letter: "Your view that one cannot ask a friend who
has put aside the recognized conventions about marriage to
one's house because of outsiders and servants seems to me incomprehensible. You, for example, accept a religion which I
and my servants, who are both agnostics, think wrong and
indeed pernicious. Am I therefore to forbid you to come here
for my servants sake? . . . I could not let you come here with-

out saying first that I entirely sympathise with Vanessa's views and conduct. If after this you like to come . . . by all means do; and I will risk not only my own morals but my cook's."

The reckless moment—it lasted hardly longer than that—when Virginia and Lytton Strachey were engaged to marry is forgotten now and they have settled into what Cyril Connolly has called "a Solomon-Sheba relationship," which was to last until his death. Her letters to him, brilliant as they are, are the only ones in which we might see a touch of self-consciousness. Virginia didn't write drafts for letters, but she may have taken a little more trouble with Lytton's, to make them flash in his face.

When he sends her an essay for his forthcoming *Eminent Victorians*, she writes him of her admiration for ". . . how you weave in every scrap—my God what scraps!—of interest to be had, like (you must pardon the metaphor) a snake insinuating himself through innumerable golden rings—(Do snakes?—I hope so.)"

She needed a little time to adjust to his fame, which blazed up when the book appeared. "I think fame has changed him, as love might," she writes to Vanessa. "He is immensely appreciative, even tender; jumps up and seizes withered virgins like Vernon Lee, and leaves them gibbering with ecstasy." A little later: "He's doing a grand season, with Cunards, Asquiths, and all the rest; completely happy; still, he assures us his soul is untouched; and I think it is."

An envy she recognizes in herself, mocks, but continues to feel enters into this and into other letters. But she had something to be envious about in other writers; not their work, but their time. She had reason for envy in the unfairness of life which robbed her, with abominable suffering, of years of the work she passionately wanted to do, as well as of the children she and Leonard had both wanted to have. (And in reading the letters, we cannot do her the disservice of ignoring what falls between them, when the continuity breaks off and the gap appears like a black fissure in bright landscape.)

Recovery was always slow. She wrote to E. M. Forster, in

1922: "Writing is still like heaving bricks over a wall . . . I should like to growl to you about all this damned lying in bed and doing nothing, and getting up and writing half a page and going to bed again. I've wasted 5 whole years (I count) doing it; so you must call me 35—not 40—and expect rather less from me. Not that I haven't picked up something from my insanities and all the rest. Indeed, I suspect they've done instead of religion. But this is a difficult point."

Virginia Woolf did not use a letter to a friend as a vent for her constant preoccupation with her writing in progress. Her self-discoveries, analyses, her elations and fears, her devastating suffering over every one of her books in turn, all went into the privacy of her diaries, which she had started during this period and was to keep up for the rest of her life. But a passing remark makes a flash in the air sometimes ("I daresay one ought to invent a completely new form [of the novel]," she says to the beginning David Garnett).

It is significant that when she most generously and ardently spoke her mind on writing itself, it was to the young. The marvelous letter she wrote to Gerald Brennan, a young man, new friend, whose letter she was answering on Christmas Day, 1922, comes just at the last of this book. It reads in part:

"One must renounce, you say . . . Ah, but I'm doomed! . . . It is not possible now, and never will be, to say I renounce. Nor would it be a good thing for literature were it possible . . . The human soul, it seems to me, orientates itself afresh every now and then. It is doing so now. No one can see it whole, therefore. The best of us catch a glimpse of a nose, a shoulder, something turning away, always in movement. Still, it seems better to catch this glimpse, than to sit down with Hugh Walpole, Wells, etc. etc. and make large oil paintings of fabulous fleshy monsters complete from top to toe . . . I mean, life has to be sloughed: has to be faced: to be rejected; then accepted on new terms with rapture. And so on, and so on; till you are 40, when the only problem is how to grasp it tighter and tighter to you, so quick it seems to slip, and so infinitely desirable it is.

". . . One must renounce, when the book is finished; but not before it is begun . . . I was wondering to myself why it is that though I try sometimes to limit myself . . . to the things I do well, I am always drawn on and on, by human beings, I think, out of the little circle of safety, on and on, to the whirlpools; when I go under."

(1976)

E. B. WHITE'S
Charlotte's Web

⊸ṣ

If I had the qualifications (a set of spinnerets and the know-how), I'd put in tonight writing "Adorable" across my web, to be visible Sunday morning hung with dewdrops for my review of *Charlotte's Web*.

Mr. E. B. White has written his book for children, which is nice for us older ones, as it calls for big type. It has liveliness and felicity, tenderness and unexpectedness, grace and humor and praise of life, and the good backbone of succinctness that only the most highly imaginative stories possess.

Most of *Charlotte's Web* takes place in the Zuckerman barn, through the passing of the four seasons.

> Life in the barn was very good—night and day, winter and summer, spring and fall, dull days and bright days. It was the best place to be, . . . with the garrulous geese, the changing seasons, the heat of the sun, the passage of swallows, the nearness of rats, the sameness of sheep, the love of spiders, the smell of manure, and the glory of everything.

The characters are varied—good and bad, human and animal, talented and untalented, warm and cold, ignorant and intelligent, vegetarian and blood-drinking—varied, but not opposites; they are the real thing.

Wilbur is of a sweet nature—he is a spring pig—affectionate, responsive to moods of the weather and the song of the crickets, has long eyelashes, is hopeful, partially willing to try anything, brave, subject to faints from bashfulness, loyal to friends, enjoying a good appetite and a soft bed, and a little likely to be overwhelmed by the sudden chance for freedom. He changes the subject when the conversation gets painful, and a buttermilk bath brings out his beauty. When he was a baby the sun shone pink through his ears, endearing him to a little girl named Fern. She is his protector, and he is the hero.

Charlotte A. Cavitica ("But just call me Charlotte") is the heroine: a large gray spider "about the size of a gumdrop." She has eight legs, and can wave them in friendly greeting. On her friends' waking up in the morning, they see what she's written for them—"Salutations!"—though it may have kept her working all night. She tells Wilbur right away that she drinks blood, and Wilbur on first acquaintance begs her not to say that.

"Why not? It's true, and I have to say what is true," says Charlotte. "I am not entirely happy about my diet of flies and bugs, but it's the way I'm made. A spider has to pick up a living somehow or other, and I happen to be a trapper. I just naturally build a web and trap flies and other insects. My mother was a trapper before me. Her mother was a trapper before her. All our family have been trappers . . . I have to think things out, catch what I can, take what comes. And it just so happens, my friend, that what comes is flies and insects and bugs."

Charlotte cannot stand hysterics. ("Slowly, slowly," says Charlotte. "Never hurry, and never worry.") She knows how many eggs are in her egg sack because she got started counting one night and couldn't stop (594). She saves Wilbur's life, because she can write—can and does. "It is not often that someone comes along who is a true friend and a good writer. Charlotte was both."

There is Templeton, the rat that lives under Wilbur's

trough—well, he constitutes somebody to talk to. "Talking with Templeton was not the most interesting occupation in the world, but it was better than nothing." "The rat had no morals, no conscience, no scruples, no consideration, no decency, no milk of rodent kindness, no compunction, no higher feeling, no friendliness, no anything." Templeton grudges his help to others, then brags about it, can fold his hands behind his head, and sometimes acts like a spoiled child.

There is the goose, who knows barnyard ways. "It's the old pail-trick, Wilbur . . . He's trying to lure you into captivity-ivity. He's appealing to your stomach." The goose always repeats everything. "It is my idio-idio-idiosyncrasy."

I do not intend to spoil the story for anybody by giving away the plot—how Charlotte sets in to save Wilbur's life. (Wilbur is grateful and says, "Don't fail to let me know if there's anything I can do to help, no matter how slight.") How Charlotte's own life was saved by a rotten goose egg. ("I'm delighted," gabbled the goose, "that the egg was never hatched.") How the Zuckermans take Wilbur to the Fair to enter him for the prize, and Charlotte hides in the crate ("We can't tell what may happen at the Fair Grounds. Somebody's got to go along who knows how to write") and so does Templeton, once he hears about the spoils of the midway. ("Is this appetizing yarn of yours true? I like high living, and what you say tempts me.")

What the book is about is friendship on earth, love and affection, adventure and miracle, life and death, trust and treachery, night and day and the seasons. As a piece of work it is just about perfect, and perfectly effortless and magical, as far as I can see, in the doing. Here is Charlotte, working through the night at her writing and talking to herself to cheer herself on: "Now for the R! Up we go! Attach! Descend! Pay out line! Whoa! Attach! Good! Up you go! Repeat! Attach! Descend! Pay out line! Whoa, girl! Steady now! Attach! Climb! Over to the right! Pay out line! Attach! Now right and down and swing that loop around and around! . . . Good girl!"

What the book "proves"—in the words the minister in the

story hands down to his congregation on the Sunday after Charlotte writes "Some Pig" in her web—is "that human beings must always be on the watch for the coming of wonders." Dr. Dorian has this to say: "Oh, no, I don't understand it. But for that matter I don't understand how a spider learned to spin a web in the first place. When the words appeared, everyone said they were a miracle. But nobody pointed out that the web itself is a miracle." The author will only say: "Charlotte was in a class by herself."

"At-at-at, at the risk of repeating myself," as the goose says, I will say *Charlotte's Web* is an adorable book.

(1952)

WILLIAM FAULKNER'S
Intruder in the Dust

What goes on here? Grave-digging. "Digging and undigging."
What's in the grave? One body or maybe another, maybe
nothing at all—except human shame, something we've done to
ourselves. Who digs? Who but the innocent, the young—and
the old and female, their burning-up energy generating a
radiance over Yoknapatawpha County and its concerns? Not
forgetting the Gowrie twins—like the vaudeville team that
follows behind the beautiful stars with its hilarious, mechanical
parody, the Gowries from the hills dig too.

Intruder in the Dust is a story of the proving of innocence,
this proof a maddening physical labor and a horrendous, well-
nigh impossible undertaking, full of riddles and always starting
over. The real innocents are the provers, the technical innocent
is old, black Lucas Beauchamp in danger of lynching for
murder of a white man—and Lucas is a lightless character,
high-and-mighty and gorgeously irritating, who would be so
temptingly guilty if he weren't so irrevocably innocent, just
the kind of man to get in just this kind of fix, who has been
building up to it all his life, and now, by hints, condescends to
be saved, offering cash fees, and requiring a receipt. The
provers, exhumers that they have to be, are Miss Eunice Habersham, "a practical woman" in her seventies, who "hadn't

taken long . . . to decide that the way to get a dead body up out of a grave was to go out to the grave and dig it up," and the sixteen-year-olds, Charles Mallison, white, Aleck Sander, colored, who end up dog-tired and a step along in man's wisdom. Gavin Stevens, the articulate uncle who by his character partly forecasts and foretells for Charles, and the sighing mother—wonderfully done—are near at hand, summoned or pushed back, and beyond and dipping down is the menacing fringe of the Gowries from the ridges of wild Beat Four. Out of the diggings comes a solution and an indictment, defining a hope, prayer, that we·should one day reach that point where it will be *Thou shalt not kill at all*, where Lucas Beauchamp's life will be secure not despite the fact that he is Lucas Beauchamp but because he is.

The action of *Intruder* is frantic—and meditative, not missing a minute. The more-than-possible failure of the task overhangs it like a big cliff. The suspense is of the chase—sometimes slow-motion, sometimes double-time; leg-work, horses, mules ("unspookable" for this business), pickup trucks, on up to a fast Sheriff's auto, bear the characters toward their grave-robbing with greater and greater urgency. The setting is the open country at night lighted by "a thin distillation of starlight," and a few dusky interiors, smelly. (How Faulkner can show us that making things out in the dark is a quality of perception as well as a quantity!) In counterpoint is the Square, back in Jefferson, with the face of its crowd, the immobile, inflexible crowd around which sentience strives and threads and skirts, until the crowd's final whizzing away like a battery of witches·on brooms. Even when Old Man Gowrie gets his Vinson back, brushes the quicksand off and takes him home to bury again tomorrow, is this story going to stop? "This time Hampton and his uncle could go out there tomorrow night and dig him up" is the boy's sleepy valediction that night.

Intruder is marvelously funny. Faulkner's veracity and accuracy about the world around keeps the comic thread from ever being lost or fouled, but that's a simple part of the matter. The complicated and intricate thing is that his stories aren't decked out in humor, but the humor is born in them, as much their blood and bones as the passion and poetry. Put one of his stories into a single factual statement and it's pure outrage—so would life be—too terrifying, too probable and too symbolic too, too funny to bear. There has to be the story, to bear it— wherein that statement, conjured up and implied and demonstrated, not said or the sky would fall on our heads, is yet the living source of his comedy—and a good part of that comedy's adjoining terror, of course.

It doesn't follow that *Intruder*, short, funny, of simple outline, with its detective-story casing, is one of the less difficult of Faulkner's novels. Offering side-by-side variations of numerous words, daringly long, building ever-working sentences (longer than *The Bear*'s, maybe, if anybody is counting), moods and moments arrested, pulled up to peaks, willfully crowned with beauty and terror and surprise and comedy, Faulkner has at once reexplored his world with his marvelous style that can always search in new ways, and also appeared to use from beginning to end the prerogatives of an impromptu piece of work. It could be that to seem impromptu is an illusion great art can always give as long as profundities of theme, organization and passionate content can come at a calling, but the art of what other has these cadenzas? Even the witty turns and the perfect neatness of plot look like the marks of a flash inspiration. If *Intruder* did come intruding in a literal way, shaped from the dust into life before the eyes, then we have a special wonder here; but it's none of our business, and the important thing is the wonder, special or not.

Time shifts its particles over a scene now and then, past and future like seasoning from a shaker, and Yoknapatawpha County we know now too, while the new story in its year, month, and ticking hour of day and night, emerges in that illumination and shading which Faulkner supplies to the last inch and the ultimate moment. The political views in *Intruder*, delivered outright as a speech, are made, rightly enough, another such shading to the story.

As in all Faulkner's work, the separate scenes leap up on their own, we progress as if by bonfires lighted on the way, and the essence of each scene takes form before the eyes, a shape in the fire. We see in matchless, "substituteless" (Faulkner's word for swearing) actuality and also by its contained vision: "Miss Habersham's round hat on the exact top of her head such as few people had seen in fifty years and probably no one at any time looking up out of a halfway rifled grave." Every aspect of vision is unique, springs absolute out of the material and the moment, only nominally out of "character" or "point of view," and so we see hats and happenings and every other thing, if not upward from a half-rifled grave, then down the road of the dark shuttered cabins, or up a jail stair, from the lonely ridge where Gowries come; or see in accompaniment with the smell of quicksand (a horse is there to get the smell and rear up), by the light even of impending conflagrations. Old Man Gowrie turning over a body that's the wrong body, not his son's, becomes "only an old man for whom grief was not even a component of his own but merely a temporary phenomenon of his slain son, jerking a strange corpse over onto its back not in appearance to its one mute indicting cry not for pity not for vengeance not for justice but just to be sure he had the wrong one, crying cheery abashless and loud, 'Yep it's that damned Montgomery damned if it ain't!' " The boy's feverish dream of Miss Habersham trying to drive around the mob to get back to her own house, a vision of How the Old Woman Got Home, is this writer's imagination soaring like the lark.

Of course it's a feat, this novel—a double and delightful feat, because the mystery of the detective-story plot is being raveled out while the mystery of Faulkner's prose is being spun and woven before our eyes. And with his first novel in eight years, the foremost critics are all giving cries as if (to change the image) to tree it. It's likely that Faulkner's prose can't be satisfactorily analyzed and accounted for, until it can be predicted, God save the day. Faulkner's prose, let's suspect, is intolerantly and intolerably unanalyzable and quite pure, something more than a possum in a tree—with its motes bright-pure and dark-pure falling on us, critics and non-critics alike.

(1949)

Selected Letters of William Faulkner

Edited by Joseph Blotner

William Faulkner's wife and daughter had said he "would not have wanted such a volume. His personal letters were never remotely intended for publication," and Faulkner himself had written (to Malcolm Cowley): "I dont like having my private life and affairs available to just any and everyone who has the price of the vehicle it's printed in." Thus Joseph Blotner writes in his introduction to this volume. "So a book of selected Faulkner letters was a logical next step."

The logic has shifted from Faulkner's to his biographer Blotner's, but while I suppose we can have little doubt that this fierce guardian of his own privacy would have abominated the publication of his letters, we can doubt, too, that he would have been much surprised at its being done anyway. Publishing personal letters of a genius gone to his grave is a human act of man. And plainly, in Blotner's case, even a reverent act.

Therefore it is good to have the book done by an editor and a publisher who cared about Faulkner the man as well as Faulkner the artist. It's been assembled and edited with taste, the responsible, devoted and thorough job we would expect after the 1974 biography.

Jill Faulkner Summers gave Blotner access and permission to

publish letters in her possession, a number of which he'd drawn upon or already published in the biography. Some recipients of letters withheld theirs, in whole or in part. Mr. Blotner doesn't say what proportion of the existing body of letters this absence represents, or name any of their recipients, if indeed he knows all these facts himself. In the letters published, a row of dots indicates where something is omitted, though without a clue as to how much—a sentence or half the letter; we aren't told whether it was the recipient or the editor who has cut it. (Blotner says he has excised some things.) "The editor and biographer must take what he can get," he says.

The letters are in chronological order, but not numbered, and not bracketed in any way; there is no sectioning by period of time of life or place—it's Oxford to New Orleans to Paris, Hollywood, New York, Stockholm, Egypt, Virginia and all the rest, and home again, from page 3 to page 465, all without an extra one-line space between. (There are brief explanatory notes to introduce some of the correspondents, and a good index, which will help you to find your place.) If this plan lacks something in imagination, still it is uninterfering.

Faulkner's letters are not "literary"; but they are very much letters about writing. They are the letters of a man living in the midst of his own world and his own society and kin, a man who was ardently and all by himself trying to do the thing he most passionately wanted to do, and by necessity earn the family living by it. The greatest number of the letters we have are those to his publishers and agents. "Yours to hand," he customarily begins them. Intimacy was no part of them; they were factual business letters, as telegraphic as an SOS, which they often were. We cannot miss the sound of desperation so often underneath: these were letters of life-and-death, about the wherewithal to survive, to keep alive his genius; he was so pressed that often he sent them off without signing them.

In 1932 he writes to his agent Ben Wasson: "I hope to hell Paramount takes Sanctuary. Dad left Mother solvent for only about a year. Then it is me."

In 1934 he is working on two novels, and writing one short story each month, trying to sell to the *Post*. "As I explained to you before," he writes Harrison Smith, "I have my own taxes and my mother's, and the possibility that Estelle's people will call on me before Feb. 1 and also my mother's and Dean's support, and occasional demands from my other two brothers which I can never anticipate . . . Then in March I have . . . insurance and income tax."

He writes agent Morton Goldman in 1935: "The man who said that the pinch of necessity, butchers and grocers bills and insurance hanging over his head, is good for an artist, is a damned fool."

From the start, Faulkner could look at his work, and thought an artist ought to, with the objectivity of (as he liked to say) a carpenter who'd built a henhouse. What he *thought* and *felt*, had worked in anguish to convey, must make its appearance in the work itself—it was the hen in the henhouse. But he had to look at all he wrote with recognition of its earning possibilities. "By God I've got to."

He steps up his pace to two short stories a week—"I dont know how long I can keep it up"—and still prophesies that his insurance premiums "will be difficult to meet and perhaps even impossible, unless I should produce a book which the movies would want—which God Himself could not promise Himself to write."

Through all this, when a publisher's comprehension of his problems was so vital, Faulkner's editors at Random House met his letters with unfaltering willingness to advance him money against the future. Faulkner appreciated his luck, which brought him in the course of time to Harrison Smith, Robert K. Haas, Saxe Commins, Bennett Cerf and Albert Erskine. In Hollywood, where he'd gone to buy himself time, he wrote to Harold Ober: "If they [Warner's] had any judgment of people, they would have realized before now that they would get a damn sight more out of me by throwing away any damned written belly-clutching contract and let us work together on simple good faith and decency, like with you and Random House." Ober, it ought to be said, must have been the most understanding of agents, as well as the most patient.

By 1940 Faulkner writes: "But maybe a man worrying about money can't write anything worth buying." To Haas he says: "I had planned, after finishing THE HAMLET, to try to earn enough from short stories by July 1 to carry me through the year, allow me six months to write another novel. I wrote six . . . the sort of pot boilers which the Post pays me $1,000.00 each for, because the best I could hope for good stories is 3 or 4 hundred . . . but only one of them has sold yet. Now I have not only wasted the mental effort and concentration which went into the trash, but the six months . . . as well as the time since March 15 which I have spent mortgaging my mares and colts one at a time to pay food and electricity and washing and such, and watching each mail train in hopes of a check. Now I have about run out of mules to mortgage."

Then he replies to Harold Ober in 1941 that no, he has no carbon of the story he'd sent. It was a story rewritten from a chapter of a novel under way and sent "first draft and in haste because I need money badly . . . In hopes that Post will take it and I can get a check next week, I am trying to make the revision desired from memory, without waiting to get back your copy. If it does not fit, please return your copy, and the revision by AIR MAIL and I will get it back the same day. Please sell it for something as soon as you can. I am in a situation where I will take almost anything for it or almost anything else I have or can write."

The *Post* found the rewrite acceptable and the story appeared in May, 1942. It was "The Bear."

But threats of oblivion were only increasing, and it was during the course of his being rescued from it that Faulkner put down the best things he ever said about his writing in a series of letters to Malcolm Cowley. The correspondence between the two men, later good friends, who had then never met, began in 1944 when Cowley put to Faulkner his idea of a

Viking Portable Faulkner, to be compiled and edited by him. The story, like all Faulkner's life, is well known now, but it remains suspenseful. We know that had it not been for the reemergence of Faulkner's work in the triumphant organization Cowley made of it for this volume, and Cowley's fresh literary insight, which called forth Faulkner's composition of the Compson genealogy called "Appendix/Compson 1699–1945," all Faulkner's work, already out of print then, might be worse than only out of print now—it might be half forgotten.

"I would like the piece," Faulkner initially replies to Cowley, "except the biography part. You are welcome to it privately, of course. But I think that if what one has thought and hoped and endeavored and failed at is not enough, if it must be explained and excused by what he had experienced, done or suffered, while he was not being an artist, then he and the one making the evaluation have both failed."

Then to the letter that's the masterpiece: "I'm trying primarily to tell a story, in the most effective way I can think of, the most moving, the most exhaustive. But I think even that is incidental to what I am trying to do . . . I am telling the same story over and over, which is myself and the world . . . I am trying to go a step further [than Thomas Wolfe] . . . I'm trying to say it all in one sentence, between one Cap and one period. I'm still trying to put it all, if possible, on one pinhead. I don't know how to do it. All I know to do is to keep on trying in a new way . . . Life is a phenomenon but not a novelty . . . Art is simpler than people think because there is so little to write about. All the moving things are eternal in man's history and have been written before, and if a man writes hard enough, sincerely enough, humbly enough, and with the unalterable determination never never never to be quite satisfied with it, he will repeat them, because art like poverty takes care of its own, shares its bread."

On April 23, 1946, he has the book: "Dear Cowley: The job is splendid. Damn you to hell anyway. But even if I had beat you to the idea, mine wouldn't have been this good. By God,

I didn't know myself what I had tried to do, and how much I had succeeded."

We have to fillet this story from where it lies embedded in the chronological pages, spread over a section fifty-one pages long. It's alongside letters like the kind one to Miss Lida, his mother-in-law, about the flowers in California, their likeness to and difference from the flowers in Mississippi, just because it comes next—telling us something about Faulkner's character and manners but holding us up when we want the next letter to Cowley. The letters, the best in Blotner's book, can still better be read in Cowley's own 1966 *Faulkner-Cowley File*, where they appear, along with the other side of the correspondence, in uninterrupted sequence, and where, so read, they can move you to tears.

But there are values in the chronological order of a special kind. When you read the letters above, embodying all Faulkner has taught himself about what he's doing, you can remember those he wrote back in 1925, when he walked over France in the greatest exuberance, planning to make his reputation abroad. He writes to his mother: "I have just written such a beautiful thing that I am about to bust—2000 words about the Luxembourg gardens and death."

The letters make us variously aware of Faulkner's Oxford, so often their background. A letter dated December 31, 1948, to the president of the American Academy of Arts and Letters, which had been trying in vain to let Faulkner know he had been elected a member on November 23, explains it perfectly: "The letter must have become mislaid after it reached my home, since I did not receive it. I was in a deer hunting camp on Nov. 23. Telegrams are a casual business here; the office in town telephones them out and if you are not there to answer the phone, nothing else is done about it unless the operator happens to meet or pass you in the street and happens to remember to tell you a telegram came for you two or three weeks ago, did you get it?"

To Malcolm Cowley he remarks: "My whole town spent

much of its time trying to decide just what living men I was writing about, the one literary criticism of the town being 'How in the hell did he remember all that, and when did that happen anyway?' "

And to Phil Mullen, of the Oxford *Eagle*, after the Nobel Prize award: "I fear that some of my fellow Mississippians will never forgive that 30,000$ that durn foreign country gave me for just sitting on my ass and writing stuff that makes my own state ashamed to own me."

But away from it, in Hollywood, he writes to A. P. Hudson: "I dont like this damn place any better than I ever did. That is one comfort, at least I cant be any sicker tomorrow for Mississippi than I was yesterday."

It was all the same emotion, and what it was, the books made us know.

I have reported mostly on those letters that have to do with Faulkner's writing because Mr. Blotner says in his introduction that "The main purpose of this collection is to provide a deeper understanding of the artist, to reveal as much as possible what one can see in the letters about his art—its sources, intentions, the process of creation . . ." and also because I believe concentrating on letters about his work to be truest to Faulkner. Those letters that directly speak of his work are marvelous, and so are others that do so obliquely. All make clear that it remained the gift—not its cost in the work or its anguish, but the gift he had—that came first with him.

He writes to Joan Williams in 1953: ". . . And now, at last, I have some perspective on all I have done. I mean, the work apart from me, the work which I did, apart from what I am . . . And now I realize for the first time what an amazing gift I had: uneducated in every formal sense, without even very literate, let alone literary, companions, yet to have made the things I made. I dont know where it came from. I dont know why God or gods, or whoever it was, selected me to be the vessel. Believe me, this is not humility, false modesty: it is simply amazement."

Neither was it self-centered. Faulkner's marked sensitivity to others, to their pain, their needs of affection, encouragement, moral support, might have been taken for granted from the evidence of his work. What might not have been so easily guessed was that their gifts as artists brought about a profound response in him.

In the occasional—even rare—letter to a literary peer, his feeling for, appreciation of, the other writer's gift—not shop-talk—is almost sure to be the subject. Just as it is to a young unknown black poet whose manuscripts Faulkner read and helped him with: "Put the passion in it, but sit on the passion. Dont try to say to the reader what you want to say, but make him say it to himself *for* you. I will edit the second one and send it to you when I get it right . . . Your idea in both is all right." ("All right" emerges in Faulkner's letters as his strongest, surest term of praise.) He apparently fell in love with Joan Williams, but the very touching letters to her all carry the current of a continuing wish to encourage her talent—she was in her twenties, just beginning to try to break away from the constrictions of family and write. He gave her his handwritten manuscript of *The Sound and the Fury*—a different sort of present from a bunch of roses.

Faulkner's letters show honesty, fairness and largeness of mind, genuine consideration for others, and compassion; also exhilaration and also despair. They pull no punches. They are in turn funny, sad, angry, desperate, tender, telegraphic, playful, quick in arithmetic and perfect in courtesy, unhappy. But these qualities, in one combination or another, and in some measure, can be found in the letters of a lot of human beings who didn't write *The Sound and the Fury*, "Spotted Horses," "The Bear." It would deny the author's whole intent, in a lifetime of work and passion and stubborn, hellbent persistence, to look in his letters for the deepest revelations he made.

No man ever put more of his heart and soul into the written word than did William Faulkner. If you want to know all you can about that heart and soul, the fiction where he put it is still right there. The writer offered it to us from the start, and when we didn't even want it or know how to take it and understand it; it's been there all along and is more than likely to remain. Read that.

(1977)

E. M. FORSTER'S
Marianne Thornton

Miss Marianne Thornton of Battersea Rise, 1797–1887, had the good fortune and good sense (both characteristic of her family) to have for a great-nephew Mr. E. M. Forster; her benevolence, characteristic too, gave him a comfortable start on his way toward becoming a writer. Here is fresh cause for rejoicing: a "domestic biography," the perspicacity, the virtue and the persuasion of which could hardly be overestimated. The subject: Marianne.

The daughter of Henry Thornton, M.P., and Marianne Sykes Thornton, she was born the eldest child of nine into a household characterized by "affections, comfort, piety, integrity, intelligence, public activity, private benevolence; and transcending them all an unshaken belief in a future life where the members of the household would meet again and would recognize each other and be happy eternally." Marianne's Papa, a prosperous banker and a man of outstanding intellect, "was fertile in devices for improving her." He had provided for her happiness before she was born by building Battersea Rise, in Clapham Common; the house is the heart of the book, as it came to be the heart of Marianne.

There will never be another Battersea Rise. To [the Thorntons] it was a perfect playground and in after years a sacred shrine. It satisfied in them that longing for a particular place, a home, which is common amongst our upper classes, and some of them transmitted that longing to their descendants, who have lived on into an age where it cannot be gratified.

We see it—with its beautiful oval library that William Pitt designed, with the garden beyond its glass doors, and its thirty-four bedrooms and the nursery upstairs—brimming with life and good spirits. Here is the family assembled for prayers, here they are at table. ("Prayers before plenty, yes. But plenty.") The neighbors—William Wilberforce the famous abolitionist, the Zachary Macaulays (little Tom was a terror in tableaux), or some of the "able and alarming Stephen family"—are likely to be guests for the evening, for we are very much in the thick of the Clapham Sect. Conversation races around the table—foreign missions, abolition, education, *infant* education, politics, the Apocrypha, Napoleon; and the irrepressible young daughters of the house are going to set the best of it down in diaries before they go to bed. "To distinguish six maidens is never easy, especially when the sound of their laughter is gone," says Mr. Forster, but he knows that any of them can call up Jane Austen today. There are always crowds of friends in—"The Bishop of Limerick has just come, *crying* with joy"—and there are teaching excursions ("the carriage stops, the pious occupants get out and teach, and drive on"), there are philosophic fetes—considered successful —and the May Meetings . . . "On the whole the way of life they discovered worked, and they could pursue it to the glory of their God without self-torture or torturing others."

Marianne grew up with a first-rate mind and an affectionate heart, and inclined to accept the responsibilities of both. She had seriousness, gaiety, exemplary judgment in conduct, faith in reason and God; she was unsuspicious of a world that could do so well with improvement, and unshocked and unscared by its bugbears; she rose to a crisis, she rose higher into detachment; she came down to earth and enjoyed fun and nonsense; she could throw herself into the joys of travel; she gave and received love. She took her understanding from the domestic orbits, none more instructive or demanding; she could reason out from those into the wider circles of society and human nature, which she saw as reaching toward heaven. Really a child of the eighteenth century, she lived almost the length of the nineteenth, and the numerous acts of her good life, indeed each of her letters, she launched like so many little lighted boats on the stream of continuity, going confident into the night. They would be safely received at the other end.

The Clapham Sect could have hardly failed to be a primary force in her life. "Wherever she walked the child found herself surrounded by assorted saints"; especially two. "The friend of friends," William Wilberforce, is given a full-length domestic portrait in these pages; no public portrait of any man could be half so remarkable. "It is with the saintly, gay and innocent side of his character that [Marianne's] recollections deal; they ignore the cleverness and astuteness which are evident in his public life and sometimes remind us of Gandhi." When Wilberforce went as one of a deputation of three from the House of Commons to persuade Queen Caroline to give up being crowned and the lady "all but kicked them downstairs," it was to the garden of Battersea Rise that he repaired for the sight of a moss rose: "Oh the beauty of it. Oh the goodness of God in giving us such alleviations in this hard world ... And oh how unlike the Queen's countenance."

Hannah More, "that bishop in petticoats," when she was not at Battersea Rise, could be descended upon in Somerset, "where the two cats called 'Non-resistance' and 'Passive obedience' were fed by us all day long ... Crowns of flowers were made for ourselves, garlands for the sheep ... We were fed with strawberries and cream and told to lie down in the hay whilst Charles the coachman made us a syllabub under the cow." "Unlike Wilberforce," says Mr. Forster, "she never married and so she never altered. Childless herself, she became the family life that does not die with death." And so, we are brought to feel, did Marianne.

We move with Marianne through her successive phases of daughter, sister, aunt, great-aunt. "She passes into spinsterhood without regret." The crises of her long, full life were few in number; its daily animation and its depth had purer, less accessible sources. The fabric of the family (for others married, and produced as many as ten children) remains strong, consistent in quality, the same on both sides, and exactly what it seems, goodness itself. It is given a variation in sheen by the occasional introduction of rainbow threads, for example, the Reverend Charles Forster, who married Marianne's sister Laura and turned out to be E. M. Forster's grandfather.

It is toward the end of Marianne's life that Imagination, with a radiant, inquisitive five-year-old face, takes its first real look at the family. It belongs to the author of, at the moment, "Chambermaids under the clothesline." Edward Morgan Forster, that dragonfly of a little boy, the son of Edward Forster and Alice Clara Whichelo, darted across Marianne's last days, and with the evident satisfaction he brought her (he had to wear corkscrew curls for her pleasure) was born some inkling perhaps of what she was not to see for herself in life. She left a bequest. This made possible Cambridge, then travel, "which inclined me to write." It was staying with "Aunt Monie" that the little boy had made at the age of four at least one discovery that would have confounded a Thornton: he was already able to read to himself. "From that moment I never looked back . . . No one taught me to read and no one managed to teach me to write."

The family papers on which this work is based are copious, varied, and descended from a number of hands old and young; they date from about 1750 to 1900, and only those of a domestic nature have been drawn upon: there are others of a different importance. Framed by the rest are Marianne's own— a lifetime's letters and her Recollections which she began writing out for young Edward Morgan Forster when she was an old lady. Time, kinship and the female human heart—formidable combination—have not now held out against him. Marianne appears, a human being—waving whatever useful domestic implement she happens to have in her hand, possibly her quill. We shall never forget her. So, while he has been about it, have appeared a great many other vigorous, attractive and irreplaceable people out of Marianne's world.

Mr. Forster has created them all out of, or in spite of, an inheritance of remarkable family papers. What the choices must have cost him! On every hand he produces the tangible, the direct, the explicit, the spark that catches fire; he shows the letter, high-minded or gossipy, with the spirit still intact, like the gentian that was folded in Marianne's letter from Switzerland, still blue. And when the evidence of the age "will not travel," when Marianne writes the account of her father's death "as if the spirit of the age, which adored deathbeds, was speaking through her lips," then he has translated to make it clear that "inside all this cocoonery of words there was love, there was pain."

What Marianne Thornton, who believed in personal immortality, would think of being provided with an earthly brand of it is an aunt's business. The reader, who has fallen in love with Marianne on account of the book, can only feel how beautifully she persists in pages so thronging with all that signified life to her: her family around her and extending in both directions, Battersea Rise and the tulip tree that Napoleon never succeeded in invading England to cut down, the beloved friends, the visits and parties and jauntings, the May Meetings and France, the crises and their resolutions, the letters and sketches and books and babies, everybody who ever was drawn into the whirl and sweep of the Thornton galaxy, from Nurse Hunter to the Mohawk who was persuaded to dance and sing when he happened in to pay his respects one day—all in a marvelously ordered account of cloudless focus, felicitous and witty and wise. Perhaps it's all no more and no less than she would take for granted from an angel.

To the Thornton mind, imagination threatened a danger a good deal less calculable than that of Napoleon; neither did the Thorntons possess the sense of mystery or of poetry. I don't refer to Mr. Forster's best gifts here in order to belittle theirs—what could be more inappropriate?—but to suggest that they are exactly what is needed to comprehend human beings who *have been* real, as well as those who (as fictional characters) are going to be. The novelist as biographer is doubly valuable if his subjects have been both real and good; triply valuable if they are receding rapidly in time but are still able to give evidence through their effects and if the effects are miscellaneous. Here Mr. Forster, a very great novelist, has employed powers Marianne might not knowingly have countenanced, but she has not been hurt: she has been celebrated and loved. Continuity has been taken care of, and we are the gainers.

(1956)

E. M. FORSTER'S

The Life to Come, and Other Stories

❧

"The Life to Come" is the title of a short story that was written seventy years ago by E. M. Forster and is receiving its first publication today. The author himself valued it: it "came more from my heart than anything else I have been able to turn out," containing "a great deal of sorrow and passion that I have myself experienced." But because the sorrow and passion had a homosexual nature, the story has gone unpublished. Upon Forster's death, not quite three years ago, it was bequeathed to King's College, Cambridge, along with his other unpublished papers: two novels in "substantial fragments" (in addition to *Maurice*), and stories, plays, poems, essays, letters, notebooks, diaries. Of the total work of Forster, who lived to be ninety-one, the reading public saw during his lifetime no more than perhaps one half. Now "The Life to Come" is giving its title to one volume of what is being published in England as a new and "as nearly as possible" complete edition of E. M. Forster.

Oliver Stallybrass, who is editor of the Abinger Edition (so named for a place of long association with Forster's family), has included in this book all the completed stories that Forster did not include in *The Celestial Omnibus* (1911) and *The Eternal Moment* (1928). Of the fourteen, only two have been published before; the rest were rejected by magazines or with-held by the author. They range in date of composition from 1903 to 1958; seven were written after the publication of *A Passage to India*: upon completing that novel, Forster said in a letter, "My patience with ordinary people has given out."

For the texts here, the editor has followed a course of going as scrupulously as he can by Forster's "latest intentions"; the manuscripts he has found to be in an untidy state. The hand-writing is puzzling, the punctuation slapdash—Forster so rarely remembered to close his quotation marks—and more than one version turns up of most of the stories, "The Other Boat" in variations Mr. Stallybrass had to label from (a) to (g). At least one story seems to have risen from the ashes. What writer could live with his unpublished pages and let them alone?

And "How dependent on approval!" Forster wrote of him-self in his diary. Going unpublished, he tried out his stories on a circle of his friends. How much did they help matters? we wonder. While Lytton Strachey thought "The Life to Come" was good, T. E. Lawrence gave it a laugh. Goldsworthy Lowes Dickinson's disgust at a "Rabelaisian" story was enough to put Forster off his work on *Maurice*. The young William Plomer, allowed to read a story and not caring for it, was never shown another.

Forster, worshipper of sylvan places and the sunlit open, of freedom of every kind, felt obliged to keep his work put away in the drawer. But works of fiction—growths of the mind, the green shoots of feeling—need air and circulation to give them nourishment. They need the world. These stories often show cramp and strain, understandably, for not having reached the good light of acceptance.

All the stories in *The Life to Come*, like the familiar ones, are fantasies. The form suited Forster's temperament and was flexible to his needs. The title story, laid in a savage country, tells of the mistaking by "the wildest, strongest, most stubborn of all the inland chiefs" of an erotic passion that he feels for a British missionary for the love of Christ. "Dr. Woolacott" is the story of an ill young man who suffers from daydreams "of the kind forbidden"; in spite of Dr. Woolacott, "who treats everybody," he is in love with death and longs for its coming. But when he has received a portentous visitor at last, "he was left with a human being who had somehow trespassed and been caught, and blundered over the furniture in the dark, bruising his defenceless body, and whispering 'Hide me.'"

This story, too, meant much to Forster; and in it comes a touching passage in which the genius of all these stories might be musing:

A violin had apparently been heard playing in the great house for the last half-hour, and no one could find out where it was. Playing all sorts of music, gay, grave and passionate. But never completing a theme. Always breaking off. A beautiful instrument. Yet so unsatisfying . . . leaving the hearers much sadder than if it had never been performed. What was the use (some asked) of music like that? Better silence absolute than this aimless disturbance of our peace.

"Arthur Snatchfold" is less mysterious, a straightforward account of the "netting" of a jolly young milkman in a yellow shirt. It opens with a view of the conventional world characteristic of all these stories, here as a country house on a Sunday morning, "with so much ahead to be eaten, and so little to be said": *something is missing*, which has left the world empty or asleep or simply waiting. It appears at the turning point in "The Other Boat"— the best story in the book and, one is glad to note, the latest written, dated 1958. Young Lionel, after an exhausting scene with his young native lover "Cocoanut" down in the cramped cabin of a P.&O. liner, has come up on deck "to recover his poise and his sense of leadership":

The deck was covered with passengers who had had their bedding carried up and now slept under the stars. They lay prone in every direction, and he had to step carefully between them on his way to the railing. He had forgotten that this migration happened nightly as soon as a boat entered the Red Sea; his nights had passed otherwise and elsewhere. Here lay a guileless subaltern, cherry-cheeked; there lay Colonel Arbuthnot, his bottom turned. Mrs. Arbuthnot lay parted from her lord in the ladies' section . . . How decent and reliable they looked, the folk to whom he belonged! He had been born one of them, he had his work with them, he meant to marry into their caste. If he forfeited their companionship he would become nobody and nothing. The widened expanse of the sea, the winking lighthouse, helped to compose him, but what really recalled him to his sanity was this quiet sleeping company of his peers.

But this recalling is the herald of the murder and suicide with which the story ends. Like most of the stories, it is carrying a heavy burden of emotion with nowhere to go. As Forster saw, the stories were homosexual daydreams; like all daydreams, they go rushing toward the sanctuaries of extremes, and can end only in violence.

According to Forster's biographer, P. N. Furbank, it was the facetious homosexual stories rather than these serious ones that caused him misgivings. Mr. Stallybrass quotes Forster's diary entry for 8 April, 1922: "Have this moment burnt my indecent writings or as many as the fire will take. Not a moral repentance, but the belief that they clogged me artistically. They were written not to express myself but to excite myself . . . I am not ashamed of them. It is just that they were a wrong channel for my pen."

Without being able to account for their coming through the flames, Mr. Stallybrass has produced three for this book. "What Does It Matter? A Morality" is one, moving at slapstick speed, about a mythical kingdom, with an *agent provocateur*, winking policemen, doors popping open onto mismatched lovers, a concealed microphone under the mattress. The old facetiousness dances like a skeleton.

Clearly, nothing has got away from Mr. Stallybrass, and I consulted Forster here, turning to what he had to say about the Chapman Edition of Jane Austen, a writer whom he loved as much as I love Forster. Yes, he says, all scraps are for bringing forth, because they "throw light." Print anything, however trivial, that will help in the "final estimate." (And heaven knows, it was having to keep his work *away* from view that had been the affliction of his life.)

And so we have "Three Courses and a Dessert: Being a New and Gastronomic Version of the Game of Consequences," an outstanding example of a scrap. It's a composite story written by four friends for a magazine called *Wine and Food*; it saw print in 1944 and never did anybody any harm. Forster contributed the fish course.

But one misses comedy (as distinct from glee), so familiar a part of his fiction—to see at once the reason for its absence: when the women went out of his stories, they took the comedy with them. (And they were also a cause of much of the beauty of his work; they afforded him a good deal of his irony; and he has not got a thoroughly good sounding board without them.) Those women allowed to remain can be got down in a phrase ("that vengeful onswishing of skirts . . .!") or by a tag ("She was one of those women who behave alternately well and badly"). Perpetua, in "The Torque," belongs to the familiar sisterhood of Forster old maids, though she is the only one he disposed of by reducing her to ashes with a bolt of lightning. (Her brother "duly mourned his distinguished sister and collected what could be found of her in an urn. But what a relief not to have her about!") Central place is perhaps occupied by Lionel's mother, in "The Other Boat," not in person but seen in Lionel's thoughts: "Blind-eyed in the midst of the enormous web she had spun—filaments drifting everywhere, strands catching. There was no reasoning with her or about her, she understood nothing and controlled everything. She had suffered too much and was too high-minded to be judged like other people, she was outside carnality and incapable of pardoning it."

There are flaws in these stories, and they show; but (women aside) they are never flaws of feeling. Herein lies their relationship with Forster's other stories.

None have attempted the broader proportions of "The Road from Colonus," nor do they reach that story's nobility. When the traveler in Greece, who had felt only that "something great was wrong" and, vowing that "I will pretend no longer," steps inside the hollow tree, it is to find that "from its living trunk there gushed an impetuous spring." What all these stories say in part is here said perfectly. Here, Forster is writing about all human desire, and its epitome in the defiance of one half-helpless old man: he would cling to life at its most meaningful point, just where he had found it, never willingly to let himself be torn away.

It will be sad if the aspect of homosexuality, which kept Forster's stories from reaching print in his own day, turns out to be their only focus of interest for today's readers. It will be sadder if it reanimates the "re-evaluators," who, upon the debut of *Maurice*, a novel then aged fifty-seven, wanted a go at the whole of Forster's work on the basis of news freshly received by them concerning his private life. Have we been as ready for Forster's honesty as we thought we were?

Forster, whose greatness surely had root in his capacity to treat all human relationships seriously and truthfully, has Clive in that novel speak of homosexual love as "a passion we can direct, like any other, to good or bad." And of course, the best realized of the homosexual stories dovetail perfectly into the best of all his work. Even the earliest and most ephemeral of them will be recognized as the frailer embodiments of the same passionate convictions that made for the moral iron in his novels.

What engaged Forster was not the issue of respectability versus homosexuality, but that of respectability versus Apollo. The weights in the balance are always spiritual life, spiritual death.

As for the light thrown by the present volume, it has given us more knowledge about a writing life of immense fidelity—it was to be the truth or nothing—that from its beginning was difficult and sad, though lit with comic glints. It is much along the lines of a Forster novel, which continues to unwind itself after his death and is now heading for its ironic conclusion.

Since "The Trustees of the Late E. M. Forster" have been listed as the author's copyright holders, two new publishers have been added to the American publishers of his lifetime: Norton brought out today's book and *Maurice;* and Liveright, in between, brought out *Albergo Empedocle and Other Writings*, edited by George H. Thomson, a sort of grab bag of 1910–1915 ephemera containing the one prize. The reader, noting in the American Introduction that *The Life to Come* corresponds to Volume 8 of the Abinger Edition—Mr. Stallybrass foresees twenty in all—wonders at this point how much more we can expect to see of the complete, and how we shall see it, and when.

The Abinger Edition will not be the measure of Forster's achievement except in pound-weight; the complete is not answerable to standards, is as blind to excellence as to the lack of it, and passion counts for exactly the same as punctuation, although the latter can be corrected. But the complete has its own excuse for being. Knowing that it is to exist, Forster readers here will find it hard to settle for the occasional parcel. We must hope.

If Forster himself could have the last word on the destination of his books, that word might well be "Eternity." He spoke of Eternity often and in familiar terms, and it was indeed upon her that he placed his reliance for that final estimate. And will there be a reader who won't see, in each of these books being launched, the paper boat in *The Longest Journey*? It is being lighted and set into the stream at last, taking the current, going under the bridge—to be watched, from wherever we stand, "still afloat, far through the arch, burning as if it would burn forever."

(1973)

S. J. PERELMAN'S

The Most of S. J. Perelman; Baby, It's Cold Inside

❦

Give him a cliché and he takes a mile. "The color drained slowly from my face, entered the auricle, shot up the escalator, and issued from the ladies' and misses' section into the housewares department." "I sent him groveling. In ten minutes he was back with a basket of appetizing fresh-picked grovels. We squeezed them and drank the piquant juice thirstily." Spring returns to Washington Square: "It lacked only Nelson Eddy to appear on a penthouse terrace and loose a chorus of deep-throated song, and, as if by magic, Nelson Eddy suddenly appeared on a penthouse terrace and . . . launched into an aria. A moment later, Jeanette MacDonald, in creamy negligee, joined the dashing rascal, making sixty-four teeth, and the lovers began a lilting duet."

Our garden of prose has no more been the same since a certain silky party put in an appearance than the Garden of Eden after the Serpent called. S. J. Perelman—for it was indeed he—has this to say by way of a concluding note to this collection of thirty years' work:

> If I were to apply for a library card in Paris, I would subscribe myself as a *feuilletoniste*, that is to say, a writer of little leaves. I may be in error, but the word seems to

me to carry a hint of endearment rather than patronage. In whatever case . . . I should like to affirm my loyalty to it as a medium. The handful of chumps who still practice it are as lonely as the survivors of Fort Zinderneuf; a few more assaults by television and picture journalism and we might as well post their bodies on the ramparts, pray for togetherness, and kneel for the final annihilation. Until then, so long and don't take any wooden rhetoric.

"There has never been a year like this for the giant double-flowering fatuity and gorgeous variegated drivel," Mr. Perelman said in "Caution—Soft Prose Ahead" and that was back in the thirties. If the only trouble is that all he's lampooned has now caught up with its parody, it's anybody's fault but S. J. Perelman's.

The book is put together chronologically, which is as good a way as any to see what was going on, prosewise, from 1930 and the Odets parody "Waiting for Santy" to 1958 when Louella Parsons, whose syntax Mr. P. recommends for its narcotic value ("You don't even need a prescription") sets him the scene for "Nirvana Small by a Waterfall." Each reader will make a leap for his own favorites. Here's "Strictly from Hunger," the masterpiece on Hollywood (" 'Have a bit of the wing, darling?' queried Diana solicitously, indicating the roast Long Island airplane with applesauce.") Here's "Farewell, My Lovely Appetizer," the one that gets Raymond Chandler right between the private eyes, both of a dusty lapis lazuli; and "Genuflection in the Sun," in which a gourmet journeys to pay his respects to the author of a piece of fountain-menu prose—"the finest thing since Baudelaire's *The Flowers of Evil*." (" 'Did you ever get any figures from Liggett's? Were there many conversions?' ") Here's "Nesselrode to Jeopardy," an intrigue—Eric Amblerish, almost Tom Swiftian—of the Macy's food taster aboard the S.S. *Dyspepsia*. ("The real Colonel Firdausi is reposing at this instant in the Bosporus, in a burlap sack weighted with stale nougat.")

Shall I not simply list some of the old friends you will find again here? The Schrafft hostess "well over nine feet tall, with ice mantling her summit." Mrs. Lafcadio Mifflin—of "Kitchenware, Notions, Lights, Action, Camera!"—"seated at the console of her Wurlitzer, softly wurlitzing to herself." And Mr. Mifflin, "in a porous-knit union suit from Franklin Simon's street floor, stretched out by the fire like a great, tawny cat. Inasmuch as there is a great, tawny cat stretched out alongside him, also wearing a porous-knit union suit, it is not immediately apparent which is Mifflin." And, as a matter of fact, Gisele Mifflin, who delivers that indelible speech about the shades her wedding *tailleur* comes in at Altman's—"among them wine, russet, beige, peach, grackle, stone, liver, lover, blubber, blabber and clabber."

There is "my escort, a Miss Chicken-Licken"; "Pandemonium, the upstairs girl" (she entered on a signal); "my hostess, Violet Hush" (of Los Angeles, of course); "my brokers, Whitelipped and Trembling"; "kindly old Professor Gompers, whose grizzled chin and chiseled grin had made his name a byword at Tunafish College for Women." "John J. Antennae, spiritual father to millions, . . . fox-nosed, sallow, closely related to God on his mother's side." Manual Dexterides, who knows a lot about Tommy Manville; Hyacinth Beddoes Laffoon, "queen-pin of the pulp oligarchy embracing Gory Story, Sanguinary Love, Popular Dissolution, and Spicy Mortician." There is Rosy Fahrleit (she plays over your face), and old man Huysmans, owner of a delicatessen. ("In slicing Huysman's brisket," it comes to be asked, "does one go with or against the grain?")

These also have I loved: the Vulturine and Serpentine National Bank; the San Culotte, "a rather dusty family hotel in the West Forties"; "The Skin Around Us," a popular medical book; and that rollicking song they sing in Asia Minor, "Sohran and Rustum Were Lovers."

Here are the well-known biopsies of the fashion magazines —a certain June issue of *Vogue* "was certainly a serious contender for the ecstasy sweepstakes." "Cloudland Revisited" is here, those vignettes of the twenties—Dr. Fu Manchu and victims to the left, Theda Bara and victims to the right. Here are the plays about (I mean, anent) the advertising world. "You mean that the finger of suspicion points to Loose-Wiles, the Thousand Window Bakeries, whose agents have recently been skulking about in dirty gray caps and gooseneck sweaters?" Here is "Westward, Ha!" and "Acres and Pains." Here in the Hollywood pieces we find him among colleagues "listening to the purr of their ulcers," or noting how the movie *Stanley and Livingstone* "by an almost unbelievable coincidence was released the very same day luminal was first synthesized." Groucho Marx, for whom, of course, Mr. Perelman has done his share of writing, seems imminent here and once appears in person; we get an intimate glimpse of him indulging "his passionate avocation, the collecting and cross-fertilization of various kinds of money." As always, Mr. Perelman's sources are allowed to play about upon each other. When he, "together with five hundred other bats, hung from the rafters at Loew's Strabismus to see Joan Crawford's latest vehicle," we are shot from there into a parody of a Ventura column on a Barbara Hutton story.

In my dictionary is an engraving of most intricate design, labeled "Human Ear." When I consulted it recently, in connection with this review, I was forced to exclaim, "But this must be the ear of S. J. Perelman!" When I looked up the ear also in my *Nouveau Petit Larousse* (under "*feuilletoniste*") and found the very same picture of the very same ear, I think I may quietly say it can hardly be laid any longer to mere coincidence. Mr. Perelman misses no mad word we write or say, and its image and essence he translates back to us with an artistry acute, brilliant, devastating, and, heaven keep preserving him, funny.

Now for the sequel.

It can do no harm to tell it now. At the age of fifteen, this reviewer fell hopelessly in love with S. J. Perelman. It was from afar, for I was sitting in Jackson (Mississippi) High School in Cicero class. While the others were studying "How long, O Catiline, must we endure your orations?" I was taking in " 'Gad, Lucy, You're Magnificent!' Breathed the Great Painter," drawing and caption by S. J. Perelman, from a copy of *Judge* on my lap. S. J. Perelman filled the whole copy of that now-forgotten magazine every week—drawings (in the style of a woodcut), sketches, playlets. I didn't guess he was just a jump ahead of me in school himself at the time. I only knew what any child with a grain of prophecy would know— that here was one of the extraordinary wits of our time, who would come to be known, loved and feared by all. Well, it happened in less than a minute.

. . . *Baby, It's Cold Inside* has the brilliance we expect. If the insouciance of the early Perelman—"I had gone into a Corn Exchange bank to exchange some corn"; "I have Bright's disease and he has mine"—is not as evident here, nobody could keep up *that* effervescence. (And if he could, he'd run into trouble today, with, at least, the Bright's disease people.) In its place is a mood very much of its times, and all the more telling in its effects.

Folly is perennial, but something has happened to parody. Life has caught up with it. When Mr. Perelman wrote the superbly hilarious pieces of the thirties and forties, our misuse of the language was in its own vintage years, or so it seems in retrospect. The misuse had its natural place in the movie dialogue, the advertising pages and the sentimental fiction of the day.

Now the misuse has proliferated and spread everywhere, and, to make it more menacing, it is taken seriously. Promoters of products, promoters of causes, promoters of self have a common language, though one with a small vocabulary.

. . . The value of the word has declined. Parody is one of the early casualties of this disaster, for it comes to be no longer recognizable apart from its subject. Parody makes its point by its precision and strictness in use of the word, probing to expose the distinction between the true and the false, the real and the synthetic. It's a demanding and exacting art, and there are few with the gift of penetration, and the temerity, let alone the wit and the style, to practice it. Right now it's in danger of becoming a lost cause. The only writer I know who can save it is the author of this book. He stands alone. We already owe him a great deal for years of delight, but we owe him even more now.

Not for nothing is the new book called *Baby, It's Cold Inside*. Back of some of these pieces, and not very far, lies deep sadness, lies outrage. What an achievement Mr. S. J. Perelman makes today, that out of our own sadness and outrage we are brought, in these pieces, to laugh at ourselves once more.

(1958; 1970)

ARTHUR MIZENER'S

The Saddest Story: A Biography of Ford Madox Ford

◈

What the reader hopes most to see in a biography is the work of the intelligent scholar who also feels an affinity for his subject. For Ford Madox Ford—who had greatness, who did so much for the cause of letters, who was intuitively kind to other writers everywhere but to whom unkindness has often been done in return—for Ford in particular his reader would hope he would fall into good hands.

Mr. Mizener's work has taken him, not surprisingly, six years. He has read and considered everything Ford ever wrote in his incredibly productive life. He has put his longest and most probing scrutiny, of course, into *The Good Soldier* and the four novels of *Parade's End*, but, we must believe, he has skimped nowhere, left nothing out. Yet for all his intelligence and his devotion to his task, the book as I see it falls short. A little more imagination might have made all the difference.

Ford's heritage was a double one, and indeed his life was almost always under a double pressure of some kind, forces pulling him in opposite directions. His father, Francis Hueffer, was German, Catholic, a London music critic and composer; his mother, Kathy Brown, was the daughter of one of the formidable Pre-Raphaelites, the painter Ford Madox Brown.

He himself grew up with a double alarm sounding in his ears: one, that he was "a patient but exceedingly stupid donkey" (this was his father talking) and the other, that he was expected to be nothing less than a genius (that came from Grandfather Brown). But perhaps the admonition that reached his deepest heart was something else that his grandfather told him: "Fordy, never refuse to help a lame dog over a stile . . . Beggar yourself rather than refuse assistance to any one whose genius you think shows promise of being greater than your own." Ford not only remembered this; he acted upon it times without number.

He lived very much in the imagination—to the point of hallucination sometimes when he read (as a child he could see, could *watch* Captain Kidd; after he was forty, as a World War soldier in France, he looked up from *The Red Badge of Courage* and saw around him on the battlefield soldiers dressed in blue, not khaki). He was also uncompetitive, deeply unself-confident; in fact, he showed as a child both the strengths and the weaknesses that would stay with him all his life. And, of course, he began in his cradle filling the capacious, wonderful and romantic memory that did him both service and disservice in his life and art.

Ford soon developed, as is well known, a tender susceptibility toward women and a deep need for them. At twenty-one he eloped with a seventeen-year-old girl, Elsie Martindale. When some years later he tried to persuade her to divorce him so that he could marry Violet Hunt, she would not, and the affair breaking into print made a scandal that left its scars on all involved. The long, exhausting and bitter ordeal (in telling which, Mizener goes to equally exhausting lengths) damaged Ford severely.

Violet was the oddest soul, a lady writer who was somewhat in vogue at the time. Henry James had called her his "Purple Patch," but when the scandal broke he had to write to detach himself from her acquaintance, signing himself "Believe me, then, in very imperfect sympathy, . . ." Ford had humbly thanked Violet for loving him, but then he almost never saw the last of her. She liked to track down her predecessors in love and move in with them, and she moved in on Elsie; and she kept up with her own successor with Ford, Stella Bowen, by peeping at her through a fence. With Stella Bowen, who had warmth of heart and sanity of mind, Ford had a daughter, and a life in France, and a garden. His later, and last, strong alliance was with Janice Biala, and in this country (where he had moved), she seems to have offered him strength and comfort. They remained together for the rest of his life. The touching, almost never realized hope of Ford's relationships with women seems all the way through to have been for domestic peace—"rest."

It is not surprising that from time to time Ford suffered with neurasthenia. What he usually did for it was to run over to Germany to see his Tante Emma, who was an advice giver. Other, more drastic, treatments were visited on him too; almost none of them ever helped. "I live," he said during the first of these illnesses, "in a state of hourly apprehension of going mad."

Mr. Mizener sees Ford's illnesses as "a product of the destructive clash between his dreams of glory and the actualities of his existence." Whatever they are called, Ford survived them, as he survived emotional crises, financial troubles and all the complications of his literary life. In the last, at any rate, he held for a long while a central place.

Ford wrote eighty-one books during his life, thirty-two of them novels. "These books were the purpose of his existence," says Mr. Mizener in his Foreword, "the one commitment of his life that nothing—disaster, illness, despair—was allowed to interfere with. They are the meaning of his life, and its most valuable product. Some of them are important books; some are imperfect . . . ; some are failures. But every one of them shows something about a human imagination perhaps not radically different from other men's but made to seem so by being revealed to us in unusual detail by these books, and every one of them helps us to understand the process by which Ford slowly learned to reveal his imagination."

Thus the biography opens with promise of the kind of criticism we would most wish to see. But this reader does not find its promise very well fulfilled.

Part of the trouble has to come from the writing. Mr. Mizener's is a rather coarse-grained prose without the compensating liveliness that sympathy can sometimes give. This is a typical Mizener sentence: "Gradually during the winter of 1913–14, Ford succeeded in inventing a conception of himself and his motives that explained his recent conduct in a way that satisfied the imagination." He is referring to the writing of *The Good Soldier*. The heaviness of his own style seems always to show most when he comes up against Ford's imagination; that seems to burden him. "The right cadence," so central in Ford's style and in his own test of good writing, is lacking in his biographer. A good ear would have helped the biographer and critic of Ford almost as much as a deeper feeling for the man and his work: perhaps the two qualities are related. This calls insistent attention to itself, for situated among the paragraphs of Mizener are the many quotations from Ford. To read while they alternate is like being carried in a train along the southern coast of France—long tunnel, view of the sea, and over again.

Mr. Mizener is fully able, by astute use of the rich help available to him, to present a good scene, and the book is full of them. There is, for example, the one in which we see Ford and Conrad, their collaborative novel *Romance* finished, taking it up to London in the train, Conrad reading the proofs down on his stomach on the floor because the train was jolting, so deeply absorbed that when Ford tapped him on the shoulder to tell him they had reached Charing Cross, "he sprang to his feet and straight at my throat."

And we see Wyndham Lewis "in an immense steeple-crowned hat and an ample black cape of the type that villains in . . . melodramas throw over their shoulders when they

say 'Ha-ha!'" appearing to Ford for the first time, having
marched upstairs to find him in the bathroom taking a bath,
and producing "crumpled . . . rolls" of manuscript from all
over his person as if he were a sleight-of-hand artist, he announced himself a genius and proceeded to read them aloud.

The extraordinarily large population that filled Ford's life
is lively here too; and not many are of an undemanding presence in their own right. The book is thronging with vivid
personalities, by no means all of them Pre-Raphaelites; it has
to concern itself with the literary great of three generations.
I think Mr. Mizener has handled this surge of people very
well. The trouble is that when he comes to the great rock in
the middle of them, the heart of his work, Ford himself, his
powers seem to weaken.

He is at his best on Ford as editor. In *The English Review*,
"the most obvious measure of Ford's editorial skill is perhaps
the fact that, even today, none of these writers except [two]
needs identifying." Ford published James, Galsworthy, Hudson, Tolstoy, Wells, Conrad, Hardy, Pound, Yeats, Forster,
Joyce . . . London took Ford to its bosom, to its clubs, even;
and shouts could be heard going up from restaurant tables,
"Hurray, Fordie's discovered another genius! Called D. H.
Lawrence!" It was electrifying.

". . . If Ford's commitment to the highest standards together
with his complete lack of business sense pretty well assured
financial disaster," says Mr. Mizener, "that same commitment,
with the support of his remarkable powers of selection, made
it certain that as long as the Review survived it would be a
great magazine."

But Ford's creative power, which I think must be Mr.
Mizener's trouble, is something else. It was a mountain with
many springs running through, sources he could tap at different times, at different levels—some near the surface, some
deeper. The most profound was hidden until he reached the
age of forty, its existence perhaps even unsuspected, until he
wrote *The Good Soldier*.

To that Rosetta stone of a novel Mr. Mizener gives full and earnest study, but he still seems to feel that the only safe way to approach the novel is with a dossier and a timetable and a firmly literal grip. It is, in fact, a dangerous way to approach *The Good Soldier*, full of traps.

Except for the timetable. It is interesting and useful (and how hard it must have been to make it!) as a parallel to the shifting times of the story. But Mr. Mizener's assumption that he must trace the characters to real people and by that means lay a finger on their fictional meaning has put him in trouble; to start with, he finds Ashburnham to be Ford's "image of himself" and the narrator Dowell to be Ford and therefore his own author.

The fact is, Mr. Mizener never makes the essential leap of mind to discover the novel as a complete entity, a world in itself and quite freed of its author.

Mr. Mizener refers to Ford's revolutionary and brilliantly developed technique as "the defensive air" he adopted "about factual inaccuracy that would eventually become a whole theory of literary art, which he would call 'Impressionism.'" "Thus Ford sought to make a virtue out of his habit of representing his memories and impressions of an experience rather than the experience itself." Mr. Mizener's apparent unwillingness or inability to see further into Ford's greatest achievement seems to me a most serious defect.

I believe Mr. Mizener treats the construction of *The Good Soldier* as a riddle, and if he can't get the answer, he'd like to get the best of it. Another reader might see the novel as a prism suspended by a thread and turning on it. Set in motion— forward, backward—at the delicate control of the author, it turns its faces to us, and the present moment moves into time past or time future. In so doing, it constructs a pattern out of its own fractured light, reflections and shadows; they glance, crisscross, pass through and modulate one another. Ford the Impressionist was breaking up human experience by his technique of the time-shift in order to show the inner life of that experience, its essential mystery. The reader slowly learns the meaning of the novel from this pattern; we *watch* it being revealed.

But Mr. Mizener consistently treats the inventions of fiction as Ford's barefaced attempts to get away with something in his personal life by foisting these false versions upon the public. "This is the novel's improved version of Ford's involvement with Gertrud Schlabowsky," he says of *The New Humpty Dumpty*. In effect he implies that all that's not "real life" is inferior to it, that fiction is at best secondhand life, that fiction is in fact not honest, for it has been stolen from life and is capable of being returned to its original state by reliable critics.

Does Mr. Mizener not recognize Ford's subjects? Pain, going-to-pieces, loneliness, courage, honor, horror, hope, most of all, passion? And *these* are real life; they do not need Gertrud Schlabowsky's identity to make them real.

When Mr. Mizener does admire, we know it only by a quote from somebody else. On *Buckshee* we hear via Robert Lowell: "In these reveries, Ford has at last managed to work his speaking voice, and something more than his speaking voice, into poems—the inner voice of the tireless old man, the old master still in harness, confiding, tolerant, Bohemian, newly married, and in France." If only the biographer himself could ever give us an expression of feeling, something of his own! We are not sure, as it is, that he ever feels any more than he can say.

The biography is written entirely from the outside. The book is one whole, huge compilation of details from outside. And so it is voluminous without being generous, just as it is lengthy but short on tolerance. One original insight would have equaled the force of a dozen of these pages.

Ford's life was sad. The scandal over the divorce is pitiable, and the more so because another time in history would have let it go by without a ripple. Ford was never lucky in his timing. But there was a worse scandal that was done to *him*, which no difference in times or manners could excuse. He

came out of the war gassed and in trouble—his memory itself
was threatened—to find himself forgotten on the literary
scene. He suffered neglect and indifference, even scorn; he
was quite callously hurt by a number of people to whom he
had been good and for whom he always bore the best will
in the world. Mr. Mizener has this to say of that time: "During
Christmas week he came to London for a party at the French
embassy for the English writers who had supported France
during the war . . . and no one recognized him. He had expected as much. 'It was seven years,' he said with superb
impressionistic inaccuracy, 'since I had written a word.' "

This may serve to suggest why, in this reader's opinion,
Mr. Mizener's biography is in some fundamental respect an
antagonistic work. If affinity between biographer and subject
is impossible, at the very least there had better be personal
tolerance.

Ford's vulnerabilities, which were scaled to the rest of him,
too large to miss, appear to have the fascination of guilty
secrets for Mr. Mizener. Ford's condescension, Ford's "Tory
gentleman" notions, Ford's overestimation of some of his work
and his fantasies about his reputation, Ford's confusion in
money matters, Ford's handwriting—they *all* exasperate him.
The assertions of his own grandeur did come, however, from
a man of painfully little self-confidence, very often of none
at all. Surely Mr. Mizener might see in this not the lie but the
connection. I think it is hard, too, to accept his interpretation
of Ford's innumerable acts of generosity as vanity, as he sometimes presents them.

By all accounts of those who knew him, Ford was a man of
exceedingly sweet nature, utterly without malice, bearing no
thought of a grudge, an uncondemning man. All his life, when
he heard that a friend was in trouble, he *went*. Sometimes it
was at a risk to himself. He sat up with other people's sick
children, he got out a book of a woman's poems when money
was needed to pay her funeral expenses. When fire destroyed
an installment of a novel Conrad had written for *Blackwood's*,

Ford found him a house nearby and worked along with him day and night to write it all over again.

Ford's lifetime broached three generations of writers and readers who were affected by him and his work. He could remember, as a little boy of three in his grandfather's house, pulling out a chair for Mr. Turgenev, and toward the other end of his life the young Hemingway was pulling out *his* editorial chair—and taking it. In between those times—and to less extent up until his death—practically every writer of serious substance in Britain or America moved through his life and gained from his mind and presence. How generously Ford offered both! There is no sign that he ever ran out of kindness.

Mr. Mizener calls Ford's life "The Saddest Story" because of what Ford might have done and didn't do. Ford did undeniably waste his gifts and fail to live up to his greatest powers. But it is, to say the least, unavailing to blame a man— and the man who had done, in spite of this, so much for the cause of literature—for what most certainly had to be a cause of pain and frustration to himself.

It has to be expected that a biographer who is unimaginative about a man's work will be unimaginative about his life, and vice versa; but if this is the saddest story, then of all ways to write it, the unimaginative is the saddest way. Mr. Mizener fairly records in his Introduction that in the opinion of Janice Biala the book does him injustice.

At bottom, Mr. Mizener puts blame on Ford as a man who could never face the truth; and apparently, in one sense, that can fairly be said. But at the same time Mizener's truth of harsh fact is not Ford's truth. Ford said that the novelist "is a sensitised instrument, recording to the measure of the light vouchsafed him what is—what *may* be—the Truth." Ford not only faced but found inner truths that confound such statements as Mr. Mizener's or show them to be beside the point of his fiction.

"An old man mad about writing." This brief self-portrait of

Ford at the end of his life contains at once the soberest and the most inspiriting truth he could teach us.

The honor that is due him I think this book pays in part. But a larger response is also due him; there are many who believe as this reader does that the response of love is the true and the right one.

(1971)

ROSS MACDONALD'S

The Underground Man

&

Curled up, with an insulted look on his upturned face, and wearing a peppermint-striped shirt, the fresh corpse of a man is disclosed in a hole in the ground. From the scene of the crime the victim's little boy is carried off, nobody knows why, by a pair of troubled teen-agers. And at the same time, a deadly forest fire gets its start in these hills above Santa Teresa: whoever murdered Stanley Broadhurst must have caused him to drop his cigarillo into the dry grass. So opens the new novel by Ross Macdonald, *The Underground Man*. It comes to stunning achievement.

A Forest Service man looks into the killing to find out who was responsible for the fire; but Lew Archer goes faster and further into his own investigation, for a personal reason. That morning he had met that little boy; they fed blue jays together. He promises the young widow, the child's mother, to find her son and bring him back.

The double mystery of Santa Teresa cries urgency, but is never going to explain itself in an ordinary way. For instance, it looks as if the victim himself might have dug the hole in which he lies. ("Why would a man dig his own grave?"— "He may not have known it was going to be his.") With the fire coming, Archer has to work fast. The corpse must be

quickly buried again, or be consumed with his murder un-
solved. This, the underground man of the title, waits the book
halfway out—the buried connection between present threat
and something out of the past.

"I don't believe in coincidences," Archer says, as the investigation leads him into a backward direction and he sees
the case take on a premonitory symmetry. And it is not coincidence indeed, or anything so simple, but a sort of spiral of
time that he goes hurtling into, with an answer lying fifteen
years deep.

He is to meet many strange and lonely souls drawing their
inspiration from private sources. On the periphery are those
all but anonymous characters, part of the floating population
of the city, evocative of all the sadness that fills a lonely
world, like some California versions of those Saltimbanques of
Picasso's ("even a little more fleeting than ourselves") drifting
across the smoke-obscured outskirts. They are the sentinels of
a case in which everybody has something to lose, and most of
the characters in this time-haunted, fire-threatened novel lose
it in the course of what happens—a son, or a husband, or a
mountain retreat; a sailing boat, a memory; the secret of fifteen
years or the dream of a lifetime; or a life.

Brooding over the case is the dark fact that for some certain
souls the past does not let go. They nourish the conviction
that its ties may be outlived but, for hidden reasons, can be
impossible to outgrow or leave behind.

Stanley Broadhurst died searching for his long-lost father.
The Oedipus story, which figured in Mr. Macdonald's *The
Galton Case* and *The Chill*, has echoes here too. But another
sort of legend takes a central place in *The Underground Man*.
This is the medieval tale of romance and the fairy.

It is exactly what Archer plunges into when he enters this
case. Finding his way, through their lies and fears, into other
people's obsessions and dreams, he might as well be in a fairy
tale with them. His investigation is a parallel to just that. The
mystery has handed him what amounts to a set of impossible

tasks: Find the door that opens the past. Unravel the ever-tangling threads of time. Rescue the stolen child from fleeing creatures who appear to be under a spell and who forbid him to speak to them. Meet danger from the aroused elements of fire and water. And beware the tower.

But Archer's own role in their fairy tale is clear to him: from the time he fed the blue jays with the little boy, he never had a choice. There is the maze of the past to be entered and come out of alive, bringing the innocent to safety. And in the maze there lives a monster; his name is Murder.

But all along the way, the people he questions shift their stands, lie as fast as they can, slip only too swiftly out of human reach. Their ages are deceiving, they put on trappings of disguise or even what might be called transformations. As Archer, by stages, all the while moving at top speed, connects one character with the next, he discovers what makes the sinister affinity between them.

"Robert Driscoll Falconer, Jr., was a god come down to earth in human guise," the older Mrs. Broadhurst has written in a memoir of her father, and here the Spencerian handwriting went to pieces; "it straggled across the lined yellow page like a defeated army." Mrs. Crandall, the mother of the runaway girl, is "one of those waiting mothers who would sit forever beside the phone but didn't know what to say when it finally rang." Another character being questioned plays "a game that guilty people play, questioning the questioner, trying to convert the truth into a shuttlecock that could be batted back and forth and eventually lost." And the violence and malice of another character "appeared to her as emanations from the external world."

"She kissed the money. 'I can really use it, it's my ticket out of here.' But she looked around the room as if it were a recurrent nightmare she had." Instead of leaving Room 7 of the Star Motel, this girl gets "strung out on an Einstein trip." That is "when you go all the way out, past the last star, and space loops back on you."

These people live in prisons of the spirit, and suffer there. The winding, prisonlike stairs that appear and reappear under Archer's hurrying feet in the course of the chase are like the repeated questionings that lead most often into some private hell.

In this company, human age is an ambiguity. The occupant of the Star Motel is "muffled in a quilted pink robe, and I couldn't tell if she was a well-preserved middle-aged woman or a dilapidated girl," says Archer. ("I don't keep good track of time, I've got too much on my mind," she says.) He has seen Mrs. Broadhurst "young and forceful, then sick and doddering. I needed something to fill up the gap between these versions of her."

Time pressing, time lapsing, time repeating itself in dark acts, splitting into two in some agonized or imperfect mind—time is the wicked fairy to troubled people, granting them inevitably the thing they dread.

An old letter that Archer turns up from a pastor of a Santa Teresa church advises the recipient: "The past can do very little for us—no more than it has already done, for good or ill—except in the end to release us. We must seek and accept release, and give release." Good advice, as Archer notes, but Stanley didn't take it. Stanley was murdered.

And of course unreality—the big underlying trouble of all these people—was back of the crime itself: the victim was obsessed with the lifelong search for his father; oblivious of everything and everybody else, he invited his own oblivion. In a different way unreality was back of the child-stealing. "As you can see, we gave her everything," says the mother standing in her runaway daughter's lovely white room. "But it wasn't what she wanted." The home environment of the girl and others like her, Archer is brought to observe, was "an unreality so bland and smothering that the children tore loose and impaled themselves on the spikes of any reality that offered. Or made their own unreality with drugs."

Indeed, it is not the secrets of those once violent and now

defeated or dead so much as those of the living young, the drifting, unreachable teen-agers, that present Archer with the most inscrutable riddles. "I want to talk to you seriously. You're in trouble."—"Go to hell."

Jean, who is the little boy's mother and who is never anything but young and beautiful—for both of which reasons Archer suspects he is half in love with her—is the only character in the novel who knows how to be helped. She is accessible to human kindness, and so conveys almost the only blessing in the book on Archer. (But not the only blessing, or the greatest.)

The plot is intricate, involuted and complicated to the hilt; and this, as I see it, is the novel's point. The danger derives from the fairy tales into which people make their lives. In lonely, fearful or confused minds, real-life facts can become rarefied into private fantasies. The danger is that the *intensities* remain the same. And when intensity is accepted—welcomed— as the measure of truth, how can the real and the fabricated be told apart?

We come to a scene where the parallel with the fairy tale is explicit—and something more. It is the best in the book—I can give but a part: "I made my way up the washed-out gravel drive. The twin conical towers standing up against the night sky made the house look like something out of a medieval romance. The illusion faded as I got nearer. There was a multi-colored fanlight over the front door, with segments of glass fallen out, like missing teeth in an old smile . . . The door creaked open when I knocked."

Here lives a lady "far gone in solitude," whose secret lies hidden at the heart of the mystery. She stands there in "a long full skirt on which there were paint stains in all three primary colors." She is a painter—of spiritual conditions, she says; to Archer her pictures resemble "serious contusions and open wounds" or "imperfectly remembered hallucinations."

" 'I was born in this house,' she said, as if she'd been waiting fifteen years for a listener." (And there are the fifteen years that have done their worst to everybody in the novel.) " 'It's interesting to come back to your childhood home, . . . like becoming very young and very old both at the same time.' That was how she looked, I thought, in her archaic long skirt—very young and very old, the granddaughter and the grandmother in one person, slightly schizo."

"There were romantic tears in her eyes" when her story is out. "My own eyes remained quite dry."

Fairy tale and living reality alternate on one current to pulse together in this remarkable scene. The woman is a pivotal character and Archer has caught up with her; they are face to face. And there comes a moment's embrace. Of the many brilliant ways Mr. Macdonald has put his motif to use, I believe this is the touch that delighted me most. For of course Archer, this middle-aging Californian who has seen everything in a career of going into impossible trouble with his eyes open, who has always been the protector of the weak and the rescuer of the helpless, is a born romantic. Here he meets his introverted and ailing opposite number—this lady is the chatelaine of the romantic-gone-wrong. He is not by nature immune, especially to what is lovely or was lovely once. At a given moment they may brush close. As Archer, the only one with insight into himself, is aware. He knows himself to be a romantic, would call it a weakness—as he calls his being a "not unwilling catalyst" for trouble; he carries the knowledge around with him—that's how he got here.

But Archer is in no way archaic himself. He is at heart a champion, but a self-questioning, often a self-deriding champion. He is of today, and one of ours.

The fairy-tale motif is brilliantly used and brilliantly appropriate. *The Underground Man* is written so close to the nerve of today as to expose most of the apprehensions we live with; it has got to one of the secrets of our ills. The problem is that of unreality, but the problem itself is real.

It is the vulnerable who *do* get exposed to danger. It is the gullible who do get told the lies, or who believe their own;

it is the lonely or the abandoned or the self-exiled, self-exalted who forever build their lives on illusion. It is the innocent who trustingly give their hands into the hands of the spoilers. Archer's cases exist ready-made in the living world of today.

We are never allowed to forget that present time has been steadily increasing its menace. Mr. Macdonald has brought the fire toward us at closer and closer stages. By the time it gets as close as the top of the hill (this is the murder area), it appears "like a brilliant omniform growth which continued to grow until it bloomed very large against the sky. A sentinel quail on the hillside below it was ticking an alarm." Next, "The fire was coming down the hill, gathering speed and size. The trees had begun to sway. From the undergrowth beneath them, a bevy of stubby-winged quail flew up fighting for altitude over the house. Smoke like billowing darkness followed them." Then, "It made a noise like a storm. Enormous and hot and wild, it leapt clumsily into the trees. The cypress that had been smoking burst into flames. Then the other trees blazed up like giant torches in a row." Then, reaching the house, "the fire bent around it like the fingers of a hand, squeezing smoke out of the windows and then flame."

By such powers of description Mr. Macdonald shows us reality—I almost said "in person." Indeed, the fire is a multiple and accumulating identity, with a career of its own, a super-character that has earned itself a character's name—Rattlesnake. Significantly, Archer says, "There was only one good thing about the fire. It made people talk about the things that really concerned them."

What really concerns Archer, and the real kernel of the book, its heart and soul, is the little boy of six, good and brave and smart. He constitutes the book's emergency; he is also entirely believable, a full-rounded and endearing character. Ronny is the tender embodiment of everything Archer is by nature bound to protect, infinitely worthy of rescue.

When Archer plunges into a case his reasons are always personal reasons (this is one of the things that make us so much for Archer). The little boy for as long as he's missing will be Archer's own loss. And without relinquishing for a moment his clear and lively identity, the child takes on another importance as well: "The world was changing," says Archer, "as if with one piece missing the whole thing had come loose and was running wild."

Indeed, this little boy may well represent all we have left— being pure enough and good enough and beautiful enough, and amusing enough, too—to qualify as the cause and object of the chivalry of any age, the innocence worth protection with one's life, or the fragile symbol of a future that one can believe in; or however you would like to put it. It is this little boy who is the blessing to Archer, whose own reward would be to see the mother and child together in the same room, so that she can look at her son "as if his round skull contained the secret meaning of her life."

If it is the character of the little boy that makes the case matter to Archer, so it is character of Archer, whose first-person narrative forms the novels, that makes it matter to us. Archer from the start has been a distinguished creation; he was always an attractive figure, and in the course of the last several books has matured and deepened in substance to our still greater pleasure. Possessed even when young of an endless backlog of stored information, most of it sad, on human nature, he tended once, unless I'm mistaken, to be a bit cynical. Now he is something much more, he is vulnerable. As a detective and as a man he takes the human situation with full seriousness. He cares. And good and evil both are real to him.

In our day it is for such a novel as *The Underground Man* that the detective form exists. I think it also matters that it is the detective form, with all its difficult demands and its corresponding charms, that makes such a novel possible. What gives me special satisfaction about it is that no one but a good writer —*this* good writer—could have possibly brought it off. *The Underground Man* is Mr. Macdonald's best book yet, I think. It is not only exhilaratingly well done; it is also very moving.

Ross Macdonald's style, to which in large part this is due, is one of delicacy and tension, very tightly made, with a spring in it. It doesn't allow a static sentence or one without pertinence. And the spare, controlled narrative, built for action and speed, conveys as well the world through which the action moves and gives it meaning, brings scene and character, however swiftly, before the eyes without a blur. It is an almost unbroken succession of sparkling pictures.

The style that works so well to produce fluidity and grace also suggests a mind much given to contemplation and reflection on our world. Mr. Macdonald's writing is something like a stand of clean, cool, well-branched, well-tended trees in which bright birds can flash and perch. And not for show, but to sing.

A great deal of what this writer has to tell us comes by way of these beautiful and audacious metaphors. "His hairy head seemed enormous and grotesque on his boy's body, like a papier-mâché saint's head on a stick": and the troubled teenager's self-absorption, his sense of destiny—theatrical but maybe in a good cause—along with the precise way he looks and carries himself, are given us all in one. At the scene of evacuation from the forest fire, at the bottom of a rich householder's swimming pool, "lay a blue mink coat, like the headless pelt of a woman." A sloop lying on her side, dismantled offshore, "flopped in the surge like a bird made helpless by oil." The Snows, little old lady and grown son: "The door of Fritz's room was ajar. One of his moist eyes appeared at the crack like the eye of a fish in an underwater crevice. His mother, at the other door, was watching him like a shark."

Descriptions so interpretive are, of course, here as part and parcel of the character of Archer, who says them to us. Mr. Macdonald's accuracy of observation becomes Archer's detection—running evidence. Mr. Macdonald brings characters into sudden sharp focus too by arresting them in an occasional archetypical pose. The obsessed Stanley is here in the words of his wife: "Sometimes he'd be just sitting there shuffling through his pictures and his letters. He looked like a man counting his money." And Fritz in the lath house, where Archer is leaving him, complaining among his plants: "The striped shadow fell from the roof and jailbirded him."

(1971)

ISAK DINESEN'S
Last Tales

Isak Dinesen has the straight-out gift for performing illusion, and the resources of mind and heart of a great lady who has lived for a good many years in many different parts of the world. In her tales, one of the extraordinary things is that the spell—for they lie in the realm of magic and romance—gets done by the speed of wit, takes its turn within the circle of morality, and keeps its hold through irony, which usually attends on learning and experience, not enchantment. But I haven't found anything out, for the spells work, too, through the pure delight of the senses.

Isak Dinesen a long time ago made herself master of the tale. Austerely objective in their execution, true to her credo of the storyteller's story, her tales are also extremely personal in their point of view, in their great style. They have a vigor which persuades us that vigor perfectly solves the secret of delicacy, for her stories are the essence of delicacy. She has a marvelous gaiety, and what makes it more marvelous still are its transpositions, true gaiety's other key. Her tales are glimpses out of, rather than into, an extraordinary mind. Sometimes one feels that Isak Dinesen's stories come toward one like the flashes and signal-beams from a lighthouse on a strange and infrequently sighted coast—a coast beautiful and precarious, for it may be the last outreach of magic, but resting on bedrock.

Like all her tales, these twelve are like no other tales. They range from country to country, the north to the south—from point to point in time, from here to there in reality. There are tales joined onto other tales, tales inlaid in tales, and one long, disturbingly beautiful, unfinished Gothic tale called "The Caryatids." What is their inner relation and their true domain? In "Night Walk," a story happening in Italy some centuries ago, a betrayer of his friend who afterward cannot sleep is told that if he walks through the streets of the city, proceeding always from the larger street into the smaller and narrower, until he can turn no further, he will find sleep at the end. He reaches the place: "This moment was a return and a beginning. He stretched out his hand, took care to draw his breath lightly twice, and opened the door. By a table in a little, faintly lit room, a redhaired man was counting his money."

Her tales all have a start in other tales—for a tale must have its "start," as good bread must; as good flowers must, proliferate how they may. Her "starts" are the fables, the fairy tales, stories from the Bible and the Arabian Nights and Ancient Greece and Rome. Sometimes they can be felt to be passing, like a procession not more than one street over; sometimes we see their old rich banners and colors, catch their songs, and sight their retinues of seraphic or diabolic origin; and sometimes that procession and the procession of her story cross and mingle, they may even dance, and all the queens and lovers then, the magicians and children and beasts and hunters and wives and gypsies and country-gods and artists and angels are of a company together.

"The divine art is the story," a storyteller says in one of these tales. "In the beginning was the story . . . Where the storyteller is loyal, eternally and unswervingly loyal to the story, there, in the end, silence will speak . . . We, the faithful, when we have spoken our last word, will hear the voice of silence."

Remembering her *Out of Africa*, surely one of the most sensitive personal accounts written in our time, we are moved to think how it is the same eye that saw the Giant Forest Hog on the path in the Ngong Forest that sees the primeval boar in the Gypsy's spell of the water wheel in her tale "The Cary-atids," and to realize so clearly that they are visions both, even perhaps of the same thing: one life gave to her and one a story gave to her. Both visions she has let us see, but kept them two.

Let Isak Dinesen remember that she said it herself: "God likes a *da capo*." Under any other title than *Last Tales*, it would be enough to open this book and start reading:

It was a lovely spring day, and the almond trees were blossoming . . . From the terrace at the top there was a wide view over the landscape, and all the shapes and colors within it . . . in the cool of the evening were as beautifully harmonious as if an angel had stood behind the shoulder of the observer and poured out it all from his flute.

"Are you sure," a lady asks a storyteller in this book, "that it is God whom you serve?"

The Cardinal looked up, met her eyes and smiled very gently. "That," he said, "that, Madame, is a risk which the artists and priests of the world have to run."

(1957)

PATRICK WHITE'S

The Cockatoos

These are six stories (a few are more like short novels) to do
with lives often driven or hopeless, but what they are ultimately
about is what might have been. They bring together the possibilities and the impossibilities of human relationship. They
happen in Australia, Egypt, Sicily, Greece, where they go off
like cannons fired over some popular, scenic river—depth
charges to bring up the drowned bodies. Accidentally set free
by some catastrophe, general or personal—war, starvation, or
nothing more than a husband's toothache—Patrick White's
characters come to a point of discovery. It might be, for instance, that in overcoming repugnancies they are actually yielding to some far deeper attraction; the possibilities of a life have
been those very things once felt as its dangers. Or they may
learn, in confronting moral weakness in others, some flaw in
themselves they've never suspected, still more terrifying.

The common barriers of sex, age, class, nationality *can*, in
uncommon hands, operate as gates, which open (for his characters) to experience beyond anything yet traveled, hope of
which may have beckoned from earliest years and gone ignored, only haunting dreams and spoiling the day at hand.
Passing us through these barriers is what Mr. White is doing
in his writing.

All these stories are studies of ambiguities, of which the greatest is sex. A middle-aged couple, long married, traveling after his retirement, find themselves rather peculiarly put back in touch with two old friends out of their respective pasts—a man for him, a woman for her—representing to each a different turn which had offered itself to their young lives. The wife's wifely solution is simple and disastrous (her bothersome guilt for her own inadequacy is set at rest if she can rearrange other people's lives): instead of letting these two make things awkward, why not marry the misfits off to each other?

This is Mr. White's longest (eighty-six pages) and in some ways the most sinister of his stories treating of the realities and the unrealities of developing human relationships. It is highly symbolic, presided over by peacocks. (According to fable, a peacock's flesh is incorruptible, which made it a symbol of the Resurrection; here it assumes the meaning of liberation from captivity.) In this story, too, the irony lies most clearly in the fact that the true and guiding relationships of our lives—for whatever inhibiting reasons—may never achieve the reality credited the ones that are acknowledged and binding but remain superficial and daunting.

"The Full Belly," a short novel laid in Athens during the German occupation, takes us deep into the humiliations and terrible intimacies of starving to death as a family: the excruciating pressures of competing unselfishness, the demanding self-sacrifice. Aunt Pronoë radiates "a kind of hectic gaiety" as they dine off boiled dandelions. Aunt Maro takes to her bed, declining ever to eat or drink again: "Remember the children. Who am I to deny them food?" The young boy in question is a musical prodigy, with his ticket to Paris still at the bottom of his handkerchief drawer; he goes on practicing ("Play to me, Costika," says the determined martyr, "music is more nourishing than food"), and sees everything "with a vividness which only sickness or hunger kindles." Away from the house, there are the temptations coming out of doorways and the cautionary sights lying in the gutters: one old woman greedy for a boy's hand in her bosom—she'd give him a fresh egg; the next old woman lying dead in her decent dress, with her emptied purse beside her and her shoes already taken from her feet.

Hunger and shame merge into a single monster. A terrible scene, in front of Aunt Maro on her dying day, spoils her victory for her: the boy and Aunt Pronoë come to desperate grappling over the plate of sacrificial rice lying untouchable before the icon, struggling together, smashing the plate and losing it all, then Costa down on the carpet. "If only the few surviving grains. Sometimes fluff got in. Or a coarse thread. He licked the grains. He sucked them up. The splinters of porcelain cutting his lips. The good goo. The blood running. Even blood was nourishment."

"Five-Twenty" is the time a certain car passes in the traffic line every afternoon. The scene is a front porch where sit an aging and childless married couple, a man now an invalid in a wheelchair and imperious as ever, and his wife, a plain woman whose marriage has been one long deprivation of love, which she has taught herself to handle as best she can: she finds it easier now, being a nurse. She fastens on the five-twenty car as something to watch for and point out: it makes her day. Inevitably, the strands converge. It happens down on the garden path, after the husband leaves her a widow. A flower garden like hers, that's been overtended, and a love like hers, gone unnourished too long, may burst out alike into the overwhelming and monstrous.

The characters in most of these stories are men and women whose predicaments are rooted in their past, to whom fresh pressure is put by the predicaments of growing old. In "The Night the Prowler," we are plunged into the world of a seventeen-year-old girl whose state of being has everything to do with today. When Felicity was raped, she hadn't been afraid: she'd even hoped something real and revealing might be going to occur, but the rapist is a failure and pathetic. She sees that her conventional parents, in the shock of what's happened, think mostly of themselves, and that the conventional boy she'd been about to marry is relieved to get his ring back, and she enters into a secret life of her own. Beginning by breaking in and wreaking havoc on a house near hers and like hers, she goes on the loose into the city night with its derelicts, drunks and hoods. She remains alone, roaming the park, kicking at lovers, accusing and punishing all the world, shouting up at God "for holding out on me," calling out only to others like herself for guidance, so they can give each other "the strength to face ugliness in any form," which might offer some kind of revelation. She herself becomes the night the prowler. As we see her "whirling in the air above her head a bicycle chain she had won from a mob of leather-jackets," she is like some saint-to-be of the Troubled Young. This story with all the rawness of today in it is not without its old progenitors. Felicity's progress through the scarifying world of Sydney night life is also a path of self-mortification. She is divested of that pride too; when she comes in the final scene to an abandoned house and finds there a naked, diseased, dirty, solitary old man lying on a mattress at point of death, she has her revelation. It is a stunning story.

A middle-aged Australian couple is on holiday, in "Sicilian Vespers," when the husband gets stuck in their hotel with toothache. Ivy would will herself to feel the pain for him: she believes in the efficacy of love, but suspecting her husband (with his "honest, un-Sicilian eyes") believes in it only theoretically, doesn't confess it to him: "She did not want to damage his affection for her: it was too precious." She is held back in her life, too, by a ghost out of her girlhood riding with her still—her father. There seems nothing for it but a deliberate act of adultery with a repugnant American (another hotel guest). In the Cathedral of San Fabrizio, she drags him from the crowd into a side chapel and down onto the marble floor.

If nearly all the stories do end up on the floor, it is, after all, the natural place for humiliation, degradation, lust, despair and hunger to reach their limit. "The Cockatoos" does not—it ends with a smell of cake.

A flock of wild cockatoos makes a descent upon a residential neighborhood, alighting first at one house, then another, arousing jealousies, coveting, intent to murder, and other things, even causing a husband and wife who haven't spoken for years in the same house to break silence—"trapped into comforting each other," they fall into bed "with laughing mouth on mouth." The characters are wayward, rather than driven. Passions fly thick and fast, but on a neighborhood level, like the cockatoos themselves, selecting the house they'd like to visit and making their choice of feeding places, setting up no more than a neighborhood commotion.

"The Cockatoos," the only story here that's a comedy, is also the only one in which the sexual aggressor is a man. As Mick (the husband who doesn't speak to his wife) sits straddling the lady who lives down the street (it's Busby LeCornu, who waits for him every day leaning on her gate, and the only time he puts on a hat is to walk through it), they exchange these words—the subject of course is the cockatoos:

"See here, Busby . . . I didn't tell you about me birds to have you seduce um away from me."

She sighed from within the crook of her arm. "I don't see why we can't share what doesn't belong to either of us."

He was already getting back into his clothes. "The wife would be disappointed," he said.

(1975)

ELIZABETH BOWEN'S
Pictures and Conversations

୬ଟ୍ଟ

Spencer Curtis Brown, Elizabeth Bowen's literary agent and friend of many years, whom she made her literary executor, writes in his affecting and helpfully informative Foreword to this collection the circumstances of the appearance here of *Pictures and Conversations*. Miss Bowen, who died in February, 1973, had talked over this book with him, and he prints here some notes she made for her publishers before she began it.

She did not intend it to be an autobiography in the accepted sense. (It got its title from *Alice in Wonderland*.) It was not to follow a time sequence, and "it will be anything but all-inclusive." Rather, "the underlying theme—to which the book will owe what it is necessary that a book *should* have, continuity—will be the relationship (so far as that can be traceable, and perhaps it is most interesting when it is apparently not traceable) between living and writing. Dislike of pomposity inhibits me from saying, 'the relationship between life and art' (meaning my own.)"

That is to say, instead of the "personal" (in the accepted sense), we were to be given the more revealing findings she herself could bring out of her life and her work, calling for the truer candor, the greater generosity—a work to do reader, as well as writer, honor.

Entering into her decision to write it was the unnervement factor: seeing some studies and analyses of herself and her work by others. "While appreciative of the honor done me and of the hard work involved, I have found some of them wildly off the mark. To the point of asking myself, if anybody *must* write a book about Elizabeth Bowen, why should not Elizabeth Bowen?"

Then she became ill. She wrote into her last year for as long as she could, and the last words she was able to speak were to Mr. Curtis Brown, for whom she'd sent in the hospital: "I want it published."

That wanting was an act of passionate good faith in the intuition of a lifetime, as I see it. (Here I must speak as her friend as well as her reader.) She believed that what she had managed to set down in however small part would carry a strength to make known to her readers what was to have been the burden of the whole. Her fragment is all-affirmative and she was right. Most of her readers will feel less pain in there being so little completed for the radiance of what is here: this is what would have permeated the book we shall never see.

It fairly ripples with life.

In the sections called "Origins," "Places" and "People," we are meeting an enchanting little girl, the Elizabeth Bowen of age seven recently transplanted from Ireland to England, in her prophetic relationship to the woman and the writer she was to become. We find it possible everywhere and time after time to make the jump.

What she says about the Irish is as wonderful as what she has made clear dramatically in her stories. All Irish share in inborn traits such as belligerence ("poles apart from aggressiveness": "Your belligerent person tends to sail through life in excellent spirits"); the passion for virtuosity of all kinds; the ability to strike root wherever set down, a peculiarity of the Anglo-Irish—which of course she is. And there is writing: "To that we have taken like ducks to water." But, she goes on to say, "Possibly, it was England made me a novelist," because, with the move, there was to be "a cleft between my heredity and my environment—the former remaining, in my case, the more powerful." "If you began in Ireland, Ireland remains the norm: like it or not." "What had to be bitten on was that two entities so opposed, so irreconcilable in climate, character and intention, as Folkestone and Dublin should exist simultaneously, and be operative, in the same life-time, particularly my own."

England affected her as a child "more in a scenic way than in any other—and still does." After Ireland ("repetitive eighteenth-century interiors with their rational proportions and faultless mouldings, evenly day-lit, without shadow, curiousness or cranny"), "release, to the point of delirium, awaited me." "Everything struck me as having been recently put together . . . *would* it last? The edifices lining the tilted streets . . . seemed engaged in just not sliding about. How much *would* this brittle fabric stand up to? My thoughts dallied with land-slides, subsidences, tidal waves."

The schools she was sent to nourished further what was to be her lifelong love affair with other people's houses, for, she says, "Never had I the misfortune to be educated in any building erected for that purpose." Digging, the leader of her companions, through walls and into foundations of some former rectory, on speculation of secret passages quite naturally turned into writing stories about houses a little later. "For all that," she says, "it was the foreground I stood upon that possessed me. Underfoot, it lost nothing by being *terra firma*: actual and tangible, it remained magic."

"I have thriven, accordingly, on the changes and chances, the dislocations and . . . the contrasts which have made up so much of my life," she says; and her imagination was most fired by the unfamiliar. "I am not a 'regional' writer in the outright sense"—but she is in another: "Since I started writing, I have been welding together an inner landscape, assembled anything but at random."

Not people and places in their own identities, but people and places that experience called up in her became her stories and novels. They represent her reactions to experience, her "beholding afresh." All kinds of characters materialized so, many of them highly magnetic (a sign of their validity to her), some of them not in the least lovable. Vitality is the overriding principle. Evil, then, may move out in front; and innocence in self-absorption may find itself able to lay devastation about on all sides.

Least of all did this writer see reflections of herself everywhere. She saw—a "sensationalist" as she has always described herself—the living and changing and enigmatic and alluring world—the place she was in at that moment of transit, and the people it had, to her eyes, succeeded in magnetizing to itself.

One is made aware in these pages of the scattering of seeds due for later flowering into *The Death of the Heart, The Little Girls, Eva Trout,* and other fiction. And well does one recognize this child. There is the same sense of expectation, the willingness to join in, take part, that gives its special strength and delight to her writing. She was a prime responder to this world. It was almost as if she'd been *invited* here. Some great pleasure lay deep inside her great sophistication—and here she was, at the top of her form, arrived to do it honor: a romantic, of course—self-described. A romantic with a particularly penetrating power of observation, and a joyous—and unconflicting—sense of the absurd.

Her understanding of a wide range of relationships might easily have been rooted in what she describes in her childhood nature as "outgoing." Later on, her grown-up generosity might have been a form of concentration almost psychic, and in her writing, this may have become the novelist's gift of quick perception, and a working tool. Fascination with the outside world, in retrospect, and through the intensity of writing fiction, becomes sharp scrutiny. A highly conscious ability to imagine herself in another's place is a writer's power too—in her case, to precipitate a highly complex plot and call up a full house of vivacious characters to play it out.

In the notes she had made, we see that the section next to be written would be called "Genesis": "Remarks on the growth a book makes while being written." One longs for that, especially when she comments: "I shall know more about this book when I am under way with it."

Pictures and Conversations was important to Elizabeth Bowen. Published, it is important to her readers, for, fragment that it is, it is whole in its essence, which survives interruption to the page. That relationship between her life and her art—and here I use, for her, the word she forbore to use for herself—she *has* divined in its spontaneous and still-mysterious source, and has traced it partway at least toward its broadening stream. What is here holds a particular blessing for those who loved Elizabeth, for they will not be able to read any sentence of it without being brought the cadence of her voice and the glow of her company.

As autobiography (in the Bowen sense), the chapters will fall into natural place beside the enchanting *Seven Winters* (for the first seven years of her life, the summers were spent in Bowen's Court, the winters in Dublin); the brilliant Introduction to the republished *Early Stories*; and of course the book *Bowen's Court*: here *is* the chronology, here in the house, the family, the land and the history: Elizabeth Bowen abides in that book, deeply in it, and while it was not designed to tell us of herself as apart from it, it joins in, all joins in together now.

There was to have been a new Bowen novel, too. We have its opening chapter. Entitled "The Move-In," it gets straight down to business with the arrival at a (somehow chosen) strange house of a carload of young people and a banging at the door. We are in at the systematic onset of outrage upon a house, of whose already existing, internal, outrages we are receiving hints in counterpoint.

One of the number in the car—a young man—and one of the number in the house—the not-at-all young Agatha, coming outside with her "virulent violet shaggy jersey" around her— meet, on the porch, while both camps look on, insiders through the windows, outsiders climbing from the car, short in patience.

There is not a safe square inch in any of this chapter of

preposterous conversation for a single character to move. The dangers signaled in the setting (a sort of lodge at road's end, high up, overlooking a lake, the stuffy heat of a July evening growing dark) are the deep psychological tensions that this highly contemporary situation is rapidly and impartially connecting up into an alarm system which the first touch will let loose.

There's enough of it to let us see again how expert Elizabeth Bowen is with the young and rebellious. These appear to be very much today's boys and girls, hauling about their dirty shirts "waiting for a dip," clawing at the insect bites they picked up passing through Spain. And how wittily she slots them into the present here: taking a look through the dining-room windows of the unsuspecting house, they see what they easily suppose may be a piece of ectoplasm in motion; and it is in fact "only one degree less occult"—the cap of a parlor-maid waiting at table, a species supposed by them to be long extinct.

The chapter—a packed ten pages—ends with Agatha insisting:

"... Anyway, my house is completely full, and will be fuller tomorrow. I have no room for you."

"What's that, then?" asked the girl, pointing to the uninhabited wing.

"Rats and bats. Ruinous. No—impossible!"

Her last opening scene leaves us thoroughly engaged and tantalized: that rare hypnotic power never lost its hold.

"Bergotte," written at the request of Peter Quennell for a symposium and never published before among Elizabeth Bowen's own works, treats again, in another form, of the relationship that springs into existence and persists in growing between a novelist and his characters. Here the author is of course Proust and his character Bergotte another author. In the Bowen confrontation with a Proustian confrontation, we are guided through the kind of dream-construction that fiction is, a house full of interconnecting rooms and crossing passages, finally being stopped by its secret door.

What was Bergotte's origin? He wrote *romans psychologiques*—"but so did many: France cradled those." He was based on Anatole France, some said. Some said Ruskin (the passion for cathedrals). "I cannot see him," says Elizabeth Bowen. "One must stop somewhere." He is composite, she concludes. Like the other, very different, writer Saint-Loup, he has "group-origin." But Saint-Loup "is the more completely perceived, for this reason: in Saint-Loup there is nothing of Proust; in Bergotte there is much. Bergotte is a stand-in, scapegoat, whipping boy for his creator . . . Just as he transferred his homosexuality to Charlus, Proust shifted on to Bergotte his literary guilt, with its nexus of ignominies, self-searchings and anxieties." She has a haunting final sentence: "Proust while dying thought about Bergotte's death—there was something, he made known, that he wanted to add."

"Notes on Writing a Novel" was a piece contributed to John Lehmann's *Orion II* in 1945. Later, Elizabeth Bowen says, she came not to like "their peremptory tone"—but to this reader it seems the natural tone for a writer firing off working directions to herself from the thick of things. They are probing, unadorned, and succinct to the point where they could almost serve as passwords between writers. They have the currency today, as far as I can see, of pure gold. "Plot is the knowing of destination." Its object is "the non-poetic statement of a poetic truth." They are provocative to imagination. Characters, she thought, pre-exist for the novelist. "They are *found*. They reveal themselves slowly to the novelist's perception—as might fellow-travellers seated opposite one in a very dimly-lit railway carriage." Among the things I learned that startled me with their truth: "Nothing physical can be invented."

Mr. Curtis Brown says he has included the Nativity Play because, while it had been suggested to him by others that he not do so, "because it is so different from the work expected from Elizabeth Bowen," this seemed to him "a most excellent reason for including it. Herself a many-faceted person, her gifts were many-faceted, too . . . and I think she would have liked to know it was in print."

It was written for her friends near Bowen's Court, neighbors who wanted a nativity play to perform with organ, chorus and trumpets, with narrators, actors speaking and in pantomime, in Limerick Cathedral. The treatment is very much her own and imaginative in its inventions. When I first read it in Ireland, it seemed to me very Irish; I see now how she made skillful dramatic use of the Irish country people, in Mary and Joseph, the Shepherds, and the Children who come to worship the Child, in contrast to the Three Kings met in their royal tent in the desert, who are austere philosophers and speak as intellectuals ("We three/who have come to a standstill"); and in contrast again, to them, the heavenly members of the drama, ranks of Angels and Smaller Angels.

Even behind the wish to make a gift to the neighbors in her play might there have lain another impulse? One remembers Elizabeth's telling, in *Seven Winters*, of the frequent reminders from her mother of angels and her Guardian Angel, and the picture on her nursery wall of the Herald Angels. "My mother wished me to care for angels: I did."

(1975)

IV

PERSONAL AND OCCASIONAL PIECES

A Sweet Devouring

When I used to ask my mother which we were, rich or poor, she refused to tell me. I was then nine years old and of course what I was dying to hear was that we were poor. I was reading a book called *Five Little Peppers* and my heart was set on baking a cake for my mother in a stove with a hole in it. Some version of rich, crusty old Mr. King—up till that time not living on our street—was sure to come down the hill in his wheelchair and rescue me if anything went wrong. But before I could start a cake at all I had to find out if we were poor, and poor *enough*; and my mother wouldn't tell me, she said she was too busy. I couldn't wait too long; I had to go on reading and soon Polly Pepper got into more trouble, some that was a little harder on her and easier on me.

Trouble, the backbone of literature, was still to me the original property of the fairy tale, and as long as there was plenty of trouble for everybody and the rewards for it were falling in the right spots, reading was all smooth sailing. At that age a child reads with higher appetite and gratification, and with those two stars sailing closer together, than ever again in his growing up. The home shelves had been providing me all along with the usual books, and I read them with love—but snap, I finished them. I read everything just alike—snap. I even came to the

Tales from Maria Edgeworth and went right ahead, without feeling the bump—then. It *was* noticeable that when her characters suffered she punished them for it, instead of rewarding them as a reader had rather been led to hope. In her stories, the children had to make their choice between being unhappy and good about it and being unhappy and bad about it, and then she helped them to choose wrong. In *The Purple Jar*, it will be remembered, there was the little girl being taken through the shops by her mother and her downfall coming when she chooses to buy something beautiful instead of something necessary. The purple jar, when the shop sends it out, proves to have been purple only so long as it was filled with purple water, and her mother knew it all the time. They don't deliver the water. That's only the cue for stones to start coming through the hole in the victim's worn-out shoe. She bravely agrees she must keep walking on stones until such time as she is offered another choice between the beautiful and the useful. Her father tells her as far as he is concerned she can stay in the house. If I had been at all easy to disappoint, that story would have disappointed me. Of course, I did feel, what is the good of walking on rocks if they are going to let the water out of the jar too? And it seemed to me that even the illustrator fell down on the characters in that book, not alone Maria Edgeworth, for when a rich, crusty old gentleman gave Simple Susan a guinea for some kind deed she'd done him, there was a picture of the transaction and where was the guinea? I couldn't make out a feather. But I liked *reading* the book all right—except that I finished it.

My mother took me to the Public Library and introduced me: "Let her have any book she wants, except *Elsie Dinsmore*." I looked for the book I couldn't have and it was a row. That was how I learned about the Series Books. The *Five Little Peppers* belonged, so did *The Wizard of Oz*, so did *The Little Colonel*, so did *The Green Fairy Book*. There were many of everything, generations of everybody, instead of one. I wasn't coming to the end of reading, after all—I was saved.

Our library in those days was a big rotunda lined with

shelves. A copy of *V.V.'s Eyes* seemed to follow you wherever you went, even after you'd read it. I didn't know what I liked, I just knew what there was a lot of. After *Randy's Spring* there came *Randy's Summer, Randy's Fall* and *Randy's Winter.* True, I didn't care very much myself for her spring, but it didn't occur to me that I might not care for her summer, and then her summer didn't prejudice me against her fall, and I still had hopes as I moved on to her winter. I was disappointed in her whole year, as it turned out, but a thing like that didn't keep me from wanting to read every word of it. The pleasures of reading itself—who doesn't remember?—were like those of a Christmas cake, a sweet devouring. The "Randy Books" failed chiefly in being so soon over. Four seasons doesn't make a series.

All that summer I used to put on a second petticoat (our librarian wouldn't let you past the front door if she could see through you), ride my bicycle up the hill and "through the Capitol" (shortcut) to the library with my two read books in the basket (two was the limit you could take out at one time when you were a child and also as long as you lived), and tiptoe in ("Silence") and exchange them for two more in two minutes. Selection was no object. I coasted the two new books home, jumped out of my petticoat, read (I suppose I ate and bathed and answered questions put to me), then in all hope put my petticoat back on and rode those two books back to the library to get my next two.

The librarian was the lady in town who wanted to be it. She called me by my full name and said, "Does your mother know where you are? You know good and well the fixed rule of this library: *Nobody is going to come running back here with any book on the same day they took it out.* Get both those things out of here and don't come back till tomorrow. And I can practically see through you."

My great-aunt in Virginia, who understood better about needing more to read than you *could* read, sent me a book so big it had to be read on the floor—a bound volume of six or eight issues of *St. Nicholas* from a previous year. In the very first pages a serial began: *The Lucky Stone* by Abbie Farwell Brown. The illustrations were right down my alley: a heroine so poor she was ragged, a witch with an extremely pointed hat, a rich, crusty old gentleman in—better than a wheelchair—a runaway carriage; and I set to. I gobbled up installment after installment through the whole luxurious book, through the last one, and then came the words, turning me to *un*lucky stone: "To be concluded." The book had come to an end and *The Lucky Stone* wasn't finished! The witch had it! I couldn't believe this infidelity from my aunt. I still had my secret childhood feeling that if you hunted long enough in a book's pages, you could find what you were looking for, and long after I knew books better than that, I used to hunt again for the end of *The Lucky Stone*. It never occurred to me that the story had an existence anywhere else outside the pages of that single green-bound book. The last chapter was just something I would have to do without. Polly Pepper could do it. And then suddenly I tried something—I read it again, as much as I had of it. I was in love with books at least partly for what they looked like; I loved the printed page.

In my little circle books were almost never given for Christmas, they cost too much. But the year before, I'd been given a book and got a shock. It was from the same classmate who had told me there was no Santa Claus. She gave me a book, all right—*Poems by Another Little Girl*. It looked like a real book, was printed like a real book—but it was *by her*. Homemade poems? Illusion-dispelling was her favorite game. She was in such a hurry, she had such a pile to get rid of—her mother's electric runabout was stacked to the bud vases with copies—that she hadn't even time to say, "Merry Christmas!" With only the same raucous laugh with which she had told me, "Been filling my own stocking for years!" she shot me her book, received my Japanese pencil box with a moonlight scene on the lid and a sharpened pencil inside, jumped back into the car and was sped away by her mother. I stood right where they had left me, on the curb in my Little Nurse's uniform, and read that book, and I had no better way to prove when I got through than I had when I started that this was not a real book. But of course it wasn't. The printed page is not absolutely everything.

Then this Christmas was coming, and my grandfather in Ohio sent along in his box of presents an envelope with money in it for me to buy myself the book I wanted.

I went to Kress's. Not everybody knew Kress's sold books, but children just before Christmas know everything Kress's ever sold or will sell. My father had showed us the mirror he was giving my mother to hang above her desk, and Kress's is where my brother and I went to reproduce that by buying a mirror together to give her ourselves, and where our little brother then made us take him and he bought her one his size for fifteen cents. Kress's had also its version of the Series Books, called, exactly like another series, "The Camp Fire Girls," beginning with *The Camp Fire Girls in the Woods*.

I believe they were ten cents each and I had a dollar. But they weren't all that easy to buy, because the series stuck, and to buy some of it was like breaking into a loaf of French bread. Then after you got home, each single book was as hard to open as a box stuck in its varnish, and when it gave way it popped like a firecracker. The covers once prized apart would never close; those books once open stayed open and lay on their backs helplessly fluttering their leaves like a turned-over June bug. They were as light as a matchbox. They were printed on yellowed paper with corners that crumbled, if you pinched on them too hard, like old graham crackers, and they smelled like attic trunks, caramelized glue, their own confinement with one another and, over all, the Kress's smell—bandannas, peanuts and sandalwood from the incense counter. Even without reading them I loved them. It was hard, that year, that Christmas is a day you can't read.

What could have happened to those books?—but I can tell you about the leading character. His name was Mr. Holmes. He was not a Camp Fire Girl: he wanted to catch one. Through every book of the series he gave chase. He pursued Bessie and

Zara—those were the Camp Fire Girls—and kept scooping
them up in his touring car, while they just as regularly got
away from him. Once Bessie escaped from the second floor of
a strange inn by climbing down a gutter pipe. Once she
escaped by driving away from Mr. Holmes in his own auto-
mobile, which she had learned to drive by watching him. What
Mr. Holmes wanted with them—either Bessie or Zara would
do—didn't give me pause; I was too young to be a Camp Fire
Girl; I was just keeping up. I wasn't alarmed by Mr. Holmes—
when I cared for a chill, I knew to go to Dr. Fu Manchu, who
had his own series in the library. I wasn't fascinated either.
There was one thing I wanted from those books, and that was
for me to have ten to read at one blow.

Who in the world wrote those books? I knew all the time
they were the false "Camp Fire Girls" and the ones in the
library were the authorized. But book reviewers sometimes say
of a book that if anyone else had written it, it might not have
been this good, and I found it out as a child—their warning is
justified. This was a proven case, although a case of the true
not being as good as the false. In the true series the characters
were either totally different or missing (Mr. Holmes was missing), and there was too much time given to teamwork. The
Kress's Campers, besides getting into a more reliable kind of
trouble than the Carnegie Campers, had adventures that even
they themselves weren't aware of: the pages were in wrong.
There were transposed pages, repeated pages, and whole sections in upside down. There was no way of telling if there was
anything missing. But if you knew your way in the woods at
all, you could enjoy yourself tracking it down. I read the
library "Camp Fire Girls," since that's what they were there
for, but though they could be read by poorer light they were
not as good.

And yet, in a way, the false Campers were no better either.
I wonder whether I felt some flaw at the heart of things or
whether I was just tired of not having any taste; but it seemed
to me when I had finished that the last nine of those books

weren't as good as the first one. And the same went for all Series Books. As long as they are keeping a series going, I was afraid, nothing can really happen. The whole thing is one grand prevention. For my greed, I might have unwittingly dealt with myself in the same way Maria Edgeworth dealt with the one who put her all into the purple jar—I had received word it was just colored water.

And then I went again to the home shelves and my lucky hand reached and found Mark Twain—twenty-four volumes, not a series, and good all the way through.

(1957)

Some Notes
on River Country

A place that ever was lived in is like a fire that never goes out.
It flares up, it smolders for a time, it is fanned or smothered
by circumstance, but its being is intact, forever fluttering
within it, the result of some original ignition. Sometimes it gives
out glory, sometimes its little light must be sought out to be
seen, small and tender as a candle flame, but as certain.

I have never seen, in this small section of old Mississippi River
country and its little chain of lost towns between Vicksburg
and Natchez, anything so mundane as ghosts, but I have felt
many times there a sense of place as powerful as if it were visible and walking and could touch me.

The clatter of hoofs and the bellow of boats have gone, all
old communications. The Old Natchez Trace has sunk out of
use; it is deep in leaves. The river has gone away and left the
landings. Boats from Liverpool do not dock at these empty
crags. The old deeds are done, old evil and old good have been
made into stories, as plows turn up the river bottom, and the
wild birds fly now at the level where people on boat deck once
were strolling and talking of great expanding things, and of
chance and money. Much beauty has gone, many little things
of life. To light up the nights there are no mansions, no celebrations. Just as, when there were mansions and celebrations,

there were no more festivals of an Indian tribe there; before the music, there were drums.

But life does not forsake any place. People live still in Rodney's Landing; flood drives them out and they return to it. Children are born there and find the day as inexhaustible and as abundant as they run and wander in their little hills as they, in innocence and rightness, would find it anywhere on earth. The seasons come as truly, and give gratefulness, though they bring little fruit. There is a sense of place there, to keep life from being extinguished, like a cup of the hands to hold a flame.

To go there, you start west from Port Gibson. This was the frontier of the Natchez country. Postmen would arrive here blowing their tin horns like Gabriel where the Old Natchez Trace crosses the Bayou Pierre, after riding three hundred wilderness miles from Tennessee, and would run in where the tavern used to be to deliver their mail, change their ponies, and warm their souls with grog. And up this now sand-barred bayou trading vessels would ply from the river. Port Gibson is on a highway and a railroad today, and lives on without its river life, though it is half diminished. It is still rather smug because General Grant said it was "too pretty to burn." Perhaps it was too pretty for any harsh fate, with its great mossy trees and old camellias, its exquisite little churches, and galleried houses back in the hills overlooking the cotton fields. It has escaped what happened to Grand Gulf and Bruinsburg and Rodney's Landing.

A narrow gravel road goes into the West. You have entered the loess country, and a gate might have been shut behind you for the difference in the world. All about are hills and chasms of cane, forests of cedar trees, and magnolia. Falling away from your road, at times merging with it, an old trail crosses and recrosses, like a tunnel through the dense brakes, under arches of branches, a narrow, cedar-smelling trace the width of a horseman. This road joined the Natchez Trace to the river. It, too, was made by buffaloes, then used by man, trodden lower and lower, a few inches every hundred years.

Loess has the beautiful definition of aeolian—wind-borne. The loess soil is like a mantle; the ridge was laid down here by the wind, the bottom land by the water. Deep under them both is solid blue clay, embalming the fossil horse and the fossil ox and the great mastodon, the same preserving blue clay that was dug up to wrap the head of the Big Harp in bandit days, no less a monstrous thing when it was carried in for reward.

Loess exists also in China, that land whose plants are so congenial to the South; there the bluffs rise vertically for five hundred feet in some places and contain cave dwellings without number. The Mississippi bluffs once served the same purpose; when Vicksburg was being shelled from the river during the year's siege there in the War Between the States, it was the daily habit of the three thousand women, children and old men who made up the wartime population to go on their all-fours into shelters they had tunneled into the loess bluffs. Mark Twain reports how the Federal soldiers would shout from the river in grim humor, "Rats, to your holes!"

Winding through this land unwarned, rounding to a valley, you will come on a startling thing. Set back in an old gray field, with horses grazing like small fairy animals beside it, is a vast ruin—twenty-two Corinthian columns in an empty oblong and an L. Almost seeming to float like lace, bits of wrought-iron balcony connect them here and there. Live cedar trees are growing from the iron black acanthus leaves, high in the empty air. This is the ruin of Windsor, long since burned. It used to have five stories and an observation tower—Mark Twain used the tower as a sight when he was pilot on the river.

Immediately the cane and the cedars become more impenetrable, the road ascends and descends, and rather slowly, because of the trees and shadows, you realize a little village is before you. Grand Gulf today looks like a scene in Haiti. Under enormous dense trees where the moss hangs long as ladders, there are hutlike buildings and pale whitewashed sheds; most of the faces under the straw hats are black, and only narrow jungly paths lead toward the river. Of course this is not Grand Gulf in the original, for the river undermined that and pulled it whole into the river—the opposite of what it did to Rodney's Landing. A little corner was left, which the Federals burned, all but a wall, on their way to Vicksburg. After the war the population built it back—and the river moved away. Grand Gulf was a British settlement before the Revolution and had close connection with England, whose ships traded here. It handled more cotton than any other port in Mississippi for about twenty years. The old cemetery is there still, like a roof of marble and moss overhanging the town and about to tip into it. Many names of British gentry stare out from the stones, and the biggest snakes in the world must have their kingdom in that dark-green tangle.

Two miles beyond, at the end of a dim jungle track where you can walk, is the river, immensely wide and vacant, its bluff occupied sometimes by a casual camp of fishermen under the willow trees, where dirty children playing about and nets drying have a look of timeless roaming and poverty and sameness . . . By boat you can reach a permanent fishing camp, inaccessible now by land. Go till you find the hazy shore where the Bayou Pierre, dividing in two, reaches around the swamp to meet the river. It is a gray-green land, softly flowered, hung with stillness. Houseboats will be tied there among the cypresses under falls of the long moss, all of a color. Aaron Burr's "flotilla" tied up there, too, for this is Bruinsburg Landing, where the boats were seized one wild day of apprehension. Bruinsburg grew to be a rich, gay place in cotton days. It is almost as if a wand had turned a noisy cotton port into a handful of shanty boats. Yet Bruinsburg Landing has not vanished: it is this.

Wonderful things have come down the current of this river, and more spectacular things were on the water than could ever have sprung up on shores then. Every kind of treasure, every kind of bearer of treasure has come down, and armadas and flotillas, and the most frivolous of things, too, and the most pleasure-giving of people.

Natchez, downstream, had a regular season of drama from 1806 on, attended by the countryside—the only one in English in this part of the world. The plays would be given outdoors, on a strip of grass on the edge of the high bluff overlooking the landing. With the backdrop of the river and the endless low marsh of Louisiana beyond, some version of Elizabethan or Restoration comedy or tragedy would be given, followed by a short farcical afterpiece, and the traveling company would run through a little bird mimicry, ventriloquism and magical tricks in-between. Natchez, until lately a bear-baiting crowd, watched eagerly "A Laughable Comedy in 3 Acts written by Shakespeare and Altered by Garrick called Catherine & Petrucio," followed by "A Pantomime Ballet Called a Trip through the Vauxhall Gardens into which is introduced the humorous song of Four and Twenty Fiddlers concluding with a dance by the characters." Or sometimes the troupe would arrive with a program of "divertisements"—recitations of Lochinvar, Alexander's Feast, Cato's Soliloquy of the Soul, and Clarence's Dream, interspersed with Irish songs by the boys sung to popular requests and concluding with "A Laughable Combat between Two Blind Fiddlers."

The Natchez country took all this omnivorously to its heart. There were rousing, splendid seasons, with a critic writing pieces in the newspaper to say that last night's Juliet spoke just a *bit* too loudly for a girl, though Tybalt kept in perfect character to delight all, even after he was dead—signed "X.Y.Z."

But when the natural vigor of the day gave clamorous birth to the minstrel show, the bastard Shakespeare went; and when the showboat really rounded the bend, the theatre of that day, a child of the plantation and the river, came to its own. The next generation heard calliopes filling river and field with their sound, and saw the dazzling showboats come like enormous dreams up the bayous and the little streams at floodtime, with whole French Zouave troops aboard, whole circuses with horses jumping through paper hoops, and all the literal rites of the minstrel show, as ever true to expectations as a miracle play.

Now if you pick up the Rodney Road again, through twenty

miles of wooded hills, you wind sharply round, the old sunken road ahead of you and following you. Then from a great height you descend suddenly through a rush of vines, down, down, deep into complete levelness, and there in a strip at the bluff's foot, at the road's end, is Rodney's Landing.

Though you walk through Rodney's Landing, it long remains a landscape, rather than a center of activity, and seems to exist altogether in the sight, like a vision. At first you think there is not even sound. The thick soft morning shadow of the bluff on the valley floor, and the rose-red color of the brick church which rises from this shadow, are its dominant notes—all else seems green. The red of the bricks defies their element; they were made of earth, but they glow as if to remind you that there is fire in earth. No one is in sight.

Eventually you see people, of course. Women have little errands, and the old men play checkers at a table in front of the one open store. And the people's faces are good. Theirs seem *actually* the faces your eyes look for in city streets and never see. There is a middle-aged man who always meets you when you come. He is like an embodiment of the simplicity and friendliness not of the mind—for his could not teach him— but of the open spirit. He never remembers you, but he speaks courteously. "I am Mr. John David's boy—where have you come from, and when will you have to go back?" He has what I have always imagined as a true Saxon face, like a shepherd boy's, light and shy and set in solitude. He carries a staff, too, and stands with it on the hill, where he will lead you—looking with care everywhere and far away, warning you of the steep stile . . . The river is not even in sight here. It is three miles beyond, past the cotton fields of the bottom, through a dense miasma of swamp.

The houses merge into a shaggy fringe at the foot of the bluff. It is like a town some avenging angel has flown over, taking up every second or third house and leaving only this. There are more churches than houses now; the edge of town is marked by a little wooden Catholic church tiny as a match-box, with twin steeples carved like icing, over a stile in a flowery pasture. The Negro Baptist church, weathered black with a snow-white door, has red hens in the yard. The old galleried stores are boarded up. The missing houses were burned—they were empty, and the little row of Negro inhabitants have carried them off for firewood.

You know instinctively as you stand here that this shelf of forest is the old town site, and you find that here, as in Grand Gulf, the cemetery has remained as the roof of the town. In a mossy wood the graves, gently tended here, send up mossy shafts, with lilies flowering in the gloom. Many of the tombstones are marked "A Native of Ireland," though there are German names and graves neatly bordered with sea shells and planted in spring-flowering bulbs. People in Rodney's Landing won silver prizes in the fairs for their horses; they planted all this land; some of them were killed in battle, some in duels fought on a Grand Gulf sand bar. The girls who died young of the fevers were some of them the famous "Rodney heiresses." All Mississippians know descendants of all the names. I looked for the grave of Dr. Nutt, the man who privately invented and used his cotton gin here, previous to the rest of the world. The Petit Gulf cotton was known in England better than any other as superior to all cotton, and was named for the little gulf in the river at this landing, and Rodney, too, was once called Petit Gulf.

Down below, Mr. John David's boy opens the wrought-iron gate to the churchyard of the rose-red church, and you go up the worn, concave steps. The door is never locked, the old silver knob is always the heat of the hand. It is a church, upon whose calm interior nothing seems to press from the outer world, which, though calm itself here, is still "outer." (Even cannonballs were stopped by its strong walls, and are in them yet.) It is the kind of little church in which you might instinctively say prayers for your friends; how is it that both danger and succor, both need and response, seem intimately near in little country churches?

Something always hangs imminent above all life—usually claims of daily need, daily action, a prescribed course of movement, a schedule of time. In Rodney, the imminent thing is a natural danger—the town may be flooded by the river, and every inhabitant must take to the hills. Every house wears a belt of ineradicable silt around its upper walls. I asked the storekeeper what his store would be like after the river had been over it, and he said, "You know the way a fish is?" Life threatened by nature is simplified, most peaceful in present peace, quiet in seasons of waiting and readiness. There are rowboats under all the houses.

Even the women in sunbonnets disappear and nothing moves at noon but butterflies, little white ones, large black ones, and they are like some flutter of heat, some dervishes of the midday hour, as in pairs they rotate about one another, ascending and descending, appearing to follow each other up and down some swaying spiral staircase invisible in the dense light. The heat moves. Its ripples can be seen, like the ripples in some vertical river running between earth and sky. It is so still at noon. I was never there before the river left, to hear the thousand swirling sounds it made for Rodney's Landing, but could it be that its absence is so much missed in the life of sound here that a stranger would feel it? The stillness seems absolute, as the brightness of noon seems to touch the point of saturation. Here the noon sun does make a trance; here indeed at its same zenith it looked down on life sacrificed to it and was worshipped.

It is not strange to think that a unique nation among Indians lived in this beautiful country. The origin of the Natchez is still in mystery. But their people, five villages in the seventeenth century, were unique in this country and they were envied by the other younger nations—the Choctaws helped the French in their final dissolution. In Mississippi they were remnants surely of medievalism. They were proud and cruel, gentlemannered and ironic, handsome, extremely tall, intellectual, elegant, pacific and ruthless. Fire, death, sacrifice formed the spirit of the Natchez' worship. They did not now, however, make war.

The women—although all the power was in their blood, and

a Sun woman by rigid system married a low-caste Stinkard and bore a Sun child by him—were the nation's laborers still. They planted and they spun, they baked their red jugs for the bear oil, and when the men came from the forests, they would throw at the feet of their wives the tongues of the beasts they had shot from their acacia bows—both as a tribute to womanhood and as a command to the wives to go out and hunt on the ground for what they had killed, and to drag it home.

The town of Natchez was named after this nation, although the French one day, in a massacre for a massacre, slew or sent into slavery at Santo Domingo every one of its namesakes, and the history of the nation was done in 1773. The French amusedly regarded the Natchez as either "*sauvages*" or "*naturels, innocents.*" They made many notes of their dress and quaint habits, made engravings of them looking like Cupids and Psyches, and handed down to us their rites and customs with horrified withholdings or fascinated repetitions. The women fastened their knee-length hair in a net of mulberry threads, men singed theirs short into a crown except for a lock over the left ear. They loved vermilion and used it delicately, men and women, the women's breasts decorated in tattooed designs by whose geometrics they strangely match ancient Aztec bowls. "*En été*" male and female wore a draped garment from waist to knee. "*En hyver*" they threw about them swan-feather mantles, made as carefully as wigs. For the monthly festivals the men added bracelets of skin polished like ivory, and thin disks of feathers went in each hand. They were painted firecolor, white puffs of down decorated their shorn heads, the one lock left to support the whitest feathers. As children, the Natchez wore pearls handed down by their ancestors—pearls which they had ruined by piercing them with fire.

The Natchez also laughed gently at the French. (Also they massacred them when they were betrayed by them.) Once a Frenchman asked a Natchez noble why these Indians would laugh at them, and the noble replied that it was only because the French were like geese when they talked—all clamoring at once. The Natchez never spoke except one at a time; no one was ever interrupted or contradicted; a visitor was always allowed the opening speech, and that after a rest in silence of fifteen or twenty minutes, to allow him to get his breath and collect his thoughts. (Women murmured or whispered; their game after labor was a silent little guessing game played with three sticks that could not disturb anyone.) But this same nation, when any Sun died, strangled his wife and a great company of loyal friends and ambitious Stinkards to attend him in death, and walked bearing his body over the bodies of strangled infants laid before him by their parents. A Sun once expressed great though polite astonishment that a certain Frenchman declined the favor of dying with him.

Their own sacrifices were great among them. When Iberville came, the Natchez had diminished to twelve hundred. They laid it to the fact that the fire had once been allowed to go out and that a profane fire burned now in its place. Perhaps they had prescience of their end—the only bit of their history that we really know.

Today Rodney's Landing wears the cloak of vegetation which has caught up this whole land for the third time, or the fourth, or the hundredth. There is something Gothic about the vines, in their structure in the trees—there are arches, flying buttresses, towers of vines, with trumpet flowers swinging in them for bells and staining their walls. And there is something of a warmer grandeur in their very abundance—stairways and terraces and whole hanging gardens of green and flowering vines, with a Babylonian babel of hundreds of creature voices that make up the silence of Rodney's Landing. Here are nests for birds and thrones for owls and trapezes for snakes, every kind of bower in the world. From earliest spring there is something, when garlands of yellow jasmine swing from tree to tree, in the woods aglow with dogwood and redbud, when the green is only a floating veil in the hills.

And the vines make an endless flourish in summer and fall.

There are wild vines of the grape family, with their lilac and turquoise fruits and their green, pink and white leaves. Muscadine vines along the stream banks grow a hundred feet high, mixing their dull, musky, delicious grapes among the bronze grapes of the scuppernong. All creepers with trumpets and panicles of scarlet and yellow cling to the treetops. On shady stream banks hang lady's eardrops, fruits and flowers dangling pale jade. The passionflower puts its tendrils where it can, its strange flowers of lilac rays with their little white towers shining out, or its fruit, the maypop, hanging. Wild wistaria hangs its flowers like flower-grapes above reach, and the sweetness of clematis, the virgin's-bower which grows in Rodney, and of honeysuckle, must fill even the highest air. There is a vine that grows to great heights, with heart-shaped leaves as big and soft as summer hats, overlapping and shading everything to deepest jungle blue-green.

Ferns are the hidden floor of the forest, and they grow, too, in the trees, their roots in the deep of mossy branches.

All over the hills the beautiful white Cherokee rose trails its glossy dark-green leaves and its delicate luminous-white flowers. Foliage and flowers alike have a quality of light and dark as well as color in Southern sun, and sometimes a seeming motion like dancing due to the flicker of heat, and are luminous or opaque according to the time of day or the density of summer air. In early morning or in the light of evening they become translucent and ethereal, but at noon they blaze or darken opaquely, and the same flower may seem sultry or delicate in its being all according to when you see it.

It is not hard to follow one of the leapings of old John Law's mind, then, and remember how he displayed diamonds in the shop windows in France—during the organization of his Compagnie d'Occident—saying that they were produced in the cups of the wildflowers along the lower Mississippi. And the closer they grew to the river, the more nearly that might be true.

Deep in the swamps the water hyacinths make solid floors

you could walk on over still black water, the Southern blue flag stands thick and sweet in the marsh. Lady's-tresses, greenish-white little orchids with spiral flowers and stems twisted like curls and braids, grow there, and so do nodding lady's-tresses. Water lilies float, and spider lilies rise up like little coral monsters.

The woods on the bluffs are the hardwood trees—dark and berried and flowered. The magnolia is the spectacular one with its heavy cups—they look as heavy as silver—weighing upon its aromatic, elliptical, black-green leaves, or when it bears its dense pink cones. I remember an old botany book, written long ago in England, reporting the magnolia by hearsay, as having blossoms "so large as to be distinctly visible a mile or more—seen in the mass, we presume." But I tested the visibility power of the magnolia, and the single flower can be seen for several miles on a clear day. One magnolia cousin, the cucumber tree, has long sleevelike leaves and pale-green flowers which smell strange and cooler than the grandiflora flower. Set here and there in this country will be a mimosa tree, with its smell in the rain like a cool melon cut, its puffs of pale flowers settled in its sensitive leaves.

Perhaps the live oaks are the most wonderful trees in this land. Their great girth and their great spread give far more feeling of history than any house or ruin left by man. Vast, very dark, proportioned as beautifully as a church, they stand majestically in the wild or line old sites, old academy grounds. The live oaks under which Aaron Burr was tried at Washington, Mississippi, in this section, must have been old and impressive then, to have been chosen for such a drama. Spanish moss invariably hangs from the live oak branches, moving with the wind and swaying its long beards, darkening the forests; it is an aerial plant and strangely enough is really a pineapple, and consists of very, very tiny leaves and flowers, springy and dustily fragrant to the touch; no child who has ever "dressed up" in it can forget the sweet dust of its smell. It would be hard to think of things that happened here without the presence of these live oaks, so old, so expansive, so wonderful, that they might be sentient beings. W. H. Hudson, in his autobiography, *Far Away and Long Ago*, tells of an old man who felt reverentially toward the ancient trees of his great country house, so that each night he walked around his park to visit them one by one, and rest his hand on its bark to bid it goodnight, for he believed in their knowing spirits.

Now and then comes a report that an ivory-billed woodpecker is seen here. Audubon in his diary says the Indians began the slaughter of this bird long before Columbus discovered America, for the Southern Indians would trade them to the Canadian Indians—four buckskins for an ivory bill. Audubon studied the woodpecker here when he was in the Natchez country, where it lived in the deepest mossy swamps along the windings of the river, and he called it "the greatest of all our American woodpeckers and probably the finest in the world." The advance of agriculture rather than slaughter has really driven it to death, for it will not live except in a wild country.

This woodpecker used to cross the river "in deep undulations." Its notes were "clear, loud, and rather plaintive . . . heard at a considerable distance . . . and resemble the false high note of a clarinet." "Pait, pait, pait," Audubon translates it into his Frenchlike sound. It made its nest in a hole dug with the ivory bill in a tree inclined in just a certain way—usually a black cherry. The holes went sometimes three feet deep, and some people thought they went spirally. The bird ate the grapes of the swampland. Audubon says it would hang by its claws like a titmouse on a grapevine and devour grapes by the bunch —which sounds curiously as though it knew it would be extinct before very long. This woodpecker also would destroy any dead tree it saw standing—chipping it away "to an extent of twenty or thirty feet in a few hours, leaping downward with its body . . . tossing its head to the right and left, or leaning it against the bark to ascertain the precise spot where the grubs were concealed, and immediately renewing its blows with fresh vigor, all the while sounding its loud notes, as if highly delighted." The males had beautiful crimson crests, the females were "always the most clamorous and the least shy." When caught, the birds would fight bitterly, and "utter a mournful and very piteous cry." All vanished now from the earth—the piteous cry and all; unless where Rodney's swamps are wild enough still, perhaps it is true, the last of the ivory-billed woodpeckers still exist in the world, in this safe spot, inaccessible to man.

Indians, Mike Fink the flatboatman, Burr, and Blennerhassett, John James Audubon, the bandits of the Trace, planters, and preachers—the horse fairs, the great fires—the battles of war, the arrivals of foreign ships, and the coming of floods: could not all these things still move with their true stature into the mind here, and their beauty still work upon the heart? Perhaps it is the sense of place that gives us the belief that passionate things, in some essence, endure. Whatever is significant and whatever is tragic in its story live as long as the place does, though they are unseen, and the new life will be built upon these things—regardless of commerce and the way of rivers and roads, and other vagrancies.

(1944)

Fairy Tale of the Natchez Trace

Led here by your president and my old friend Charlotte Capers, I stand before you as a fiction writer invited to address a gathering of historians. I'm deeply aware of the honor. I should like to rise to the occasion in a style more becoming to it, but I can do my best only by sticking to my own line of country in choosing my subject. And there's one novel I've written that can furnish it. It set its foot, lightly enough, across the border between my territory and yours, and for you I'm going to call it my historical novel.

The Robber Bridegroom, my second book, was my first novel—or novella—and different from the fiction I'd done before or was yet to do in exactly this respect: it did not spring from the present-day world, from life I could see around me, from human activities I might run into every day. My fictional characters are always imaginary—but the characters of *The Robber Bridegroom* are peculiarly so.

The novel is set in the Natchez country of the late eighteenth century, in the declining days of Spanish rule. It opens like this:

It was the close of day when a boat touched Rodney's Landing on the Mississippi River, and Clement Musgrove,

A talk before the Mississippi Historical Society.

an innocent planter, with a bag of gold and many presents, disembarked. He had made the voyage from New Orleans in safety, his tobacco had been sold for a fair price to the King's men. In Rodney he had a horse stabled against his return, and he meant to spend the night there at an inn, for the way home through the wilderness was beset with dangers.

As his foot touched shore, the sun sank into the river the color of blood, and at once a wind sprang up and covered the sky with black, yellow, and green clouds the size of whales, which moved across the face of the moon. The river was covered with foam, and against the landing the boats strained in the waves and strained again. River and bluff gave off alike a leaf-green light, and from the water's edge the red torches lining the Landing-under-the-Hill and climbing the bluff to the town stirred and blew to the left and right. There were sounds of rushing and flying, from the flourish of carriages hurrying through the streets after dark, from the bellowing throats of the flat-boatmen, and from the wilderness itself, which lifted and drew itself in the wind, and pressed its savage breath even closer to the little galleries of Rodney, and caused a bell to turn over in one of the steeples, and shook the fort and dropped a tree over the racetrack.

Holding his bag of gold in his hand, Clement made for the first inn he saw under the hill. It was all lighted up and full of the sounds of singing.*

In the first sentence, there is one word in particular that may have signaled to the reader the kind of story that this is *not*. It is the word "innocent." Used to describe Clement Mus-grove's character—and the only description allotted to him— "innocent" has nothing to do with the historical point of view; and it shines like a cautionary blinker to what lies on the road ahead.

* *The Robber Bridegroom,* Copyright 1942 by Eudora Welty.

In *The Robber Bridegroom*, the elements of wilderness and pioneer settlements, flatboats and river trade, the Natchez Trace and all its life, including the Indians and the bandits, are all to come together. The story is laid in an actual place, traces of which still exist, and in historical times—which, all of you need no reminding, have been well recorded. And you historians and scholars would be the first to recognize that this is not a *historical* historical novel.

The Robber Bridegroom does not fit anywhere that I know of into that pattern, which conventionally tends to be grand and to run to length. Nor was fitting into the pattern ever its aim. It *is* a story laid in and around Rodney just before 1798—but you had better now meet all the characters.

Clement Musgrove, on this opening night at the Rodney inn, draws two strangers for bedfellows, which was not uncommon. However, the two strangers *are*. Here speaks one of them:

"I'm an alligator!" yelled the flatboatman, and began to flail his mighty arms through the air. "I'm a he-bull and a he-rattlesnake and a he-alligator all in one! I've beat up so many flatboatmen and thrown them in the river I haven't kept a count since the Flood, and I'm a lover of women like you'll never see again . . . I can outrun, out-hop, out-jump, throw down, drag out, and lick any man in the country! . . . I can pick up a grown man by the neck in each hand and hold him out at arm's length, and often do, too . . . I eat a whole cow at one time, and follow her up with a live sheep if it's Sunday . . . I only laugh at the Indians, and I can carry a dozen oxen on my back at one time, and as for pigs, I tie them in a bunch and hang them to my belt!"

As you have recognized, the innocent planter has for one bedfellow Mike Fink, the legendary folk hero. And for the other? We see a young man: "brawny and six feet tall, dressed up like a New Orleans dandy, with his short coat knotted about

him capewise . . . His heavy yellow locks hung over his forehead and down to his shoulders . . . When he removed his
cloak, there was a little dirk hid in the knot."

And so it's a night of wondering who will succeed in robbing
or murdering whom, but Jamie Lockhart establishes himself
as the hero to the innocent planter by saving his life, and to us
as a bandit at the same time. "We shall surely meet again,"
says Jamie to Clement as they part. It's surer than history!
Knotting the sleeves of his coat about his shoulders, Jamie takes
up a Raven in his fingers, which speaks boding words:

> "Turn back, my bonny,
> Turn away home."

Jamie Lockhart's Raven—though I have let him avail himself of
it from the possession of Mike Fink—has really got here from
the same place Jamie did: the fairy tale. The Robber Bridegroom, the double character of the title, owes his existence on
the one side to history—the history of the Natchez Trace
outlaws—and on the other side to the Brothers Grimm.

It is not only the character of our hero that partakes of the
fairy tale. Mike Fink, in his bragging just now, might have
been speaking the words of Jack the Giant Killer. And here
is the planter Clement Musgrove telling Jamie the story of his
wife Salome:

> "There on the land which the King of Spain granted to
> me," said Clement, "I built a little hut to begin with. But
> when my first tobacco was sold at the market, Salome, my
> new wife, entreated me in the night to build a better
> house, like the nearest settler's, and so I did . . .
> " 'Clement,' Salome would say, 'I want a gig to drive in
> to Rodney.' 'Let us wait another year,' said I. 'Nonsense!'
> So there would be a gig. Next, 'Clement, I want a row of
> silver dishes to stand on the shelf.' 'But my dear wife,
> how can we be sure of the food to go in them?' And the

merchants, you know, have us at their mercy. Nevertheless, my next purchase off the Liverpool ship was not a new wrought-iron plow, but the silver dishes. And it did seem that whatever I asked of the land I planted on, I would be given, when she told me to ask, and there was no limit to its favors."

"How is your fortune now?" asked Jamie, leaning forward on his two elbows.

"Well, before long a little gallery with four posts appeared across the front of my house, and we were sitting there in the evening; and new slaves sent out with axes were felling more trees, and indigo and tobacco were growing nearer and nearer to the river there under the black shadow of the forest. Then in one of the years she made me try cotton, and my fortune was made."

You'll be reminded of a story in Grimm, "The Fisherman and His Wife." The Fisherman, because he kindly returned to the sea a magic Flounder he'd caught, is offered his wish; and his wife sends him to the Flounder again and again to have a new wish granted: from living in a pot, she wants to rise to be owner of a cottage, then owner of a castle, then king, then emperor, then pope, and then the Lord Almighty—at which the Flounder loses his patience.

"Next year," said Salome, and she shaded her eagle eye with her eagle claw, and scanned the lands from east to west, "we must cut down more of the forest, and stretch away the fields until we grow twice as much of everything. Twice as much indigo, twice as much cotton, twice as much tobacco. For the land is there for the taking, and I say, if it can be taken, take it."

"To encompass so much as that is greedy," said Clement. "It would take too much of time and the heart's energy."

"All the same, you must add it on," said Salome. "If we have this much, we can have more."

"Are you not satisfied already?" asked her husband.

"Satisfied!" cried Salome. "Never, until we have got rid of this house which is little better than a Kentuckian's cabin, with its puncheon floor, and can live in a mansion at least five stories high, with an observatory of the river on top of that, with twenty-two Corinthian columns to hold up the roof."

"My poor wife, you are ahead of yourself," said Clement.

(The reason she's ahead of herself, as you will know, is that she's describing Windsor Castle, out from Port Gibson, which did not get built until 1861.)

I think it's become clear that it was by no accident that I made our local history and the legend and the fairy tale into working equivalents in the story I came to write. It was my firm intention to bind them together. And the intention further directed that beyond the innocent planter, the greedy second wife, the adventurous robber, the story needed its beautiful maiden. Of these, as we know, there were plenty in that part of the world: they were known as "the Rodney heiresses." Rosamond is beautiful and young and unwed, with a devoted father and a wicked stepmother, and she is also an heiress. We see her first leaning from her window to sing a lovesick ballad out to the waiting air, "truly a beautiful golden-haired girl, locked in the room by her stepmother for singing, and still singing on." And Rosamond "did not mean to tell anything but the truth, but when she opened her mouth in answer to a question, the lies would simply fall out like diamonds and pearls." So she has every fairy-tale property. Diamonds and pearls normally fall from the lips of fairy-tale maidens because they can speak nothing but what is truthful and pure—otherwise, the result is snakes and toads—but Rosamond is a romantic girl, not a wicked one, and the lies she's given to telling are simply a Rodney girl's daydreams, not intended to do any harm: perfectly good pearls.

In several other ways her fairy-tale character has ironic modifications. Jamie Lockhart and Rosamond meet for the first time when he, now as the robber with his face disguised in berry juice, rides up to her in the woods to rob her of her fine clothes: Clement's present from New Orleans, a wonderful gown with a long train, is what she's wearing out to pick herbs.

When he has the gown—

> Then she stood in front of Jamie in her cotton petticoats, two deep, and he said, "Off with the smocks, girl, and be quick . . . Now off with the rest."
>
> "God help me," said Rosamond, who had sometimes imagined such a thing happening, and knew what to say. "Were you born of woman? For the sake of your poor mother, who may be dead in her grave, like mine, I pray you to leave me with my underbody."

Jamie will do no such thing, and—

> Rosamond, who had imagined such things happening in the world, and what she would do if they did, readily reached up and pulled the pins out of her hair, and down fell the long golden locks, almost to the ground, but not quite, for she was very young yet."

Jamie, as he gathered up the gold hairpins from France, asks politely—

> "Which would you rather? Shall I kill you with my little dirk, to save your name, or will you go home naked?"
>
> "Why, sir, life is sweet," said Rosamond, looking straight at him through the two curtains of her hair, "and before I would die on the point of your sword, I would go home naked any day."

The fairy-tale daughter, as we see, is also the child of her times, a straightforward little pioneer herself.

Jamie has to come a second time in order to steal Rosamond herself. He sweeps her up as she carries in the milk from the barn and gallops away with her on his horse. "So smoothly did they travel that not a single drop was spilled." As I read somewhere in the history books, "It was the habit of the day for heiresses to disappear."

And so the circle is joined: Jamie Lockhart the New Orleans dandy is besought by Clement Musgrove to find his lost daughter Rosamond, and Jamie Lockhart the bandit is already her enamored kidnapper. And neither lover knows who the other is.

The title of the novel is the title of the fairy tale; and it may be appropriate at this point to recall the original story of the Robber Bridegroom to mind.

In Grimm, a maiden becomes engaged to a man, and preceding her wedding day goes to his house to surprise him with a visit. There, no one seems to be at home. Only a bird speaks to her. This bird says—he's more explicit than my Raven—"Turn back, turn back, young maiden dear, 'Tis a murderer's house you enter here." On she goes. An old old woman kept prisoner deep in the lower part of the house gives the maiden the further news that her bridegroom and his gang are cannibals and make a habit of eating young girls like her. The bride-to-be hides behind a cask to await the robbers' return, and just as my Rosamond at length will do, she sees, in place of herself, another young girl dragged in to be their victim. Grimm relates: "They gave her wine to drink, three glasses full, one glass of white wine, one glass of red, and a glass of yellow, and with this her heart burst in twain." (Rosamond is given only her stepmother's poisonous insinuations.) Thereupon the robbers "cut her beautiful body in pieces and strewed salt thereon." The little finger flies out and falls into the maiden's bosom. And so with Rosamond. Only, in my story it is not Jamie's own self whom Rosamond sees perform this act of monstrosity—it's his terrible, and real-life, counterpart, the Little Harpe—who might have done it.

Nothing has stopped the maiden yet, in the very sinister tale of Grimm's, and after this revelation she goes right ahead with the wedding. And then afterward, at the feast, she has her turn: she tells the bridegroom the whole story of her visit to the house and what she saw, saying disingenuously at every stage, "My darling, I only dreamt this," until she reaches the part about the finger. "It fell in my bosom," she says, "—and here it is!" She holds it up for all present to see, and the wedding guests hold the bridegroom fast and "deliver him over to justice."

Whereas all that Rosamond is frightened into doing, after what she sees in the robbers' house, is making a direct investigation on her own. After she and Jamie are in bed and he falls asleep, she washes off those berry stains.

Jamie's berry stains, the disguise in which he carries on his work, in which he kidnaps Rosamond, and in which he has continued to keep his identity secret from her after she joins him in the robbers' house (he never lets her see his face unwashed) are conventional in Mississippi history (the bandit Mason blacked his face as a disguise) and still more widely in song and story. Bandits, adventurers, lovers and gods have the disguise in common. But girls always fall for taking it off. Psyche, in the fable, held a candle over Cupid's sleeping face— a god who only came in the dark—then let a drop of hot wax fall, and up he jumped, away he flew. Rosamond tries a mixture—her witch of a stepmother gives her the recipe, which concludes with a recipe's magic words, "It can't fail"—and she makes her version of the classic mistake.

In my novel, Jamie rises out of his bed, waked up by having his face washed.

"Goodbye," he said. "For you did not trust me, and did not love me, for you wanted only to know who I am. Now I cannot stay in the house with you."

And going straight to the window, he climbed out through it and in another moment was gone.

Then Rosamond tried to follow and climbed out after him, but she fell in the dust.

At the same moment, she felt the stirring within her that sent her a fresh piece of news.

And finally a cloud went over the moon, and all was dark night.

Actually, the fairy tale exceeds my story in horror. But even so, it isn't so much worse than what really went on during those frontier times, is it? History tells us worse things than fairy tales do. People were scalped. Babies had their brains dashed out against tree trunks or were thrown into boiling oil when the Indians made their captures. Slavery was the order on the plantations. The Natchez Trace outlaws eviscerated their victims and rolled their bodies downhill, filled with stones, into the Mississippi River. War, bloodshed, massacre were all part of the times. In my story, I transposed these horrors—along with the felicities that also prevailed—into the element I thought suited both just as well, or better—the fairy tale. The line between history and fairy tale is not always clear, as *The Robber Bridegroom* along the way points out. And it was not from the two elements taken alone but from their interplay that my story, as I hope, takes on its own head-long life.

In the strivings and carryings-on of the day, there was also, you must agree, an element of comedy. Every period has its parodists and clowns. In *The Robber Bridegroom*, Goat and his mother and flock of sisters are the clowns—folk clowns. They go scrambling about at the heels of the purposeful, and live by making sly bargains and asking "What's in it for me?" —cashing in on other people's troubles. (You could almost accuse me of unearthing some of the collateral forerunners of the family Snopes.)

Goat, who has through mutual attraction become the

familiar of Rosamond's wicked stepmother, is out to do her
bidding one day when he comes upon a certain robber sitting
out in front of his cave, and salutes him. This robber—

> blinked his eyes and smiled, for nothing pleased him on a
> fine day like a lack of brains. "Come here," he said, "I will
> give you work to do."
>
> "Gladly," replied Goat, "but I am already working for
> another, a very rich lady who wants me to see that her
> step-daughter is well kidnapped by a bandit. But I don't
> see why a young fellow like me could not take care of
> two commissions at once."
>
> "That is the way to talk," said the Little Harpe. "You
> will come up in the world."

For of course, you will have had in mind the real-life bandits
of the day, and here is the sample. The historical Little Harpe
is hiding out correctly here, very close to Rodney. He is in
possession—again correctly—of the head of his brother, the
Big Harpe, which he keeps in a trunk. He can always turn it
in and claim the reward on it—it's like money in the savings
bank.

The Little Harpe is in the novel right along with Jamie
Lockhart; a side story develops in clownish parallel to Jamie
and Rosamond's story: a ludicrous affair of hapless kidnapping
and mistaken identity between the Little Harpe and Goat's
oldest sister with a sack over her head.

For while Jamie Lockhart leads a double life by hero's necessity, clearly this isn't the only aspect of duality in the novel.
Crucial, or comical, scenes of mistaken identity take place
more or less regularly as the story unwinds. There's a doubleness in respect to identity that runs in a strong thread through
all the wild happenings—indeed, this thread is their connection, and everything that happens hangs upon it. I spun that
thread out of the times. Life was so full, so excessively charged
with energy in those days, when nothing seemed impossible

in the Natchez country, that leading one life hardly provided scope enough for it all. In the doubleness there was narrative truth that I felt the times themselves had justified.

Of the story's climax, it's sufficient to say that all the elements are caught up in one whirl together, in which identities and disguises and counter-disguises, stratagems and plans and deceits and betrayals and gestures heroic and desperate all at one time come into play.

I think I've proved my claim that mine was not a *historical* historical novel. *The Robber Bridegroom*, from the start, took another direction: instead of burying itself deep in historical fact, it flew up, like a cuckoo, and alighted in the borrowed nest of fantasy.

Fantasy, like any other form of fiction, must have its validity. Fantasy is no good unless the seed it springs from is a truth, a truth about human beings. The validity of my novel has to lie in the human motivations apparent alike in the history of a time and in the timeless fairy tale. In whatever form these emerge, they speak out of the same aspirations—to love, to conquer, to outwit and overcome the enemy, to reach the goal in view. And, in the end, to find out what we all wish to find out, exactly who we are and who the other fellow is, and what we are doing here all together.

Subservient to the needs of the fantasy, the characters may take on an exaggerated size. But to whatever scale they are drawn, they are each and every one human beings at the core. Even Little Harpe. When Jamie puts an end to him after a terrible battle that lasts all night, "the Little Harpe, with a wound in his heart, heaved a deep sigh and a tear came out of his eye, for he hated to give up his life as badly as the harmless deer in the wood."

In correct historical detail, the end of the Little Harpe was having his own head stuck on a pole. My reading tells me that the heads of Little Harpe and one of his partners, brought in for reward, were mounted on poles at the north and south

ends of the town of Old Greenville where the Natchez Trace
went by—I can't recall if it's certain who was responsible.
Naturally, in *The Robber Bridegroom*, the Robber Bridegroom himself alone is responsible. It's necessary that Jamie
Lockhart kill his evil counterpart, the Little Harpe, for the
sake of Jamie Lockhart's future and that of his love, Rosamond;
for as the novel ends—and this is the only ending possible—
the hero is to be a robber no longer.

But of course, the Robber Bridegroom's pursuit of a double
life was (like his subsequent renouncement of it) by hero's
necessity. On the one occasion when Rosamond manages to
leave the robbers' house for a visit home, Clement, her father,
says to her:

"If being a bandit were his breadth and scope, I should
find him and kill him for sure. But since in addition he
loves my daughter, he must be not one man but two, and I
should be afraid of killing the second. For all things are
double, and this should keep us from taking liberties with
the outside world, and acting too quickly to finish things
off . . . And perhaps after the riding and robbing and burning and assault is over with this man you love, he will step
out of it all like a beastly skin, and surprise you with his
gentleness. For this reason, I will wait and see; but it
breaks my heart not to have seen with my own eyes what
door you are walking into and what your life has turned
out to be."

Clement, for his good prophecy, gets his wish. Several years
later (enough for the steamboat to have been invented), on
a trip to the New Orleans market, he goes walking about,
and this is the way the novel ends:

New Orleans was the most marvelous city in the Spanish
country or anywhere else on the river. Beauty and vice
and every delight possible to the soul and body stood hos-
pitably, and usually together, in every doorway and be-

neath every palmetto by day and lighted torch by night. A shutter opened, and a flower bloomed. The very atmosphere was nothing but aerial spice, the very walls were sugar cane, the very clouds hung as golden as bananas in the sky. But Clement Musgrove was a man who could have walked the streets of Bagdad without sending a second glance overhead at the Magic Carpet, or heard the tambourines of the angels in Paradise without dancing a step, or had his choice of the fruits of the Garden of Eden without making up his mind. For he was an innocent of the wilderness, and a planter of Rodney's Landing, and this was his good.

So, holding a bag of money in his hand, he went to the docks to depart . . . And as he was putting his foot on the gangplank, he felt a touch at his sleeve, and there stood his daughter Rosamond, more beautiful than ever, and dressed in a beautiful, rich, white gown.

Then how they embraced, for they had thought each other dead and gone.

"Father!" she said. "Look, this wonderful place is my home now, and I am happy again!"

And before the boat could leave, she told him that Jamie Lockhart was now no longer a bandit but a gentleman of the world in New Orleans, respected by all that knew him, a rich merchant in fact. All his wild ways had been shed like a skin, and he could not be kinder to her than he was. They were the parents of beautiful twins, one of whom was named Clementine, and they lived in a beautiful house of marble and cypress wood on the shores of Lake Pontchartrain, with a hundred slaves, and often went boating with other merchants and their wives, the ladies reclining under a blue silk canopy; and they sailed sometimes out on the ocean to look at the pirates' galleons. They had all they wanted in the world, and now that she had found her father still alive, everything was well. Of course, she said at the end, she did sometimes miss the house in the wood, and even the rough-and-tumble of their old life when he used to scorn her for her curiosity. But the city was splendid, she said; it was the place to live.

"Is all this true, Rosamond, or is it a lie?" said Clement.

"It is the truth," she said, and they held the boat while she took him to see for himself, and it was all true but the blue canopy.

Then the yellow-haired Jamie ran and took him by the hand, and for the first time thanked him for his daughter. And as for him, the outward transfer from bandit to merchant had been almost too easy to count it a change at all, and he was enjoying all the same success he had ever had. But now, in his heart Jamie knew that he was a hero and had always been one, only with the power to look both ways and to see a thing from all sides.

Then Rosamond prepared her father a little box lunch with her own hands. She asked him to come and stay with them, but he would not.

"Goodbye," they told each other. "God bless you."

So I present them all—the characters of *The Robber Bridegroom*—to you historians in order that you may claim them. They're fanciful, overcharged with high spirits, perhaps, and running out of bounds when advisable or necessary, some of them demented—but they are legitimate. For they're children of their time, and fathered, rather proudly, by its spirit. If I carried out well enough my strongest intentions, fantasy does not take precedence over that spirit, but serves the better to show it forth. It partakes, in a direct way possible to fantasy alone, of the mood and tempo and drive of those challenging times, in the wild and romantic beauty of that place.

Some of the novel's reviewers called it a dream. I think it more accurate to call it an awakening to a dear native land and its own story of early life, made and offered by a novelist's imagination in exuberance and joy.

(1975)

A Pageant of Birds

One summer evening on a street in my town I saw two Negro
women walking along carrying big colored paper wings in
their hands and talking and laughing. They proceeded un-
questioned, the way angels did in their day, possibly, although
anywhere else but on such a street the angels might have been
looked back at if they had taken their wings off and carried
them along over their arms. I followed them to see where they
were going, and, sure enough, it was to church.

They walked in at the Farish Street Baptist Church. It stands
on a corner in the Negro business section, across the street from
the Methodist Church, in a block with the clothing stores, the
pool hall, the Booker-T movie house, the doctor's office, the
pawnshop with gold in the windows, the café with the fish-sign
that says "If They Don't Bite We Catch 'em Anyhow," and the
barbershop with the Cuban hair styles hand-drawn on the
window. It is a solid, brick-veneered church, and has no holler-
ing or chanting in the unknown tongue. I looked in at the
door to see what might be going on.

The big frame room was empty of people but ready for
something. The lights were shining. The ceiling was painted
the color of heaven, bright blue, and with this to start on,
decorators had gone ahead to make the place into a scene that

could only be prepared to receive birds. Pinned all around the walls were drawings of birds—bluebirds, redbirds, quail, flamingos, wrens, lovebirds—some copied from pictures, and the redbird a familiar cover taken from a school tablet. There was greenery everywhere. Sprigs of snow-on-the-mountain—a bush which grows to the point of complete domination in gardens of the neighborhood this time of year—were tied in neat bunches, with single zinnias stuck in, at regular intervals around the room, on the pews and along the altar rail. Over in the corner the piano appeared to be a large mound of vines, with the keyboard bared rather startlingly, like a row of teeth from ambush. On the platform where the pulpit had been was a big easy chair, draped with a red and blue robe embroidered in fleur-de-lys. Above it, two American flags were crossed over a drawing of an eagle copied straight off the back of a dollar bill.

As soon as people began coming into the church, out walked Maude Thompson from the rear, bustling and starched in the obvious role of church leader. She came straight to welcome me. Yes indeed, she said, there was to be a Pageant of Birds at seven o'clock sharp. I was welcome and all my friends. As she talked on, I was pleased to learn that she had written the Pageant herself and had not got it from some Northern YWCA or missionary society, as might be feared. "I said to myself, 'There have been pageants about everything else—why not about birds?' " she said. She told me proudly that each costume had been made by the bird who would wear it.

I brought a friend, and presently we were seated—unavoidably, because we were white—in the front row, with our feet turned sidewise by a large can of zinnias, but in the first of the excitement we were forgotten, and all proceeded as if we weren't there.

Maude Thompson made an announcement to the audience that everybody had better be patient. "Friends, the reason we are late starting is that several of the birds have to work late and haven't arrived yet. If there are any birds in the audience now, will they *kindly get on back here?*" Necks craned and eyes popped in delight when one girl in a dark-blue tissue-paper dress jumped up from a back pew and skittered out. Maude Thompson clapped her hands for order and told how a collection to be taken up would be used to pay for a piano— "not a new one, but a better one." Her hand was raised solemnly: we were promised, if we were quiet and nice, the sight of even more birds than we saw represented on the walls. The audience fanned, patted feet dreamily, and waited.

The Pageant, decidedly worth waiting for, began with a sudden complete silence in the audience, as if by mass intuition. Every head turned at the same time and all eyes fastened upon the front door of the church.

Then came the entrance of the Eagle Bird. Her wings and tail were of gold and silver tin foil, and her dress was a black and purple kimono. She began a slow pace down the aisle with that truly majestic dignity which only a vast, firmly matured physique, wholly unselfconscious, can achieve. Her hypnotic majesty was almost prostrating to the audience as she moved, as slowly as possible, down the aisle and finally turned and stood beneath the eagle's picture on the wall, in the exact center of the platform. A little Eaglet boy, with propriety her son, about two and a half feet tall, very black, entered from the Sunday School room and trotted around her with a sprightly tail over his knickers, flipping his hands dutifully from the wrist out. He wore bows on each shoulder. No smiles were exchanged—there was not a smile in the house. The Eagle then seated herself with a stifled groan in her chair, there was a strangled chord from the piano, where a Bird now sat, and with the little Eaglet to keep time by waving a flag jutting out from each wing, the congregation rose and sang "The Star-Spangled Banner."

Then the procession of lesser Birds began, and the music—as the pianist watched in a broken piece of mirror hidden in the vines—went gradually into syncopation.

The Birds would enter from the front door of the church,

portentously, like members of a bridal party, proceed in absolute and easily distinguishable character down the aisle, cross over, and take their places in a growing circle around the audience. All came in with an assurance that sprang from complete absorption in their roles—erect in their bright wings and tails and crests, flapping their elbows, dipping their knees, hopping and turning and preening to the music. It was like a dance only inasmuch as birds might dance under the circumstances. They would, on reaching the platform, bow low, first to the Eagle Bird, who gave them back a stern look, and then to the audience, and take their positions—never ceasing to fly in place and twitter now and then, never showing recognition or saying one human word to anyone, even each other. There were many more Birds of some varieties than of others; I understood that "you could be what you want to." Maude Thompson, standing in a white uniform beside the piano, made a little evocation of each variety, checking down a list.

"The next group of Birds to fly will be the Bluebirds," she said, and in they flew, three big ones and one little one, in clashing shades of blue crepe paper. They were all very pleased and serious with their movements. The oldest wore shell-rimmed glasses. There were Redbirds, four of them; two Robin Redbreasts with diamond-shaped gold speckles on their breasts; five "Pink-birds"; two Peacocks who simultaneously spread their tails at a point halfway down the aisle; Goldfinches with black tips on their tails, who waltzed slowly and somehow appropriately; Canary birds, announced as "the beautiful Canaries, for pleasure as well as profit," who whistled vivaciously as they twirled, and a small Canary who had a yellow ostrich plume for a crest. There was only one "beautiful Blackbird, alone but not lonesome," with red caps on her wings; there was a head-wagging Purple Finch, who wore gold earrings. There was the Parrot-bird, who was a man and caused shouts— everyone's instant favorite; he had a yellow breast, one green trouser-leg, one red; he was in his shirt sleeves because it was hot, and he had red, green, blue and yellow wings. The lady

Parrot (his wife) followed after in immutable seriousness—she had noticed parrots well, and she never got out of caracter: she ruffled her shoulder feathers, she was cross, she pecked at her wings, she moved her head rapidly from side to side and made obscure sounds, not quite words; she was so good she almost called up a parrot. There was loud appreciation of the Parrots—I thought they would have to go back and come in again. The "Red-headed Peckerwood" was a little boy alone. The "poor little Mourning Dove" was called but proved absent. "And last but not least, the white Dove of Peace!" cried Maude Thompson. There came two Doves, very sanctimonious indeed, with long sleeves, nurse's shoes and white cotton gloves. They flew with restraint, almost sadly.

When they had all come inside out of the night, the Birds filled a complete circle around the congregation. They performed a finale. They sang, lifting up their wings and swaying from side to side to the mounting music, bending and rolling their hips, all singing. And yet in their own and in everybody's eyes they were still birds. They were certainly birds to me.

> "And I want TWO wings
> To veil my face
> And I want TWO wings
> To fly away,
> And I want TWO wings
> To veil my face,
> And the world can't do me no harm."

That was their song, and they circled the church with it, singing and clapping with their wings, and flew away by the back door, where the ragamuffins of the alley cried "Oooh!" and jumped aside to let them pass.

I wanted them to have a picture of the group to keep and offered to take it. Maude Thompson said, "Several of the Birds could meet you in front of the church door tomorrow afternoon at four."

There turned out to be a number of rendezvous; but not all the Birds showed up, and I almost failed to get the Eagle, who has some very confining job. The Birds who could make it were finally photographed, however, Maude Thompson supervising the poses. I did not dare interfere. She instructed them to hold up their necks, and reproached the Dove of Peace for smiling. "You ever see a bird smile?"

Since our first meeting I have chanced on Maude Thompson several times. Every time I would be getting on a train, I would see her in the station; she would be putting on a coffin, usually, or receiving one, in a church capacity. She would always tell me how the Pageant was doing. They were on the point of taking it to Forrest or Mount Olive or some other town. Also, the Birds have now made themselves faces and beaks.

"This is going to be one of those things going to grow," said Maude Thompson.

(1943)

The Flavor of Jackson

❧

Most Jacksonians would agree, I think, that Jackson has always characteristically dined at home and entertained at home, and does so still by first preference. It's been our natural form of hospitality as of course it's been the most logical and economical way to live.

There was indeed, and for many years, the elegant dining room of the Edwards House ready for the important or large occasion. But we were too small a place and too far inland from the Gulf or New Orleans to have been heir to restaurants of another kind: one Mexican at his hot-tamale stand, on the corner of North West and Hamilton during the cold months, couldn't make us cosmopolitan. Rather than anything else, I think—and I like to think—the word for the Jackson flavor is "home."

It was mostly the young who went forth with any regularity for outside refreshment. After the movies, the ice cream parlor. After *The Thief of Bagdad* at the Majestic, the other dime went for the strawberry ice cream soda at McIntyre's. And wasn't it Mr. Key's Drug Store that seemed a functional part of the Century Theatre? It had purple paper grapes on

Introduction to *The Jackson Cookbook*.

a cardboard trellis overhead—almost like a part of the stage scenery to come. Just before curtain time my father took me in there and presented me with the box of Jordan Almonds—"bird eggs"—that was part of the theatre rite. Some tired road company would go through its Victor Herbert for us, but it was magic, all the same, and holding a "bird egg" in the mouth (impossible to swallow, in the excitement) was part of the magic.

When the whole family sallied forth for refreshment, it was very likely after supper on hot nights just before bedtime. They'd get in the car and drive to Seale Lily's and have ice cream cones all around; it was best to hold them outside the car and eat them through the windows, and finish fast before the last bit melted.

But parties were given at home, and they started—I believe it was true for old and young—plenty early in the afternoon. You began eating about three-thirty and kept it up until you had entirely spoiled your supper. Party food drew its praises for how pretty it was (example, Bridemaids' Salad, all white down to the white grapes) or for how much trouble the hostess went to to make it (Pressed Chicken), but it's a safe bet that all the refreshments were the successes they were because they were rich—thunderously rich.

Sometimes we branched out from home as far as Shadow Lawn. When parties were given there it wasn't in order to save the trouble at home but to offer the guests a change—an alfresco entertainment in the quiet country air of the Terry Road. Some of our high school graduation "teas" took place at Shadow Lawn. The receiving line stood there on Miss Anita Perkins's lawn, in the very early shadows, and the punch bowl waited on her porch, and there were her own delicious things to eat—frozen fruit salad was her specialty—and all was elegant. It was the era of the Madeira tea napkin. I believe I could say that more tea napkins were handed round at that high-minded time than I ever saw in my life, before or since. (And at least half of them have been monogrammed by Miss

Irene Anderson. She, too, was very much a part of the flavor
of Jackson.)

As a child I heard it said that two well-traveled bachelors of
the town, Mr. Erskine Helm and Mr. Charles Pierce, who lived
on Amite Street, had "brought mayonnaise to Jackson." Well
they might have, though not in the literal way I pictured the
event. Mayonnaise had a *mystique*. Little girls were initiated
into it by being allowed to stand at the kitchen table and help
make it, for making mayonnaise takes three hands. While the
main two hands keep up the uninterrupted beat in the bowl, the
smaller hand is allowed to slowly add the olive oil, drop-by-
counted-drop. The solemn fact was that sometimes mayonnaise
didn't make. Only the sudden dash of the red pepper onto the
brimming, smooth-as-cream bowlful told you it was finished
and a triumph.

For sure, you couldn't *buy* mayonnaise, and if you could,
you wouldn't. For the generation bringing my generation up,
everything made in the kitchen started from scratch, too. There
was a barrel of flour standing in the kitchen! Perhaps a sugar
barrel too. The household may have provided (ours did) its
own good butter (which implies a churn and, of course, a cow)
and its own eggs, and most likely it grew its own tomatoes,
beans, strawberries, even asparagus. Why, your mother called
up the butcher, talked to him, asked what was especially nice
today, and let him send it. There was communication with
butchers. And my father sometimes *saw* them, for he'd stop by
on his way from the office and come bringing home by hand
the little squared-off, roofed-over white-cardboard bucket with
the wire handles, fragrant and leaking a little—and produced
oysters for supper, just ladled out of the oyster barrel that the
butcher got in from New Orleans.

And they grated from whole nutmegs, they ground coffee
from the beans, went to work on whole coconuts with the
hatchet. Some people knew how to inveigle for the real vanilla
bean. (Vanilla must have had a central importance in those
days—think of all the cakes. Wasn't there a local lady who

made her living, and her entertainment, just selling vanilla extract over the telephone?)

Our mothers were sans mixes, sans foil, sans freezer, sans blender, sans monosodium glutamate, but their ingredients were as fresh as the day; and they knew how to make bread.

Jackson believed in and knew how to achieve the home flavor. And if ever there were a solid symbol of that spirit, one that radiates its pride and joy, it is the hand-cranked ice cream freezer. I see it established in a shady spot on a back porch, in the stage of having been turned till it won't go around another time; its cylinder is full of its frozen custard that's bright with peaches, or figs, or strawberries, its dasher lifted out and the plug in tight, the whole packed with ice and salt and covered with a sack to wait for dinner—and right now, who bids to lick the dasher?

I daresay any fine recipe used in Jackson could be attributed to a local lady, or her mother—Mrs. Cabell's Pecans, Mrs. Wright's Cocoons, Mrs. Lyell's Lemon Dessert. Recipes, in the first place, had to be imparted—there was something oracular in the transaction—and however often they were made after that by others, they kept their right names. I make Mrs. Mosal's White Fruitcake every Christmas, having got it from my mother, who got it from Mrs. Mosal, and I often think to make a friend's fine recipe is to celebrate her once more, and in that cheeriest, most aromatic of places to celebrate in, the home kitchen.

Jackson had its full plenty of recipes, but I hardly remember a cookbook. My mother had the only one I ever saw as a child, *The White House Cookbook*. I don't recall which President's wife was in headquarters at the time of our edition, but the book opened to a full-length drawing of a deer, complete with antlers, marked off with dotted lines to show how to cut it up for venison, which suggests poor Mrs. Teddy Roosevelt. The most useful thing about *The White House Cookbook* was its roomy size, for in between its pages could be stored the recipes, jotted down on scraps of paper and old envelopes, that my mother really used. They accumulated themselves over the years from friends and relations and from her own invention and a time or two from the Mystery Chef who came in over the radio. She had a cookbook within a cookbook. She had some of the making, in fact, of the very sort of cookbook that this one now is certain to be. Today there's a cookbook available for every conceivable purpose and occasion, but in this one we come full circle: we're back again to the local. Using these cherished recipes we can make and delight in the fruits of Jackson itself.

I'd like to express the pious hope that we're to find these recipes given in full. My mother's don't do me as much good as they might because she never included directions. Her reasoning, often expressed, was that any cook worth her salt would know, given a list of ingredients, what to do with them, and if she did come to a momentary loss while stirring up a dish—*taste* it! Cooking was a matter of born sense, ordinary good judgment, enough experience, materials worth the bothering about, and tasting. I had to sit on a stool while she made spoonbread and take down what I saw like a reporter, to get her recipe.

I can't resist adding this, for I think it applies. John Woodburn was a New York editor who'd come through Jackson on a scouting trip for young unknown writers and spent a night at our house. He carried my first collection of stories back with him and worked very hard trying to persuade his publisher to take them. Several years later, when he succeeded, he sent me a telegram to say, "I knew as soon as I tasted your mother's waffles it would turn out all right."

(1971)

The Little Store

❧

Two blocks away from the Mississippi State Capitol, and on the same street with it, where our house was when I was a child growing up in Jackson, it was possible to have a little pasture behind your backyard where you could keep a Jersey cow, which we did. My mother herself milked her. A thrifty homemaker, wife, mother of three, she also did all her own cooking. And as far as I can recall, she never set foot inside a grocery store. It wasn't necessary.

For her regular needs, she stood at the telephone in our front hall and consulted with Mr. Lemly, of Lemly's Market and Grocery downtown, who took her order and sent it out on his next delivery. And since Jackson at the heart of it was still within very near reach of the open country, the blackberry lady clanged on her bucket with a quart measure at your front door in June without fail, the watermelon man rolled up to your house exactly on time for the Fourth of July, and down through the summer, the quiet of the early-morning streets was pierced by the calls of farmers driving in with their plenty. One brought his with a song, so plaintive we would sing it with him:

"Milk, milk,
Buttermilk,

Snap beans—butterbeans—
Tender okra—fresh greens . . .
And buttermilk."

My mother considered herself pretty well prepared in her kitchen and pantry for any emergency that, in her words, might choose to present itself. But if she should, all of a sudden, need another lemon or find she was out of bread, all she had to do was call out, "Quick! Who'd like to run to the Little Store for me?"

I would.

She'd count out the change into my hand, and I was away. I'll bet the nickel that would be left over that all over the country, for those of my day, the neighborhood grocery played a similar part in our growing up.

Our store had its name—it was that of the grocer who owned it, whom I'll call Mr. Sessions—but "the Little Store" is what we called it at home. It was a block down our street toward the capitol and half a block further, around the corner, toward the cemetery. I knew even the sidewalk to it as well as I knew my own skin. I'd skipped my jumping-rope up and down it, hopped its length through mazes of hopscotch, played jacks in its islands of shade, serpentined along it on my Princess bicycle, skated it backward and forward. In the twilight I had dragged my steamboat by its string (this was homemade out of every new shoebox, with candle in the bottom lighted and shining through colored tissue paper pasted over windows scissored out in the shapes of the sun, moon and stars) across every crack of the walk without letting it bump or catch fire. I'd "played out" on that street after supper with my brothers and friends as long as "first-dark" lasted; I'd caught its lightning bugs. On the first Armistice Day (and this will set the time I'm speaking of) we made our own parade down that walk on a single velocipede—my brother pedaling, our little brother riding the handlebars, and myself standing on the back, all with arms wide, flying flags in each hand. (My father snapped that picture as we raced by. It came out blurred.)

As I set forth for the Little Store, a tune would float toward me from the house where there lived three sisters, girls in their teens, who ratted their hair over their ears, wore headbands like gladiators, and were considered to be very popular. They practiced for this in the daytime; they'd wind up the Victrola, leave the same record on they'd played before, and you'd see them bobbing past their dining-room windows while they danced with each other. Being three, they could go all day, cutting in:

> "Everybody ought to know-oh
> How to do the Tickle-Toe
>   (how to do the Tickle-Toe)"—

they sang it and danced to it, and as I went by to the same song, I believed it.

A little further on, across the street, was the house where the principal of our grade school lived—lived on, even while we were having vacation. What if she would come out? She would halt me in my tracks—she had a very carrying and well-known voice in Jackson, where she'd taught almost everybody—saying, "Eudora Alice Welty, spell OBLIGE." OBLIGE was the word that she of course knew had kept me from making 100 on my spelling exam. She'd make me miss it again now, by boring her eyes through me from across the street. This was my vacation fantasy, one good way to scare myself on the way to the store.

Down near the corner waited the house of a little boy named Lindsey. The sidewalk here was old brick, which the roots of a giant chinaberry tree had humped up and tilted this way and that. On skates, you took it fast, in a series of skittering hops, trying not to touch ground anywhere. If the chinaberries had fallen and rolled in the cracks, it was like skating through a whole shooting match of marbles. I crossed my fingers that Lindsey wouldn't be looking.

During the big flu epidemic he and I, as it happened, were

being nursed through our sieges at the same time. I'd hear my
father and mother murmuring to each other, at the end of a
long day, "And I wonder how poor little *Lindsey* got along
today?" Just as, down the street, he no doubt would have to
hear his family saying, "And I wonder how is poor *Eudora* by
now?" I got the idea that a choice was going to be made soon
between poor little Lindsey and poor Eudora, and I came up
with a funny poem. I wasn't prepared for it when my father
told me it wasn't funny and my mother cried that if I couldn't
be ashamed for myself, she'd have to be ashamed for me:

> There was a little boy and his name was Lindsey.
> He went to heaven with the influinzy.

He didn't, he survived it, poem and all, the same as I did. But
his chinaberries could have brought me down in my skates in
a flying act of contrition before his eyes, looking pretty funny
myself, right in front of his house.

Setting out in this world, a child feels so indelible. He only
comes to find out later that it's all the others along his way who
are making themselves indelible to him.

Our Little Store rose right up from the sidewalk; standing in
a street of family houses, it alone hadn't any yard in front, any
tree or flowerbed. It was a plain frame building covered over
with brick. Above the door, a little railed porch ran across on
an upstairs level and four windows with shades were looking
out. But I didn't catch on to those.

Running in out of the sun, you met what seemed total ob-
scurity inside. There were almost tangible smells—licorice
recently sucked in a child's cheek, dill-pickle brine that had
leaked through a paper sack in a fresh trail across the wooden
floor, ammonia-loaded ice that had been hoisted from wet
croker sacks and slammed into the icebox with its sweet butter
at the door, and perhaps the smell of still-untrapped mice.

Then through the motes of cracker dust, cornmeal dust, the

Gold Dust of the Gold Dust Twins that the floor had been swept out with, the realities emerged. Shelves climbed to high reach all the way around, set out with not too much of any one thing but a lot of things—lard, molasses, vinegar, starch, matches, kerosene, Octagon soap (about a year's worth of octagon-shaped coupons cut out and saved brought a signet ring addressed to you in the mail. Furthermore, when the postman arrived at your door, he blew a whistle). It was up to you to remember what you came for, while your eye traveled from cans of sardines to ice cream salt to harmonicas to flypaper (over your head, batting around on a thread beneath the blades of the ceiling fan, stuck with its testimonial catch).

Its confusion may have been in the eye of its beholder. Enchantment is cast upon you by all those things you weren't supposed to have need for, it lures you close to wooden tops you'd outgrown, boy's marbles and agates in little net pouches, small rubber balls that wouldn't bounce straight, frazzly kitestring, clay bubble-pipes that would snap off in your teeth, the stiffest scissors. You could contemplate those long narrow boxes of sparklers gathering dust while you waited for it to be the Fourth of July or Christmas, and noisemakers in the shape of tin frogs for somebody's birthday party you hadn't been invited to yet, and see that they were all marvelous.

You might not have even looked for Mr. Sessions when he came around his store cheese (as big as a doll's house) and in front of the counter looking for you. When you'd finally asked him for, and received from him in its paper bag, whatever single thing it was that you had been sent for, the nickel that was left over was yours to spend.

Down at a child's eye level, inside those glass jars with mouths in their sides through which the grocer could run his scoop or a child's hand might be invited to reach for a choice, were wineballs, all-day suckers, gumdrops, peppermints. Making a row under the glass of a counter were the Tootsie Rolls, Hershey Bars, Goo-Goo Clusters, Baby Ruths. And whatever was the name of those pastilles that came stacked in a cardboard cylinder with a cardboard lid? They were thin and dry, about the size of tiddlywinks, and in the shape of twisted rosettes. A kind of chocolate dust came out with them when you shook them out in your hand. Were they chocolate? I'd say rather they were brown. They didn't taste of anything at all, unless it was wood. Their attraction was the number you got for a nickel.

Making up your mind, you circled the store around and around, around the pickle barrel, around the tower of Cracker Jack boxes; Mr. Sessions had built it for us himself on top of a packing case, like a house of cards.

If it seemed too hot for Cracker Jacks, I might get a cold drink. Mr. Sessions might have already stationed himself by the cold-drinks barrel, like a mind reader. Deep in ice water that looked black as ink, murky shapes that would come up as Coca-Colas, Orange Crushes, and various flavors of pop, were all swimming around together. When you gave the word, Mr. Sessions plunged his bare arm in to the elbow and fished out your choice, first try. I favored a locally bottled concoction called Lake's Celery. (What else could it be called? It was made by a Mr. Lake out of celery. It was a popular drink here for years but was not known universally, as I found out when I arrived in New York and ordered one in the Astor bar.) You drank on the premises, with feet set wide apart to miss the drip, and gave him back his bottle.

But he didn't hurry you off. A standing scales was by the door, with a stack of iron weights and a brass slide on the balance arm, that would weigh you up to three hundred pounds. Mr. Sessions, whose hands were gentle and smelled of carbolic, would lift you up and set your feet on the platform, hold your loaf of bread for you, and taking his time while you stood still for him, he would make certain of what you weighed today. He could even remember what you weighed the last time, so you could subtract and announce how much you'd gained. That was goodbye.

Is there always a hard way to go home? From the Little

Store, you could go partway through the sewer. If your brothers had called you a scarecat, then across the next street beyond the Little Store, it was possible to enter this sewer by passing through a privet hedge, climbing down into the bed of a creek, and going into its mouth on your knees. The sewer—it might have been no more than a "storm sewer"—came out and emptied here, where Town Creek, a sandy, most often shallow little stream that ambled through Jackson on its way to the Pearl River, ran along the edge of the cemetery. You could go in darkness through this tunnel to where you next saw light (if you ever did) and climb out through the culvert at your own street corner.

I was a scarecat, all right, but I was a reader with my own refuge in storybooks. Making my way under the sidewalk, under the street and the streetcar track, under the Little Store, down there in the wet dark by myself, I could be Persephone entering into my six-month sojourn underground—though I didn't suppose Persephone had to crawl, hanging onto a loaf of bread, and come out through the teeth of an iron grating. Mother Ceres would indeed be wondering where she could find me, and mad when she knew. "Now am I going to have to start marching to the Little Store for *myself*?"

I couldn't picture it. Indeed, I'm unable today to picture the Little Store with a grown person in it, except for Mr. Sessions and the lady who helped him, who belonged there. We children thought it was ours. The happiness of errands was in part that of running for the moment away from home, a free spirit. I believed the Little Store to be a center of the outside world, and hence of happiness—as I believed what I found in the Cracker Jack box to be a genuine prize, which was as simply as I believed in the Golden Fleece.

But a day came when I ran to the store to discover, sitting on the front step, a grown person, after all—more than a grown person. It was the Monkey Man, together with his monkey. His grinding-organ was lowered to the step beside him. In my whole life so far, I must have laid eyes on the

Monkey Man no more than five or six times. An itinerant of rare and wayward appearances, he was not punctual like the Gipsies, who every year with the first cool days of fall showed up in the aisles of Woolworth's. You never knew when the Monkey Man might decide to favor Jackson, or which way he'd go. Sometimes you heard him as close as the next street, and then he didn't come up yours.

But now I saw the Monkey Man at the Little Store, where I'd never seen him before. I'd never seen him sitting down. Low on that familiar doorstep, he was not the same any longer, and neither was his monkey. They looked just like an old man and an old friend of his that wore a fez, meeting quietly together, tired, and resting with their eyes fixed on some place far away, and not the same place. Yet their romance for me didn't have it in its power to waver. I wavered. I simply didn't know how to step around them, to proceed on into the Little Store for my mother's emergency as if nothing had happened. If I could have gone in there after it, whatever it was, I would have given it to them—putting it into the monkey's cool little fingers. I would have given them the Little Store itself.

In my memory they are still attached to the store—so are all the others. Everyone I saw on my way seemed to me then part of my errand, and in a way they were. As I myself, the free spirit, was part of it too.

All the years we lived in that house where we children were born, the same people lived in the other houses on our street too. People changed through the arithmetic of birth, marriage and death, but not by going away. So families just accrued stories, which through the fullness of time, in those times, their own lives made. And I grew up in those.

But I didn't know there'd ever been a story at the Little Store, one that was going on while I was there. Of course, all the time the Sessions family had been living right overhead there, in the upstairs rooms behind the little railed porch and the shaded windows; but I think we children never thought of that. Did I fail to see them as a family because they weren't living in an ordinary house? Because I so seldom saw them close together, or having anything to say to each other? She sat in the back of the store, her pencil over a ledger, while he stood and waited on children to make up their minds. They worked in twin black eyeshades, held on their gray heads by elastic bands. It may be harder to recognize kindness—or unkindness, either—in a face whose eyes are in shadow. His face underneath his shade was as round as the little wooden wheels in the Tinker Toy box. So was her face. I didn't know, perhaps didn't even wonder: were they husband and wife or brother and sister? Were they father and mother? There were a few other persons, of various ages, wandering singly in by the back door and out. But none of their relationships could I imagine, when I'd never seen them sitting down together around their own table.

The possibility that they had any other life at all, anything beyond what we could see within the four walls of the Little Store, occurred to me only when tragedy struck their family. There was some act of violence. The shock to the neighborhood traveled to the children, of course; but I couldn't find out from my parents what had happened. They held it back from me, as they'd already held back many things, "until the time comes for you to know."

You could find out some of these things by looking in the unabridged dictionary and the encyclopedia—kept to hand in our dining room—but you couldn't find out there what had happened to the family who for all the years of your life had lived upstairs over the Little Store, who had never been anything but patient and kind to you, who never once had sent you away. All I ever knew was its aftermath: they were the only people ever known to me who simply vanished. At the point where their life overlapped into ours, the story broke off.

We weren't being sent to the neighborhood grocery for facts of life, or death. But of course those are what we were on the track of, anyway. With the loaf of bread and the Cracker Jack prize, I was bringing home the intimations of pride and disgrace, and rumors and early news of people coming to hurt one another, while others practiced for joy— storing up a portion for myself of the human mystery.

(1975)

Ida M'Toy

✑

For one human being to point out another as "unforgettable" seems a trifle condescending, and in the ideal world we would all keep well aware of each other, but there are nevertheless a few persons one meets who are as inescapable of notice as skyrockets; it may be because like skyrockets they are radiant with their own substance and shower it about regardlessly. Ida M'Toy, an old Negro woman, for a long time a midwife in my Mississippi town and for another long time a dealer in secondhand clothes in the same place, has been a skyrocket as far back as most people remember. Or, rather, she is a kind of meteor (for she is not ephemeral, only sudden and startling). Her ways seem on a path of their own without regard to any course of ours and of a somewhat wider circuit; she will probably leave a glow behind and return in the far future on some other lap of her careening through all our duller and steadier bodies. She herself deals with the rest of us in this mighty and spacious way, calling in allegories and the elements, so it is owing to her nature that I may speak a little grandly.

The slave traders of England and New England, when they went capturing, took away the most royal of Africans along with their own slaves, and I have not much doubt that Ida has come down from a race of tall black queens. I wish I might have seen her when she was young. She has sharp clever features, light-filled black eyes, arched nostrils and fine thin mobile lips, and her hair, gray now, springs like a wild kind of diadem from the widow's peak over her forehead. Her voice is indescribable but it is a constant part of her presence and is filled with invocation. She never speaks lightly of any person or thing, but she flings out her arm and points at something and begins, "Oh, precious, I'm telling you to look at that—*look* at it!" and then she invokes about it, and tolerates no interruptions. I have heard long chants and utterances on the origin and history and destination of the smallest thing, any article or object her eye lights on; a bit of candle stuck on the mantelpiece will set her off, as if its little fire had ignited her whole mind. She invokes what she wishes to invoke and she has in all ways something of the seer about her. She wields a control over great numbers of her race by this power, which has an integrity that I believe nothing could break, and which sets her up, aloof and triumphant, above the rest. She is inspired and they are not. Maybe off by themselves they could be inspired, but nobody else could be inspired in the same room with Ida, it would be too crowded.

Ida is not a poor old woman, she is a rich old woman. She accepts it that she is held in envy as well as respect, but it is only another kind of tribute as far as she is concerned, and she expects to be gaped at for being rich, for having been married in the home of a white lady, "in her bay window," and for being very wise, all these things; but she is not vain in the usual sense.

Ida's life has been divided in two (it is, in many ways, eloquent of duality); but there is a thread that runs from one part into the other, and to trace this connection between delivering the child and clothing the man is an interesting speculation. Moreover, it has some excuse, for Ida herself helps it along by a wild and curious kind of talk that sashays from one part to the other and sounds to some of her customers like "ranting and raving." It is my belief that if Ida had not been a midwife, she would not be the same kind of secondhand-clothes dealer she is. Midwifery set her off, it gave her a hand in the mysteries, and she will never let go that flying hold merely because she is engaged in something else. An ex-alchemist would run a secondhand-clothes business with extra touches—a reminiscence of glitter would cling to the garments he sold, and it is the same with Ida. So it is well when you meet her to think what she was once.

Ida's memory goes back to her beginnings, when she was, she says, the first practical nurse in Jackson at the age of twenty-one, and she makes the past sound very dark and far back. She thanks God, she says, that today Capitol Street is not just three planks to walk on and is the prettiest place on earth, but that "people white and black is too high and don't they know Ida seen them when they carried a little tin coal-oil lamp that wasn't any bigger than their little fingers?" Ida speaks of herself in the third person and in indirect discourse often and especially when she says something good of herself or something of herself long ago. She will intone, "Ida say that she was good to the poor white people as she was to the rich, as she made a bargain to nurse a poor white lady in obstetrical case for a peck of peas. Ida said no, she couldn't see her suffer, and therefore a peck of black-eyed peas would be sufficient." She wants all she says to be listened to with the whole attention, and declares she does wish it were all written down. "Let her keep it straight, darling, if she remember Ida's true words, the angels will know it and be waiting around the throne for her." But Ida's true words are many and strange. When she talks about the old days it is almost like a story of combat against evil. "Ida fitted a duel from twenty-one to fifty-six, and then they operated on her right side and she was never able to stoop down to the floor again. She was never like those young devils, that pace around in those white shoes and those white clothes and up and down the streets of an evening while their patient is calling for a drink of water down poor parched throat— though I wore those white shoes and those white clothes. Only, my heart was in another direction."

Ida said, "I was nursing ever since there was a big road in Jackson. There was only nine doctors, and they were the best in all the world, all nine, right here in Jackson, but they were weak in finance. There wasn't nary hospital nowhere—there wasn't nary brick in Jackson, not one brick, no brick walk, no brick store, no brick nothing else. There wasn't no Old Ladies' Home at the end of the street, there wasn't no stopping place but the country. Town was as black as tar come night, and praise God they finally put some gas in bottles on the corners. There wasn't no such thing in the world as a nice buggy. Never heard tell of a cotton mattress, but tore up shucks and see the bed, so high, and the hay pillow stand up so beautiful! Now they got all this electric light and other electricity. Can't do nothing without the clickety-click. And bless God they fly just like buzzards up in the air, but Ida don't intend to ride till she ride to Glory."

In those early days when Jackson seems to have been a Slough of Despond with pestilence sticking out its head in the nights as black as tar, Ida was not only a midwife, she nursed all diseases. "It was the yellow fever first, and the next after that was the worst pox that there ever was in this world—it would kill you then, in my girl-days, six or seven a day. They had to stretch a rope across the road to keep the poor sick ones apart and many's the day I've et at the rope and carried the food back to the ones suffering." Ida remembers epidemics as major combats in which she was a kind of giant-killer. She nursed through influenza "six at a blow, until the doctor told me if I didn't quit nursing by sixes I would drop dead in the room." She says the doctors wrote her a recommendation as long as where she will show you up her arm, saying that when they called, it never was too cold and it never was too hot for Ida to go, and that the whole town would bow and say Amen, from the Jews on. "Bless my patients," she says, "nary one ever did die under my nursing, though plenty were sick enough to die. But laugh here," she directs. "My husband stayed sick on me twenty-one years and cost me one thousand whole dollars, but you can't nurse the heart to do no good, and in the night he fallen asleep and left me a widow, and I am a widow still."

When Ida found she could no longer stoop to the floor she stopped being a midwife and began selling clothes. She was successful at once in that too, for there is a natural flowering-ground for the secondhand-clothes business in the small American community where the richest people are only a little richer than the poor people and the poorest have ways to save pride and not starve or go naked. In Jackson the most respectable matron, if she would like a little extra cash to buy a new camellia bush or take the excursion to New Orleans, can run over to Ida's with her husband's other suit and Ida will sell it to a customer as a bargain at five dollars and collect twenty-five percent for herself, and everybody except the husband ("Right off my back! Perfectly good suit!") will be satisfied.

It could be a grubby enough little business in actual fact, but Ida is not a grubby person, and in her handling, it has become an affair of imagination and, to my notion, an expression of a whole attitude of life as integrated as an art or a philosophy.

Ida's store is her house, a white-painted five-room house with a porch across the front, a picket fence around, and the door-yard planted to capacity in big flowers. Inside, it is a phantasmagoria of garments. Every room except the kitchen is hung with dresses or suits (the sexes are segregated) three and four times around the walls, for the turnover is large and unpredictable, though not always rapid—people have to save up or wait for cotton-money. She has assumed all the ceremonies of Business and employs its practices and its terms to a point within sight of madness. She puts on a show of logic and executive order before which the customer is supposed to quail; sometimes I think her customers take on worth with her merely as witnesses of the miracles of her workings, though that is unfair of me. Her house turns year by year into a better labyrinth, more inescapable, and she delights in its complication of aisles and curtains and its mystery of closed doors with little signs on ruled paper, "Nobody can come in here." Someday some little colored girl is going to get lost in Ida's house. The richer she gets, the more "departments" she builds and adds on to the house, and each one is named for the color of its walls, the pink department, or the blue. Even now her side yard is filled with miscellaneous doors, glass panes, planks, and little stacks of bricks that she is accumulating for a new green department she says she will build in 1943.

Her cupboards and drawers are a progressive series of hiding places, which is her interpretation of the filing system. She hides trinkets of mysterious importance or bits of paper filled with abbreviated information; she does not hide money, however, and she tells how much she has on hand ($660.60 is the latest figure), and her life insurance policy is nailed up on the wall over the mantel. Everybody knows her to be an old woman living with only a small grandchild to guard her in a house full of cash money, and yet she has not been murdered. She never will be. I have wondered what Ida would do if she saw a burglar coming after her money. I am convinced that she has no ax or gun ready for him, but a flow of words will be unstoppered that will put the fear of God in him for life; and I think the would-be burglars have the same suspicion, and will continue to keep away, not wanting so much fear of God as that.

She keeps as strict and full a ledger of transaction as the Book of Judgment, and in as enthusiastic and exalted a spirit of accuracy as an angel bookkeeper should have. The only trouble is, it is almost impossible to find in it what she is looking for—but perhaps there will be confusion on Doomsday too. The book, a great black one, which she now has little William, her grandson, to hold for her while she consults it (and he will kneel under it like a little mural figure), covers a period of twenty-six years, concerns hundreds of people, "white and black," and innumerable transactions, all noted down in a strange code full of flourishes, for Ida properly considers all she does confidential. "You could find anything in the world in this book," she says reverently, then slamming it shut in your face, "if you turn enough pages and go in the right direction. Nothing in here is wrong," she says. Loose slips are always flying out of the ledger like notes in a sibyl's book, and she sets William flying to chase them and get them inside again.

She writes her own descriptions of the garments brought to her to sell, and a lady giving over her finest white dress of last summer must not be surprised, if she looks over Ida's shoulder, to see her pen the words "Rally Day, $2.00" or note down her best spring straw hat as "Tom Boy, 75c." The customer might be right, but Ida does not ever ask the customer. After a moment of concentration Ida goes and hangs the object for sale on the wall in the room of her choice, and a tag is pinned to the sleeve, saying simply "Mrs. So-and-So." Accuracy is a passion with Ida, and so is her belief in her own conscience, and I do not know what it must have cost her to pin a tag on one poor sagging dress that has hung there year in, year out, saying "Don't know who this is."

She bears respect to clothes in the same degree as she bears it to the people from whose backs they come; she treats them like these people, until indeed it seems that dignity is in them, shapeless and even ridiculous as they have seemed at first; she gives them the space on the wall and the room in the house that correspond to the honor in which she holds the human beings, and she even speaks in the proper tone of voice when she is in the room with them. They hang at human height from the hangers on the walls, the brighter and more important ones in front and on top. With the most serene impartiality she makes up her mind about client and clothes, and she has been known to say, "For God's sake, take it back. Wouldn't a man white or black wear that suit out of here."

There is a magnificence in Ida's business, an extent and an influence at which she hints without ceasing, that undoubtedly inspire the poorest or idlest customer with almost an anxiety to buy. It is almost like an appeasement, and the one that goes off with nothing must feel mean, foolish and naked indeed, naked to scorn. "I clothe them," she says, "from Jackson to Vicksburg, Meridian to Jackson, Big Black to 'Azoo, Memphis to New

Orleans—Clinton! Bolton! Edwards! Bovina! Pocahontas! Flora! Bentonia! 'Azoo City! Everywhere. There ain't nobody hasn't come to Ida, or sooner or later will come."

If no one else had thought of the secondhand-clothes business, Ida would have originated it, for she did originate it as far as she is concerned; and likewise I am forced to believe that if there had never been any midwives in the world, Ida would have invented midwifery, so ingenious and delicate-handed and wise she is, and sure of her natural right to take charge. She loves transformation and bringing things about; she simply cannot resist it. The Negro midwives of this state have a kind of organization these days and lesser powers, they do certain things in certain book-specified ways, and all memorize and sing at meetings a song about "First we put—Drops in their eyes," but in Ida's day a midwife was a lone person, invested with the whole charge of life; she had to draw upon her own resources and imagination. Ida's constant gestures today still involve a dramatic outthrust of the right hand, and let any prominent names be mentioned (and she mentions them), and she will fling out her palm and cry into the conversation, "Born in this hand!" "Four hundred little white babies—or more," she says. "My God, I was bringing them all the time. I got 'em everywhere—doctors, lawyers, school teachers and preachers, married ladies." She has been in the clothes business for twenty-six years, but she was a midwife for thirty-five.

She herself has been married, twice, and by her first husband she had one son, "the only one I ever did have and I want his name written down: Julius Knight." Her mother (before she died) and her brothers live out in the country, and only one little grandson has lived with her for a long time. Her husband, Braddie M'Toy, whom she called Toy, is remembered collecting and delivering clothes in a wagon when he was young, and was to be seen always on some street if not another, moving very slowly on account of his heart.

Now without Toy, Ida uses a telephone down the road and a kind of deluxe grapevine service to rouse up her clients and customers. Anybody who is asked to by Ida feels it a duty to phone any stranger for her and "tell them for God's sake to come get their money and bring the change." Strange Negroes call people at dawn, giving news of a sale, white ladies call unknown white ladies, notes on small rolls or scraps of paper folded like doctors' "powders" are conscientiously delivered, and the whole town contrives in her own spirit of emergency to keep Ida's messages on their way. Ida takes twenty-five per-cent of the sales price, and if she sells your dress for a dollar, you have to take her a quarter when you go, or come back another time, for she will not make change for anybody. She will not violate her system of bookkeeping any more than she would violate her code of ethics or her belief in God—down to the smallest thing, all is absolute in Ida's sight.

Ida finds all Ornament a wonderful and appropriate thing, the proper materializing of the rejoicing or sorrowing soul. I believe she holds Ornament next to birth and somehow kin to it. She despises a drab color and welcomes bright clothes with a queenly and triumphant smile, as if she acknowledges the bold brave heart that chose that. Inferior color means inferior spirit, and an inferior person should not hope to get or spend more than four-bits for an outfit. She dearly loves a dress that is at once identifiable as either rich mourning or "rally-day" —the symbolic and celebrating kind appeal to her inevitably over the warm or the serviceable, and she will ask and (by oratory) get the finest prices for rather useless but splendid garments. "Girl, you buy this spangle-dress," she says to a customer, and the girl buys it and puts it on and shines. Ida's scale of prices would make a graph showing precisely the rise from her condemnation of the subdued and nondescript to her acclaim of the bright and glorious. It is nice on Saturdays to pass in front of Ida's house on the edge of town and see the customers emerge. With some little flash of scarf, some extra glitter of trimming for which they have paid dearly, dressed like some visions in Ida's speculations on the world, glorious or menial as befits their birth, merit and willingness, but all rampant and somehow fulfilled by this last touch of costume as though they have been tapped by a spirit when Ida's thimble rapped them, they float dizzily down the steps and through the flowers out the gate; and you could not help thinking of the phrase "going out into the world," as if Ida had just birthed them anew.

I used to think she must be, a little, the cross between a transcendentalist and a witch, with the happiness and kind of self-wonder that this combination must enjoy. They say that all things we write could be; and sometimes in amazement I wonder if a tiny spark of the wonderful Philosopher of Clothes, Diogenes Teufelsdröckh, could be flashing for an instant, and somewhat barbarically, in the wild and enthusiastic spirit of this old black woman. Her life, like his, is proudly emblematic— she herself being the first to see her place in the world. It is she literally who clothes her entire world, as far and wide as she knows—a hard-worked midwife grown old, with a memory like a mill turning through it all the lives that were born in her hand or have passed through her door.

When she stalks about, alternately clapping her hand over her forehead and flinging out her palm and muttering "Born in this hand!" as she is likely to do when some lady of the old days comes bringing a dress to sell, you cannot help believing that she sees them all, her children and her customers, in the double way, naked and clothed, young and then old, with love and with contempt, with open arms or with a push to bar the door. She is moody now, if she has not always been, and sees her customers as a procession of sweet supplicant spirits that she has birthed, who have returned to her side, and again sometimes as a bunch of scarecrows or even changelings, that she wishes were well gone out of sight. "They would steal from their own mother," she says, and while she is pinning up some purchase in a newspaper and the customer is still counting out the pennies, she will shout in a deep voice to the grandchild that flutters around like a little blackbird, "Hold the door, William."

I have never caught Ida doing anything except selling clothes or holding forth on her meditations, but she has a fine garden.

"If you want to carry me something I really like," she will say, bringing up the subject first, "carry me dallion potatoes [dahlia bulbs] *first*, and old newspapers second." Ida has the green finger from her mother, and she says, "You're never going to see any flowers prettier than these right here." She adores giving flowers away; under your protest she will cut every one in the garden, every red and white rose on the trellis, which is a wooden sunset with painted rays, the blossoms with little two-inch stems the way a child cuts them, and distribute them among all present and those passing in the road. She is full of all the wild humors and extravagances of the godlike toward this entire town and its environs. Sometimes, owing to her superior wisdom, she is a little malign, but much oftener she will become excruciatingly tender, holding, as if in some responsibility toward all the little ones of the world, the entire population to her great black cameoed breast. Then she will begin to call people "It." "It's all hot and tired, it is, coming so far to see Ida. Take these beautiful flowers Ida grew with her own hand, *that's* what it would like. Put 'em in its bedroom," and she presses forward all the flowers she has cut and then, not content, a bouquet dripping from a vase, one of a kind of everything, all into your arms.

She loves music too, and in her house she has one room, also hung with clothes, called the music room. "I got all the music in the world in here," she used to say, jabbing a finger at a silent radio and an old Gramophone shut up tight, "but what's the use of letting those contrivances run when you can make your own music?" And ignoring the humble customers waiting, she would fling down at the old pump organ in the corner and tear into a frenzy of chords. "I make my own!" she would shout into the turmoil. She would send for little William, and he knew how to sing with her, though he would give out. "Bass, William!" she would shout, and in his tiny treble he sang bass, bravely.

When Ida speaks of her mother it is in a strange kind of pity, a tender amazement. She says she knew when her mother was going to die, and with her deep feeling for events and commemorations, she gave her a fine big party. Ida would no more shrink from doing anything the grand way than she would shrink from other demands upon her greatness. "Hush now," she told me, "don't say a word while I tell you this. All that day long I was cooking dinner between niggers. I had: four turkeys, four hens, four geese, four hams, red cake, white cake, chocolate cake, caramel cake, every color cake known. The table reached from the front door to the icebox. I had all the lights burning up electricity, and all the flowers cut. I had the plates changed seven times, and three waiters from the hotel. I'd got Mama a partner. Mama was eighty years old and I got her another old lady eighty years old to march with. I had everybody come. All her children—one son, the big shot, came all the way from Detroit, riding in a train, to be at Mama's grand dinner. We had somebody play Silent Night and march music to follow later. And there was Mama: look at Mama! Mama loved powder. Mama had on a little old-fashioned hat, but she wouldn't take it off—had nice hair, too. Mama did all right for the march, she marched all right, and sat down on time at the right place at the head of the table, but she wouldn't take off her hat. So the waiters, they served the chicken soup first, and Mama says, 'Where my coffee? Bring on turnip and cornbread. Didn't you make a blackberry pie?' I said, 'Mama, you don't eat coffee first.' But she said, 'Where my coffee? Bring on turnip and cornbread. Didn't you make a blackberry pie? What's the matter with you?' Everything was so fine, you know. It took her two big sons, one on each side, to quiet her, that's the way Mama acted!" And Ida ended the story laughing and crying. It was plain that there was one person who had no recognition of Ida's grandeur and high place in the world, and who had never yielded at all to the glamour as others did. It was a cruelty for Ida, but perhaps all vision has lived in the house with cruelty.

Nowadays she is carried to such heights of business and power, and its paraphernalia crowds her so, that she is overcome with herself, and suddenly gives way to the magnitude of it all. A kind of chaos comes over her. Now and then she falls down in a trance and stays "dead as that chair for three days." White doctors love her and by a little struggle take care of her. Ida bears with them. "They took my appendix," she will say. "Well, they took my teeth." She says she has a paralyzed heel, though it is hard to see how she can tell—perhaps, like Achilles, she feels that her end is coming by entering that way. "The doctor told me I got to rest until 1945," she declares, with a lifted hand warding you off. "Rest! Rest! Rest! I must rest." If a step is heard on the front porch, she instantly cries warning from within the house, "Don't set your heels down! When you speak to me, whisper!" When a lady that was a stranger came to see her, Ida appeared, but said in haste, "Don't tell me your name, for I'm resting my mind. The doctors don't want me to have any more people in my head than I got already." Now on Saturdays if a dusty battered car full of customers from across the cotton fields draws up, one by one all the shades in the house are yanked down. Ida wishes to see no one, she wishes to sell nothing.

Perhaps the truth is that she has expended herself to excess and now suffers with a corresponding emptiness that she does not want anyone to see. She can show you the track of the pain it gives her: her finger crosses her two breasts. She is as hard to see as a queen.

And I think she lives today the way she would rather be living, directly in symbols. People are their vestures now. Memories, the great memories of births and marriages and deaths, are nearly the same as the pieces of jewelry ("$147.65 worth") she has bought on anniversary days and wears on her person. "That's Mamma's death," she says—a silver watch on a silver chain. She holds out for your admiration the yellow hands that she asserts most of this county was born in, on which now seven signet rings flash. "Don't go to church any longer," she says, "or need to go. I just sit at home and enjoy my fingers."

(1942)

One Time, One Place

These photographs are my present choices from several hundred I made in Mississippi when I had just come home from college and into the Depression. There were many of us, and of those, I was also among the many who found their first full-time jobs with the Works Progress Administration. As publicity agent, junior grade, for the State office, I was sent about over the eighty-two counties of Mississippi, visiting the newly opened farm-to-market roads or the new airfields hacked out of old cow pastures, interviewing a judge in some new juvenile court, riding along on a Bookmobile route and distributing books into open hands like the treasures they were, helping to put up booths in county fairs, and at night, in some country-town hotel room under a loud electric fan, writing the Projects up for the county weeklies to print if they found the space. In no time, I was taking a camera with me.

In snapping these pictures I was acting completely on my own, though I'm afraid it was on their time; they have nothing to do with the WPA. But the WPA gave me the chance to travel, to see widely and at close hand and really for the first time the nature of the place I'd been born into. And it gave me

Preface to *One Time, One Place*: A Snapshot Album.

the blessing of showing me the real State of Mississippi, not the abstract state of the Depression.

The Depression, in fact, was not a noticeable phenomenon in the poorest state in the Union. In New York there had been the faceless breadlines; on Farish Street in my hometown of Jackson, the proprietor of the My Blue Heaven Café had written on the glass of the front door with his own finger dipped in window polish:

> At 4:30 A.M.
> We open our doors.
> We have no certain
> time to close.
> The Cook will be
> glad to serve U
> With a 5 & 10¢
> stew.

The message was personal and particular. More than what is phenomenal, that strikes home. It happened to me everywhere I went, and I took these pictures.

Mine was a popular Kodak model one step more advanced than the Brownie. (Later on, I promoted myself to something better, but most of the pictures here were made with the first camera.) The local Standard Photo Company of Jackson developed my rolls of film, and I made myself a contact-print frame and printed at night in the kitchen when I was home. With good fortune, I secured an enlarger at secondhand from the State Highway Department, which went on the kitchen table. It had a single shutter-opening, and I timed exposures by a trial-and-error system of countdown.

This is not to apologize for these crudities, because I think what merit the pictures do have has nothing to do with how they were made: their merit lies entirely in their subject matter. I presume to put them into a book now because I feel that, taken all together, they cannot help but amount to a record of a kind—a record of fact, putting together some of the elements of one time and one place. A better and less ignorant photographer would certainly have come up with better pictures, but not these pictures; for he could hardly have been as well positioned as I was, moving through the scene openly and yet invisibly because I was part of it, born into it, taken for granted.

Neither would a social-worker photographer have taken these same pictures. The book is offered, I should explain, not as a social document but as a family album—which is something both less and more, but unadorned. The pictures now seem to me to fall most naturally into the simple and self-evident categories about which I couldn't even at this distance make a mistake—the days of the week: workday; Saturday, for staying home and for excursions too; and Sunday.

The book is like an album as well in that the pictures all are snapshots. It will be evident that the majority of them were snapped without the awareness of the subjects or with only their peripheral awareness. These ought to be the best, but I'm not sure that they are. The snapshots made with people's awareness are, for the most part, just as unposed: I simply asked people if they would mind going on with what they were doing and letting me take a picture. I can't remember ever being met with a demurrer stronger than amusement. (The lady bootlegger, the one in the fedora with the drawn-back icepick, was only pretending to drive me away—it was a joke; she knew I hadn't come to turn her in.)

I asked for and received permission to attend the Holiness Church and take pictures during the service; they seated me on the front row of the congregation and forgot me; once the tambourines were sounded and the singing and dancing began, they wouldn't have noticed the unqualified presence of the Angel Gabriel. My ignorance about interior exposures under weak, naked light bulbs is to blame for the poor results, but I offer them anyway in the hope that a poor picture of Speaking in the Unknown Tongue is better than none at all. The pictures of the Bird Pageant—this was Baptist—were made at the invitation, and under the direction, of its originator, Maude Thompson; I would not have dared to interfere with the poses, and my regret is that I could not, without worse interfering with what was beautiful and original, have taken pictures during the Pageant itself.

Lastly, and for me they come first, I have included some snapshots that resulted in portraits: here the subjects were altogether knowing and they look back at the camera. The only one I knew beforehand was Ida M'Toy, a wonderful eccentric who for all her early and middle years had practiced as a midwife. She wanted and expected her picture to be taken in the one and only pose that would let the world know that the leading citizens of Jackson had been "born in this hand."

It was with great dignity that many other portrait sitters agreed to be photographed, for the reason, they explained, that this would be the first picture taken of them in their lives. So I was able to give them something back, and though it might be that the picture would be to these poverty-marked men and women and children a sad souvenir, I am almost sure that it wasn't all sad to them, wasn't necessarily sad at all. Whatever you might think of those lives as symbols of a bad time, the human beings who were living them thought a good deal more of them than that. If I took picture after picture out of simple high spirits and the joy of being alive, the way I began, I can add that in my subjects I met often with the same high spirits, the same joy. Trouble, even to the point of disaster, has its pale, and these defiant things of the spirit repeatedly go beyond it, joy the same as courage.

In taking all these pictures, I was attended, I now know, by an angel—a presence of trust. In particular, the photographs of black persons by a white person may not testify soon again to such intimacy. It is trust that dates the pictures now, more than the vanished years.

And had I no shame as a white person for what message might lie in my pictures of black persons? No, I was too busy imagining myself into their lives to be open to any generalities. I wished no more to indict anybody, to prove or disprove anything by my pictures, than I would have wished to do harm to the people in them, or have expected any harm from them to come to me.

Perhaps I should openly admit here to an ironic fact. While I was very well positioned for taking these pictures, I was rather oddly equipped for doing it. I came from a stable, sheltered, relatively happy home that up to the time of the Depression and the early death of my father (which happened to us in the same year) had become comfortably enough off by small-town Southern standards and according to our own quiet way of life. (One tragic thing about the poor in Mississippi is how little money it did take here to gain the things that mattered.) I was equipped with a good liberal arts education (in Mississippi, Wisconsin, and New York) for which my parents had sacrificed. I was bright in my studies, and when at the age of twenty-one I returned home from the Columbia Graduate School of Business—prepared, I thought, to earn my living—of the ways of life in the world I knew absolutely nothing at all. I didn't even know this. My complete innocence was the last thing I would have suspected of myself. Anyway, I was fit to be amazed.

The camera I focused in front of me may have been a shy person's protection, in which I see no harm. It was an eye, though—not quite mine, but a quicker and an unblinking one—and it couldn't see pain where it looked, or give any, though neither could it catch effervescence, color, transience, kindness, or what was not there. It was what I used, at any rate, and like any tool, it used me.

It was after I got home, had made my prints in the kitchen and dried them overnight and looked at them in the morning by myself, that I began to see objectively what I had there.

When a heroic face like that of the woman in the buttoned sweater—who I think must come first in this book—looks back at me from her picture, what I respond to now, just as I did the first time, is not the Depression, not the Black, not the South, not even the perennially sorry state of the whole world, but the story of her life in her face. And though I did not take these pictures to prove anything, I think they most assuredly do show something—which is to make a far better claim for them. Her face to me is full of meaning more truthful and more terrible and, I think, more noble than any generalization about people could have prepared me for or could describe for me now. I learned from my own pictures, one by one, and had to; for I think we are the breakers of our own hearts.

I learned quickly enough when to click the shutter, but what I was becoming aware of more slowly was a story-writer's truth: the thing to wait on, to reach there in time for, is the moment in which people reveal themselves. You have to be ready, in yourself; you have to know the moment when you see it. The human face and the human body are eloquent in themselves, and a snapshot is a moment's glimpse (as a story may be a long look, a growing contemplation) into what never stops moving, never ceases to express for itself something of our common feeling. Every feeling waits upon its gesture. Then when it does come, how unpredictable it turns out to be, after all.

We come to terms as well as we can with our lifelong exposure to the world, and we use whatever devices we may need to survive. But eventually, of course, our knowledge depends upon the living relationship between what we see going on and ourselves. If exposure is essential, still more so is the reflection. Insight doesn't happen often on the click of the moment, like a lucky snapshot, but comes in its own time and more slowly and from nowhere but within. The sharpest recognition is surely that which is charged with sympathy as well as with shock—it is a form of human vision. And that is of course a gift. We struggle through any pain or darkness in nothing but the hope that we may receive it, and through any term of work in the prayer to keep it.

In my own case, a fuller awareness of what I needed to find out about people and their lives had to be sought for through another way, through writing stories. But away off one day up in Tishomingo County, I knew this, anyway: that my wish, indeed my continuing passion, would be not to point the finger in judgment but to part a curtain, that invisible shadow that falls between people, the veil of indifference to each other's presence, each other's wonder, each other's human plight.

(1971)

About the Author

One of America's most admired authors, Eudora Welty was born in Jackson, Mississippi, which is still her home. She was educated locally and at Mississippi State College for Women, the University of Wisconsin, and the Columbia University Graduate School of Business. She is the author of, among many other books, *The Robber Bridegroom*, *Delta Wedding*, *The Ponder Heart*, *The Optimist's Daughter*, and *Losing Battles*.

VINTAGE INTERNATIONAL

VINTAGE INTERNATIONAL

___ **Spring Snow** by Yukio Mishima	$10.95	679-72241-6
___ **Runaway Horses** by Yukio Mishima	$10.95	679-72240-8
___ **The Temple of Dawn** by Yukio Mishima	$10.95	679-72242-4
___ **The Decay of the Angel** by Yukio Mishima	$10.95	679-72243-2
___ **Cities of Salt** by Abdelrahman Munif	$12.95	394-75526-X
___ **Ada, or Ardor** by Vladimir Nabokov	$10.95	679-72522-9
___ **Bend Sinister** by Vladimir Nabokov	$8.95	679-72727-2
___ **The Defense** by Valdimir Nabokov	$8.95	679-72722-1
___ **Despair** by Vladimir Nabokov	$7.95	679-72343-9
___ **Invitation to a Beheading** by Vladimir Nabokov	$7.95	679-72531-8
___ **King, Queen, Knave** by Vladimir Nabokov	$8.95	679-72340-4
___ **Laughter in the Dark** by Vladimir Nabokov	$8.95	679-72450-8
___ **Lolita** by Vladimir Nabokov	$7.95	679-72316-1
___ **Look at the Harlequins!** by Vladimir Nabokov	$8.95	679-72728-0
___ **Mary** by Vladimir Nabokov	$6.95	679-72620-9
___ **Pale Fire** by Vladimir Nabokov	$8.95	679-72342-0
___ **Pnin** by Vladimir Nabokov	$7.95	679-72341-2
___ **Speak, Memory** by Vladimir Nabokov	$9.95	679-72339-0
___ **Strong Opinions** by Vladimir Nabokov	$8.95	679-72609-8
___ **Transparent Things** by Vladimir Nabokov	$6.95	679-72541-5
___ **A Bend in the River** by V. S. Naipaul	$7.95	679-72202-5
___ **A Turn in the South** by V. S. Naipaul	$8.95	679-72488-5
___ **Black Box** by Amos Oz	$8.95	679-72185-1
___ **The Shawl** by Cynthia Ozick	$6.95	679-72926-7
Dictionary of the Khazars by Milorad Pavić		
___ male edition	$9.95	679-72461-3
___ female edition	$9.95	679-72754-X
___ **Swann's Way** by Marcel Proust	$9.95	679-72009-X
___ **Grey Is the Color of Hope**		
by Irina Ratushinskaya	$8.95	679-72447-8
___ **Selected Poetry** by Rainer Maria Rilke	$10.95	679-72201-7
___ **Shame** by Salman Rushdie	$9.95	679-72204-1
___ **No Exit and 3 Other Plays** by Jean-Paul Sartre	$7.95	679-72516-4
___ **And Quiet Flows the Don** by Mikhail Sholokhov	$10.95	679-72521-0
___ **Ake: The Years of Childhood** by Wole Soyinka	$9.95	679-72540-7
___ **Confessions of Zeno** by Italo Svevo	$9.95	679-72234-2
___ **On the Golden Porch** by Tatyana Tolstaya	$8.95	679-72843-0
___ **The Optimist's Daughter** by Eudora Welty	$8.95	679-72883-X
___ **Losing Battles** by Eudora Welty	$8.95	679-72882-1
___ **The Eye of the Story** by Eudora Welty	$8.95	679-73004-4
___ **The Passion** by Jeanette Winterson	$7.95	679-72437-0

Now at your bookstore or call toll-free to order: 1-800-733-3000
(credit cards only).